Th

GARDEN

PRAISE FOR *THE FORSAKEN GARDEN*

"This beautifully written and conceived book investigates how to continue evolving as individuals and as a planet while maintaining a vital link to the soul and to spirit. A significant contribution to our growing understanding of psyche."
—Michael Conforti, Ph.D., author of *Field, Form and Fate: Patterns in Psyche, Mind and Matter*

"A fascinating journey. The intelligence of Nancy Ryley's inquiry and the sensitivity of her listening allows the reader to participate in intimate, revelatory conversations about soul, myth, Nature, God and Goddesses, and the universe. You will want to read this book more than once."
—Joseph Kulin, Publisher of *Parabola* Magazine

"Invites us into a garden budding with questions, courage, silences, dream and memory. The marvel Nancy Ryley brings to her four interviews and the vision she acquires are like precious seeds and rich earth and swirls of fresh rain. Helps us see that despite eco-diseases and ecological disasters, life just keeps right on sprouting."
—Chellis Glendinning, psychologist, author of *My Name is Chellis and I'm in Recovery from Western Civilization*

"Luminous conversations with four of the wisest teachers we have shine beacons of hope that the world's soul can be saved while we heal and whole ourselves."
—Jean Houston, Ph.D., author of *A Passion for the Possible* and *Manual for the Peacemaker*

"An essential and inspiring prescription for planetary health, issued by five very smart and encouraging doctors of the soul. One can only hope that it will be filled, and followed."
—Kirkpatrick Sale, author of *Dwellers in the Land* and *The Green Revolution*

"A vital book. These soulful conversations can guide us on a journey of healing for ourselves and the earth."
—Brian Swimme, author of *The Hidden Heart of the Cosmos*

"There is much that we need to attend to, for the sake of our health and the well-being of the planet. This book tells us where to start. Nancy Ryley has gathered the wisdom of four of the most thoughtful writers on psyche and nature, along with her personal insights, to give us crucial guidance for the road ahead."
> —Jonathan Young, Ph.D., Founder, Mythological Studies Department, Pacifica Graduate Institute

"Highly readable and inspiring book to tell the world of the environmental illness threatening the body and soul of all of us. A heartfelt wakeup call to this universal urgency. We are indebted to her valiant effort and brilliant achievement. Bravo!"
> —Chungliang Al Huang, Living Tao Foundation, author of *Embrace Tiger, Return to Mountain*

"A depth of extraordinary wisdom. Nancy Ryley's personal journey speaks eloquently of the changes we all need to make to restore balance and harmony in our relationship with ourselves, with each other, and with the Earth."
> —Helena Norberg-Hodge, Director, International Society of Ecology and Culture

"A beautiful book, full of the wisdom of the ages—a wisdom that must be applied to our present age if we are to survive and create and not wait for death to be our teacher."
> —Bernie Siegel, M.D., author of *Love, Medicine, and Miracles*

"The truest voice I have ever read about the problems of our world. These four brilliant people, resonating against each other on a topic of such complexity and spirituality, are absolutely wonderful. I was enriched by reading it."
> —Janet Turnbull Irving, literary agent

The FORSAKEN GARDEN

FOUR CONVERSATIONS ON THE DEEP MEANING OF ENVIRONMENTAL ILLNESS

NANCY RYLEY

AWARD-WINNING DOCUMENTARY FILMMAKER TALKS TO

LAURENS VAN DER POST
MARION WOODMAN
ROSS WOODMAN
THOMAS BERRY

ABOUT HER OWN HEALING AND THE HEALING OF THE EARTH

A publication supported by
THE KERN FOUNDATION

Quest Books
Theosophical Publishing House
Wheaton, Illinois ♦ Chennai (Madras), India

The Theosophical Publishing House
P.O. Box 270
Wheaton, IL 60189-0270

A publication of the Theosophical Publishing House,
a department of the Theosophical Society in America

LIBRARY OF CONGRESS CATALOGING-IN-PUBLICATION DATA

Ryley, Nancy.
    The forsaken garden: four conversations on the deep meaning of
environmental illness / Nancy Ryley. — 1st Quest ed.
        p.   cm.
    "A publication supported by the Kern Foundation."
    Includes bibliographical references.
    ISBN 0-8356-0771-2
    1. Environmentally induced diseases. 2. Environmental health.
    3. Human ecology.   I. Kern Foundation.   II. Title.
RB152.5.R95   1998
616.9'8—dc21   98-15996
                                                                        CIP

        4   3   2   1   *   98   99   00   01   02   03   04

                Printed in the United States of America

To David, whose love and support made this book possible

CONTENTS

PART FOUR: THOMAS BERRY
Abandoned Planet, Abandoned Souls

INTRODUCTION

THIS IS a book about the relationship between the health of our bodies and souls and the condition of the planet.

For many years I have entertained the idea that what is really at the bottom of our dismantling of the natural world is our lack of a spiritual connection to it. With this in mind, I chose four distinguished people with whom I could explore the thesis that the result of our severing of this tie to Mother Earth is that we are taking out our "divine discontent" on the planet. Because of their connection to what author Laurens van der Post calls the spiritual "life of our times," he, as well as Jungian analyst Marion Woodman, Blake scholar Ross Woodman, and theologian and cultural historian Thomas Berry are all eminently qualified to speak on this subject.

My own involvement with this book began several years ago when, after decades of urban living, I became ill and for the sake of my health moved to a country property bordering on wilderness. Suddenly environmental issues of which I had been totally ignorant became of paramount importance to me. It became obvious that humans needed a different perception of the natural world if we were going to halt our desecration of it and avoid an environmental crisis. Somehow we had to learn to see beyond our perception of the Earth as merely a source of economic benefit, and change our philosophical and cultural assumptions in order to experience nature in a more transcendent way.

As well as searching for the deeper causes of our planetary crisis, I also felt the need to re-orient my life's direction. In that sense, this book traces my quest for a path towards both a deeper commitment to the earth's well-being, as well as to more spiritually conscious values.

In the early 1980s I had been diagnosed with environmental illness—although that wasn't what it was called then. No one at that time had a name for what was beginning to plague a lot of otherwise perfectly healthy people: extreme fatigue, depression, reactive sensitivity to foods and chemicals, and a whole range of other physical and mental ailments.

What was causing these problems? The doctors didn't seem to know, but people like me were faced with symptoms that didn't go away no matter how aggressively they were treated.

In my own case, environmental illness came on relatively slowly. It started in the mid-1970s with excruciating attacks of bladder pain. For the next ten years I underwent treatments at a large hospital in downtown Toronto for inflammatory reactions to what were later discovered to be certain chemicals in my environment. Gradually symptoms began to develop in other parts of my body as well. Joint pain made walking difficult at times, and lower-back problems rivaled the bladder attacks for mind-numbing pain. Episodes of near paranoia and hysteria were even more frightening than the physical symptoms.

At first the doctors attributed all these symptoms to stress. For many years I had been working in downtown Toronto as a network television producer/director/writer for the Canadian Broadcasting Corporation (CBC). It was demanding work so it made sense that I might be suffering from extreme burnout. But when, after taking many months off to relax and escape from my heavy work load, I remained as sick as ever, I knew that this was more than just burnout.

My career had peaked in the mid-1970s when one of my documentaries was a finalist for an International Emmy in New York, and another of my films won the ACTRA Award for the best television program of the year. I couldn't have been happier about that, nor about the fact that I had married a wonderful man just preceding these successes. All in all I felt doubly blessed; my life seemed focused and complete.

Then everything changed. My immune system began to treat foods that I had been eating all my life as allergens, which meant that when I ate them they now made me ill. Gradually I had to eliminate more and more from my diet, until by 1983 I was down to a dozen foods I could tolerate and had lost 20 pounds. By this time I was spending all my time when I wasn't working coping with this disease. A typical day under these circumstances started with a mad rush to pack a lunch to take to work from foods I had specially prepared the night before. I also had to carry my day's filtered water supply with me since even the city tap water made me ill.

Diesel fumes from city buses drained my energy to such an extent that I often arrived at work exhausted. But the real hazard turned out to be the

CBC building itself. A garage in the basement leaked various noxious gases such as carbon monoxide into the poorly ventilated floors above. All kinds of outgassing was taking place as well from the film stock and equipment that I worked near every day. The result of breathing in all these fumes was that my ability to think and do my job properly was becoming severely compromised.

As a documentary filmmaker, I had to travel a fair amount. What I didn't know was that hotel and motel rooms could be sprayed with up to fifty different kinds of chemicals. In retrospect it was obvious that I was being poisoned by their residue since my bladder and mental problems worsened during every trip. Finally, on arrival for a film shoot in New Mexico, an exposure to jet fumes in the airport overwhelmed my already dysfunctional immune system, and I collapsed.

At this point I knew nothing about environmental illness or the possible effects of toxic overload on one's body. Then one day I watched two programs on the CBC entitled *Air of Death* and *The Twentieth Century Disease*. The first programs ever to address the problem of environmental pollution and its effect on human health, they would be land-mark documentaries—prophetic in their warnings about the deleterious consequences of our relentless abuse of the planet. Produced by my colleague Larry Gosnell, they really opened my eyes to the truth, and the seriousness, of my own situation.

By this time I had partially lost my bearings in the world in which I had once felt at home. Poisoned by the environment, I could no longer walk along my own street without becoming tired and weak from breathing in the pesticides and herbicides sprayed to keep the manicured lawns pest- and weed-free. The pollution from passing cars and trucks, and the myriad other sources that contaminated the city overpowered the smell of the fresh spring air in which I had once rejoiced. The world had become an implacable foe—the air unbreathable, the water lifeless, the food toxic. Nature, once my spiritual refuge, had become my enemy.

The cost to me and my husband both financially and emotionally was predictably high. We tried everything to alleviate my symptoms, in the hope that I would be able to go back to work. But as long as I stayed in the city I was virtually a prisoner in my own house. Eventually I was advised by my doctor that if my immune system was exposed to any more pollutants my health might be permanently impaired. Reluctantly my husband and I decided to leave Toronto. In 1985 we pulled up stakes and moved to the Canadian West.

In the ten years that have passed since we came here, I have been engaged in an on-going philosophical meditation about how to relate my story to what the culture and, beyond it the planet itself, are enduring. In these spacious surroundings my body has begun to heal, and in the new, unhurried pace of my life I have had time to ponder all that has happened. The seeds of this book, sown more than a decade ago in a very different environment, have now sprouted and grown into reflections that have enabled me to make the connection between the spiritual nature of this illness and our contamination of the Earth. For my soul's sake—as well as my body's—I have planted a garden on the island off Canada's West Coast where I spend my summers, and rejoiced over the years at its increasing abundance and beauty. Finally, I have sought out mentors for both my inner and outer gardens—people who have helped me nourish my spiritual and emotional well-being. It is their compassion for the planetary garden which we all share that I have tried to incorporate into this book.

I chose Laurens van der Post, Marion Woodman, Ross Woodman, and Thomas Berry to participate in my journey of exploration because when-ever I read their works, or heard them speak, I felt an invisible thread connect-ing us. Instinctively recognizing kindred spirits, I longed for the wisdom that associating with them would bring. Spiritually they had been where I was now and were lighting a path in the darkness for me to follow.

"Intuition," James Hillman writes in *The Soul's Code*, "is a clear, quick and full apprehension." We all need mentors, and intuitively I recognized that these four people were to be mine. They were to teach me to see mythically, to transform each painful experience into a meaningful, one by showing me how to respond to it symbolically. This, I am now convinced, is what we must all do so that another Reality can enter and transform our consciousness. For, as I was gradually to discover during the many months that these conversations took place, it is only by renewing ourselves imaginatively that we can hope to heal ourselves and finally cease our ravaging of the planet.

THE FORSAKEN GARDEN

IN AN essay entitled *Life Lived Backwards*, Jungian analyst James Hillman expresses his belief that within each of us there exists a *daimon*, or guiding spirit. This daimon, or "seed image" of what we have in our hearts to become, may not actually surface into our consciousness until we are near the end of our lives, although it has always been present in our imaginations. Then, when we look back, we may suddenly recognize it as the drive that "inhabited us" from the beginning which we have spent our lives unconsciously actualizing. As James Hillman says: "The oak lies in the acorn."

The daimon that inhabits us speaks to us through our fantasies. It lives in the world of our dreams and our imaginings, and we hear its voice in our moments of creativity. We really are "such stuff as dreams are made on." Our responsibility to life is to befriend these soul images, so that through them we may piece together a picture of what is moving through our psyches as the "primary determinant" of our lives.

One "seed image" for me lies in the heart of "the forsaken garden." My childhood memories are replete with lush gardens—gardens in which I played, or hid, or danced—gardens, in a word, in which I was ensouled. Since then gardens, whether in the form of pristine wilderness or cultivated plots, have provided the rich soil that has nourished my spirit and fueled my creativity.

My dreams, however, often tell a different story about gardens than my memories of them. Replete with images of ruined landscapes, and dismembered plants and animals, they seem to speak out of what today's ecopsychologists call "the ecological unconscious." With its source in the collective unconscious, this disturbing imagery carries within it the germ of a healing alternative to our present treatment of the Earth. Deeply rooted in our earliest experiences as humans on this planet, the ecological unconscious addresses our deepest concerns about the state of our reciprocal relationship with the natural environment.

Because my health was threatened by my polluted urban surroundings,

I began to see my disease as an opportunity to warn others of the danger we all face if we continue to contaminate the planet. It was as though my daimon had spoken in the most urgent way of the need for me to protest our present-day poisoning of the natural world.

The documentary films I had been making for the CBC before I became ill were biographies of artists and naturalists—men and women who, through their close aesthetic and spiritual ties to the wilderness, had indirectly protested the devastation of nature. Although I was no longer making films, I believed it was now my task to continue to explore those themes. Above all, I wanted to understand the psychological and spiritual determinants which lay at the root of our destruction of the Earth.

Intuitively I knew that I could only bring the "seed image" in my heart to fruition by listening to what my soul was saying to me through my symptoms. Aside from my physical problems, the aspect of my illness which troubled me the most was a profound sense of depression and loss. It nevertheless took me some time to realize that part of my ill health was due to my grief over what was happening to the planet. Through our contamination of the Earth we had "forsaken the garden"—causing untold suffering to its creatures, its soil, its waters, and its vegetation. We humans had betrayed and devastated a beloved organism that had not only given us life, but had generously nourished and supported us in that life.

My main anxiety about our troubled times was that our failure to protest the despoliation of the Earth had placed us in serious spiritual danger because we were all ensouled within the body of the Earth. For some time I had suffered from a sense of soul abandonment—of life having lost its meaning. My fear was that collectively we had allowed a state of separation to occur between what Laurens van der Post called "our small selves and our large Selves." We had then projected our Self-alienation onto the Earth, and were abusing her as a way of venting our sense of frustration and loss. In order to become "whole" again, we therefore had to commit ourselves not only to our own personal inner journeys, but also to the greater community of beings with whom we share the environment.

One worrisome aspect of my illness was a parasitic infection which seemed impossible to eradicate. I wondered if there was some connection between its persistent presence in my body and the multiplying numbers of humans now feeding off the body of the Earth. Then one day I came across this statement in an article about how Mother Earth is apparently utilizing killer viruses to cope with this problem.

> It is almost as if Mother Earth recognizes the human species as a threat to her well being, and her immune response is to cleanse herself of this parasite.[1]

Through my illness I could imagine how Mother Earth—Gaia—must feel with a parasitic scourge like ourselves draining all the life out of her. Interconnected as we are in the bodysoul of this planet, decimation of any part of the Earth is picked up by those who are sensitive to her suffering. The increasing number of people today who are being made ill by our sick planet bears witness to the fact that Gaia is issuing her warnings through us.

For a long time the scientific community has been alerting us to the consequences of our continuous abuse of the planet. Perhaps we don't care if we self-destruct. Perhaps we are so caught up in denial that we no longer think about what kind of world we are passing on to our children. Here is what one prominent American scientist has said about the prospects for the future of life on Earth:

> We've created chemicals now that go into the body, that go right into the center of the cell and end up in the DNA—and they latch onto the DNA and disrupt its functioning. There are 70,000 commercially marketed chemicals, and every year we add another 1,000. How many of these are actually tested? Very, very few. . . . The damage done to the DNA by these chemicals is permanent. You can't wash them off, you can't get at them—they're in the center of people, and they will be carried by the human race for a very long time. Serious birth defects have doubled in the last twenty-five years and the worst won't begin showing up for twenty years. This is what we're passing on to future generations.

> If you take one DNA molecule from everyone who ever lived in the whole planet—all the way back—and add them all together, do you know how big that is? It's one tear drop—eighty billion DNA molecules add up to one drop. Everything that's going to happen to humans in the future depends on the quality of that drop . . . and we're sprinkling genetic toxins into it. Two hundred

and sixty-four million tons of hazardous waste is what we in the United States are sprinkling into the gene pool—into the center of life—every year.[2]

The connection between soul abandonment and our destruction of life on the planet is complex, but perhaps it is best summed up in the image of that one tear drop—an image which reflects better than any words the incredible pathos which lies at the heart of modern life. If we damage that "center of life," the idea that there will be any sanctity or holiness left is wishful thinking. For as Thomas Berry points out, such deep feelings cannot be aroused in genetically defective humans. A "forsaken garden" is a desolate prospect because with it goes all hope of divine presence on the planet. As we destroy species after species, their total disappearance is irrevocable—we can never get them back. Then one day when all the grizzlies have disappeared—and all the whales, and all the song birds—and we are left in solitude to reign over what's left of life on Earth, will we finally have the humility to shed that one tear for what we have done?

One thing which the four people interviewed in this book have in common is that each has experienced the devastation of the second half of the twentieth century; each has endured harrowing events during their lifetime. But like Jonah in the belly of the whale, not only have they learned something from their trials, but "the belly" has turned out to be the belly of the Great Mother from which they were born again.

In certain cultures the Great Mother is called Kali, the Goddess who destroys life in order to create it anew. Each person interviewed here has been through his or her own process of destruction and re-creation, forging a new paradigm as a result: a new paradigm that Laurens van der Post found in the devastation of the Bushman in South Africa; that Marion Woodman realized in her encounter with the feminine; that Ross Woodman discovered in his meeting with William Blake; that Thomas Berry learned in his confrontation with life as an endangered species. Each of them has emerged from these experiences with a vision of life that, far from being ethereal, is profoundly grounded and therefore accessible to everyone born on this planet at this time.

Cosmologist Brian Swimme points out that nature in its evolution is "everything: gentle, violent, unpredictable." This could also be a description of our psyche's striving for growth which is also "gentle, violent, unpredictable"—and persistent, no matter how painful that may be for us personally. The journeys to consciousness which the people in this book have all taken can be seen as microcosms of the macrocosm in which all things push to come into greater awareness. They are expressions of what Laurens van der Post calls "the quest for wholeness." The dedication required for such an undertaking calls for an attitude that is both humble and reverent before the awesome reality of the psyche within, and the world of nature without. It demands that we consciously sacrifice *hubris*, which in this century has led us to misappropriate the powers of the gods in our attempts to control both our own and the Earth's destinies. Perhaps straightening out the mess we have made of the planet will be the final chance we have to act, not as gods, but as the humans that we are.

For each person in this book, our destruction of life on the planet constitutes the epitome of Supreme Evil. Every major extinction in the 4.5 billion years of the Earth's history has been because Nature, or God, or whatever we call the intelligence behind the creation of the universe, ordained it. This is the first time *we* have had the power to decree it. We may have been "brought up to be gods" as Marion Woodman says. But she also emphasizes that we are not gods, and in exceeding our proper human limitations we can only invite what the Greeks called *nemesis*, or retribution.

> There are unseen barriers which man who has *aidos* (reverence) in him does not wish to pass. *Hubris* passes them all. . . . *Hubris* is the insolence of irreverence: the brutality of strength. . . . nearly always it is the sin of the strong and the proud. It is born of *Koros*, or satiety—of "being too well off," and it spurns the weak and the helpless out of its path.[3]

Our exit from the mythical Garden of Eden may be interpreted as a splitting off of ourselves from any conscious sense of intimacy with matter, with the physical world. The reality is that our separation from nature has taken us into a connection with a transcendent Father-God that has nothing to do with our roots—either in the natural world, or in our own bodies and souls. For hundreds of years we have been sheltered by the security of that paternal relationship, but today the projection of a Creator onto an omnipotent father figure has died for many people. There's "Nobodaddy aloft," says William Blake.

This is not to say that, like the French philosopher Jean Jacques Rousseau, we should yearn for a return to a natural paradise in which we can vegetate in blissful unconsciousness. The struggle to consciously resolve the conflicts that arise in life due to the tension of opposites—love and hate, good and evil, pleasure and pain—is what matures us as human beings. To that end, many of us today are taking our first steps into a mature relationship with the divinities—and the devils—that rule our physical and psychic lives.

A major concern of all the participants in this book is how the planetary crisis in which we find ourselves is critically linked to our neglect of the feminine principle. "The forsaken garden" itself refers to both our abandoned feminine souls and the abandoned Earth. A garden is a living protest on behalf of Gaia against the psychic encroachments of a patriarchal and driven society. The struggle we face today is the need to reclaim our places in the natural world away from the alienated state which the values of our technological world have imposed upon us. The sundering that began with Descartes' separation of mind from body three hundred years ago continues today in our culture's failure to have any intimacy with nature beyond our button-pushing compulsion to control it. This excessive interference with the external world then creates chaos and anxiety in our inner worlds, because macrocosm and microcosm are so closely intertwined.

We have reached a point in our planetary crisis where what William Blake called the "mind-forg'd manacles," which still have a hold over our consciousness, must be broken. For it is they which prevent us from living our own authentic lives, and from protesting the rape of the environment:

> The great industrial armies, the technological systems must be hobbled in their runaway career. . . . Gaia speaks to that within each of us that wishes to be known peculiarly and personally. . . . This "song of myself" may be no more than a brief discordant tune. But sung by a sufficient number, it is enough to halt the rhythm of the great machine. In that moment we become what Charlie Chaplin's little victim-hero became in *Modern Times* when, falling out of synch on the assembly line, he wound up jamming the man-eating gears. In becoming even a small piece of ourselves, we become what the burdened planet needs: creatures with some more urgent calling, some greater joy than comes of waging war upon nature.[4]

If we are to believe William Blake that the route to our souls is through our senses, then a garden must be one of the most soulful places on earth. Where else do birds and insects, plants and mammals, congregate in such gorgeous profusion? In what other place can our senses be so rapturously engaged? To "forsake the garden" is not only to forfeit our own souls, but to forsake life itself. If we are to *survive*, a return to intimacy with the Earth and its creatures and to a celebration of the cosmos beyond, is imperative.

NOTES

[1] Brad Hunter, *The Family News*, Vol. 6, No. 11, Miami Shores: Family News Inc., 1995, p. 8.

[2] Brian Swimme, *Canticle to the Cosmos* (video), San Francisco: Tides Center, 1990, #12: *A New Prosperity.*

[3] Gilbert Murray, *The Rise of the Greek Epic*, in Edward Edinger, *Ego and Archetype*, New York: Penguin Books, 1973, p. 31.

[4] Theodore Roszak, *The Voice Of The Earth*, New York: Simon & Schuster, 1992, p. 278.

PART ONE

REDEEMING THE WASTELAND

"The war that has to be won, if another cataclysm of the world is to be prevented, is the insidious war of the mind and spirit."

LAURENS VAN DER POST

INTRODUCTION

LOSS OF SOUL

THE FIRST interview that I did for this book was with Laurens van der Post, author and chronicler of the life of the South African Bushman, and close personal friend of C. G. Jung. During our conversations, I was struck by his repetition of a phrase he used in his book *The Heart of the Hunter* to describe a spiritual malaise known to the Bushman. He called it "loss of soul," a phrase which also describes the sense of alienation which many of us keenly feel in our own time.

> The situation which I believe we are all facing in the world today is one which the primitive world, the past life of Africa, knew only too well. It is a loss of first spirit, or to put it in the old-fashioned way, a loss of soul. . . . This is the greatest calamity that could come to human beings, and the keepers of man's first spirit in Africa constantly warned against this peril. Indeed, the primitive world regarded the preservation of first spirit as the greatest, most urgent of all its tasks. It designed elaborate ritual, ceaselessly fashioned myths, legends, stories, and music, to contain the meaning and feed the fire of the creative soul.[1]

For some time I had felt at odds with the emphasis on materialistic values and the lack of meaning in my own life and in the life of my society. The phrase "loss of soul" perfectly described my own feelings of estrangement from any kind of transcendent values in our difficult times.

The necessity to reclaim my own "lost soul" through a journey to the center of my being came out of my need to deal with a disease that was consuming more and more of my life. Apart from my depression over what was happening to the planet, how was I to deal with my grief over the loss of many

15

precious years to this illness? How was I to reconcile myself to the premature end of my career, to the alienation that I felt from most people—nearly all of whom seemed either baffled, or indifferent, and in some cases really threatened—by what I was experiencing? One day I was out in the world, doing what I loved most, making films. The next day I was trying desperately to cope with adverse reactions to every morsel of food and sip of liquid that I put into my mouth. Where was I going to find the strength I needed to cope with this unprecedented feeling of vulnerability?

I have never been a religious person in any orthodox sense, so I had to turn to other sources for help. I have always loved to read and had often turned to the inspiring, soulful books of Laurens van der Post. One day I picked up his book *About Blady* in which he discussed the "privilege" of illness. Our afflictions, he said, can be our greatest gifts if we can accept them as indicators of our need for some kind of inner transformation. At first I thought what Laurens van der Post was saying was utterly masochistic—I certainly did not consider it a "privilege" to have environmental illness! Gradually, however, I began to see how this illness could transform my life by teaching me things I badly needed to know.

And so, like taking the sea journey which he describes in so many of his books as a metaphor for his own journey of self-discovery, I began to cling to the life-raft of my dreams, and faithfully record and work with them. In this way, I was able to plumb the depths of my psyche as I struggled to find a port in this particular storm. In my spiritual isolation, my journals became a repository for drawings and writings in which my soul's story was revealed.

Dreams, Laurens van der Post told me, link the divine guide within to the sacred Source without. One night I had a very important dream about him, which would ultimately change my life.

I am approaching Laurens van der Post. He is standing, beckoning to me, surrounded by a kind of eerie gray mist. It's a very beautiful image, as though he were in another world. I think to myself that I'd like to capture that image, and more images like it, on film. Finally I come into his presence. I think we're in a church. It's very modern—somewhat plain, and filled with simple wooden benches. The room is bright. There's a priest there too, dressed in ordinary clothes. Laurens van der Post and I finally meet, and he asks me what I want to do in this film. I tell him that I want to put his ideas into simple terms. He seems really interested in this idea.

What I believed this dream was saying to me was that the numinous images surrounding Laurens van der Post were ones I needed to work with in film; in other words, I needed to "project" them in some creative way into my life. This made such an impression on me that I decided that it was important for me to make every attempt to meet this man. Through a friend who knew us both, an introduction was arranged. Shortly afterward—armed for the trip with medications and a filter mask—I packed a supply of the foods that I could eat into a small suitcase and flew to London, England, where he lived. After all, other people—particularly native people—crossed continents and came halfway around the world to meet him. Why shouldn't I?

I'm not usually so impulsive, and I really couldn't afford this trip with all the medical bills piling up to be paid, but I knew it was vitally important for my soul's sake to meet this remarkable man. As it turned out, our meeting was auspicious. The interview we did together on that occasion became the first of a series of conversations for what would eventually become this book.

It was a memorable meeting for me for another reason: Laurens van der Post, through his writings, had already become an important soul-guide for me. To put his ideas "into simple terms" meant that my psyche was pointing out how important it was for me to understand the *essence* of this man's life. In a life full of outer adventure, the inner adventure—the tracking of his own "lost self"—had been the real one. I suspected that through the dream my psyche was preparing me for the sacrifices I too would have to make in order to live in a more spiritually conscious way.

Laurens van der Post was a vitally important model for me of how to do this, but so was Thomas Berry, whom I did not know at the time I had my dream. As this book unfolded I became convinced that the unconscious—so awesome in its ability to know our deepest needs—had presented me with another soul-guide in the unidentified figure of "the priest in ordinary clothes." Later on, Thomas Berry, a priest of endearing informality and writer of several books linking our spiritual lives to that of the environment's, joined Laurens van der Post as a contributor to this book, and as a major spiritual influence in my life.

Laurens van der Post was born in South Africa in 1906 and grew up on a farm in the Orange Free State. Author, explorer, film-maker, journalist, soldier, philosopher, and conservationist, inherent in all of his pursuits was an intense interest in what his close friend C. G. Jung called "modern man in search of a soul."

From early childhood, Laurens van der Post had felt a loving responsibility for the indigenous people of South Africa, who had the earliest understanding of the natural world around them, and who were his first teachers. In the 1950s, through a series of television documentaries on the Bushmen of the Kalahari Desert, he began his efforts to save these people from extinction. His films attracted an audience in England second in size only to that of the coronation of Queen Elizabeth II. Along with his books, in particular *The Lost World of the Kalahari* and *Testament to the Bushman*, they constitute an invaluable record of a vanished, prehistoric way of life.

Today the Bushman culture that Laurens van der Post championed has been submerged under the wash of "civilization." For the rest of his life, he mourned this loss of an older and deeply sacred way of life—a way of life that he felt held profound significance for our own spiritually impoverished day.

> The one outstanding characteristic of these people as I knew them, and which distinguished them from us, was that wherever they went, they felt they were known. The staggering loss of identity and meaning that we in the modern world experience was unknown to them. . . . This sense of being known has completely abandoned us in the modern world, because we have destroyed the wilderness persons in ourselves and banished the wilderness that sustained them from our lives.[2]

> There is a great lost world to be rediscovered and rebuilt, not in the Kalahari but in the wasteland of our spirit where we have driven the first things of life, as we have driven the little Bushman into the desert of southern Africa. There is indeed a cruelly denied and neglected first child of life, a Bushman in each of us.[3]

The journey that Laurens van der Post took in search of the Bushman was really a quest to find the lost soul of civilized man. There was a "wilderness man," an instinctive man in all of us, that we had lost. The loss of the real Bushman was also a tragedy for us because he was a "bridge to knowing wilderness and nature in the way in which it is known by the Creator and in which it really should be known."[4] For until the second half of this century the Bushman, like the indigenous plants and animals of his native Africa, was still living in the Garden. Contaminated as we civilized twentieth-century men and women have become by our own hubris, such completeness could only come to us in our dreams. Separated from our instinctive roots in the natural world, we share the grief that Laurens van der Post expresses for what we have lost:

> Less and less [does contemporary man] experience the process within. Less and less is he capable of committing himself body and soul to the creative experiment that is continually seeking to fire him and charge his little life with great objective meaning. Cut off by accumulated knowledge from the heart of his own living experience, he moves among a comfortable rubble of material possessions, alone and unbelonging, sick, poor, starved of meaning.

> How different the naked little Bushman, who could carry all he possessed in one hand. Whatever his life lacked, I never felt it was meaning. Meaning for him died only when we bent him to our bright twentieth-century will. Otherwise, he was rich where we were poor; he walked clear-cut through my mind, clothed in his own vivid experience of the dream of life within him. By comparison most of the people I saw on my way to the sea were blurred, and like the knights at arms in Keats' frightening allegory, "palely loitering" through life.[5]

To primitive peoples, "loss of soul" meant not only a loss of containment by one's group or tribe, it also meant a separation of one's being from the Great Powers that created and sustained the universe. Consequently, it meant a loss of one's Self because one's identity could only be found within that larger context. In Jungian terminology, "loss of soul" means a loss of connection between the ego and its larger container, the realm of the archetypes in the collective unconscious. In other words, it's a loss of contact with the numinous symbolic forms (Great Powers) both in the psyche and in the universe, which are the Source of our being and which give our lives depth and meaning. Both explanations, in essence, are saying the same thing. The South African Bushman believes "loss of soul" to be a catastrophe, and so should we.

Laurens van der Post's meeting with C. G. Jung served as a further stimulus to his pursuit of an understanding of what he often called "the life of our time." As their friendship grew, the emphasis he had placed on the importance of the soul's journey deepened.

> For me, a new phase in the life of our time began when Jung climbed the mountains and explored the valleys of the unconscious within modern man. He realized how much we had lost by neglecting our inner world—how dangerously one-sided we had become in ignoring our intuitive sides.[6]

> The great mystery of life, however, is not the existence of an unconscious, but of consciousness, and what it is in the unconscious that perennially seeks greater consciousness. It is just a fact that consciousness constantly enlarges itself, and the problem for us is that the more consciousness is enlarged, the greater our responsibility to life and the universe becomes. That is why many people shrink from it; that is why many like to be lost in the crowd—mind, identity and all—because then they have not got to carry this burden of individual responsibility.[7]

Laurens van der Post's own journey into consciousness is revealed in the more than twenty-five books he wrote, all of which attest to the remarkable odyssey he took during his lifetime. Like the earliest myths of the hero, many of his books describe a journey to a far-off place or distant land, such as the hinterland of Africa, or the steppes of Russia. Such exotic and mysterious landscapes are metaphors for the interior quest, for as he himself describes it:

> The journey itself is not a mere changing of place, an exchange of geographical locations, but a change of being, a becoming, the task indeed of traveling from the familiar being a person receives from his parents, to the distant being he has neither known nor seen in this invisible dimension of the spirit. . . . [It] begins with a state of being that we know, and the inadequacy of this state of being is symbolized by the trials and persecutions, the years in bondage or captivity in the physical world to which it is subjected.[8]

Some of the trials of his own journey included his life as a journalist in South Africa in the 1920s. There he documented abuses by the Afrikaans police against black South Africans in some of the first anti-Apartheid articles ever printed in that country. Later books describe the three and a half years during World War II that he spent in a prisoner-of-war camp in Java. As a colonel in charge of six thousand men, he both taught and lived out his philosophy of compassion and forgiveness towards his Japanese captors and tormentors. His courageous stance influenced the whole camp to such an extent that even today he is remembered with veneration by the men who were incarcerated with him. Several credit him with saving their lives—both psychically and physically.

Many of Laurens van der Post's books about this period predict the collective racial and nihilistic shadow which has fallen across the latter half of this century. In his later work, he focused again and again on how unawareness of these unconscious elements in ourselves has enabled them to become such spiritually destructive forces in our time.

Following the war, Laurens van der Post returned to active service in Indonesia on the staff of Lord Louis Mountbatten, after which he received a CBE (Commander of the British Empire) for services rendered in the field. He was knighted in 1981.

I talked to Laurens van der Post in his flat in Chelsea in London in 1993, and we remained in touch with one another until his death in December, 1996.

Chapter One

What Ails Thee?

NANCY RYLEY: Sir Laurens, many people today are very worried about the breakdown and emptiness in our society and our civilization. To what do you attribute the demoralization and spiritual bankruptcy of contemporary life?

LAURENS VAN DER POST: Well, it's always a terribly difficult question to answer, because I think all societies at all times are in a process of becoming, and transition, and of changing their character. And certain aspects of them need to be discarded because they're wasteful. So I don't think it's all breakdown and all demoralization, what's happening.

But there are certain areas of life—compared to what one reads about in other moments in history—which are peculiarly of our own time. We're facing a very new phenomenon which, at its worst, could be called demoralization, of which every nation is partaking at the moment. I think this is the first time that one knows of in history where the whole world is gripped by some kind of crisis. There is not a society which is not, in a sense, being found wanting by very large numbers, sometimes by all the people who participate in that society. And it applies to all cultures, that's the interesting thing. It doesn't matter whether it's a totalitarian country, or whether it's what we call a democracy, or whether it's a country like China, which is a formidable reality on its own. It affects the whole of Southeast Asia. It affects primitive societies. It's in Africa. It's in South America. It's everywhere. This is the crisis. And one would almost think it's in the nature of time.

And so there's a great challenge being thrown out at life—all life in a sense is inadequate in the form in which it expresses itself at the moment. There's a challenge to renew ourselves, to express human society, human beings' contribution to life, in a totally new way. And very often one fails this challenge. The little I know of the past, of the histories of civilizations, they've all ultimately collapsed because they could not renew themselves in a greater aspect of themselves.

NR: Why do you think that we're unable to renew ourselves in order to rise above our current spiritual malaise?

LvDP: Well, I think life is always reaching out into new areas of itself. It doesn't stand still. Creation is not repetitive; it's always moving, moving, moving on into larger aspects of creation and of meaning. But in this there are certain areas, I think, in which Western civilization has progressively failed itself. That is, it's become lopsided. Instead of broadening the basis of consciousness, it has narrowed the basis of consciousness.

Ever since the Renaissance, Western civilization seems to have been singularly extroverted. Its focus has been singularly projected onto the external world. You might say that the Middle Ages, the medieval world, was perhaps too introverted and that life went over into its opposite. Burckhardt, the great historian of the Renaissance, said that the moment the Renaissance began was when the poet Petrarch climbed a mountain in the Alps just for the sake of climbing it. Up to that moment people hadn't gone to the tops of mountains. They thought they were inhabited with monsters, and they weren't interested in them. But suddenly this feeling came in Petrarch, the great poet, that he had to go to the top of that mountain. And that was a sign that man was sort of coming out of himself, and that he had started to feel the challenge of his physical environment, which up until then had been shirked.

All that became a subject of research, of science. The physical world, matter—which had had, of course, a profound basis laid for it already by the alchemists and the Greeks—had been neglected. Suddenly this became the thing, the rational approach to life—extroverted, materialistic society, backed up by an enlargement of man's rational self.

And so, over time, man immeasurably increased his power in the material world. But the result has been that our societies have become infinitely more brutalized. They've became more interested in and corrupted by technological power. Today man can go to the moon, but he can also destroy forests; he can devastate the Earth. In a week he can do more of that than people did in the two thousand years before.

We've got that sort of power, but there is also this abuse in every one of us—we participate in sheer power values. There is this hubris which I think is threatening us at this moment. But the greater the power, the more important to be aware of the power, and the more one's obligation to see that the power is not abused.

I think that in the process the instinctive world, the natural world within us, instead of becoming a partner, as it were, and giving us values and a greater sense of the importance of the "whole" to correct this power of hubris, has been singularly neglected. And, in a sense, it has made an enemy of man in his searching.

NR: Do you think that by becoming too narrowly focused in our approach to life that we are corrupting ourselves in some way?

LvDP: You know, Shakespeare—I think in *Measure for Measure*—says it's excellent to have the strength of a giant but how awful to use it like a giant. He suddenly discovers this giant in himself, and also the gentleness and the love and the caring to not use it like a giant. Because this is there too. All these things are provided for in the whole of the man.

But our trouble, and our decadence if you like, our corruption, comes because we use a part of ourselves as if it were the whole, instead of using the part to discover the whole.

You know, the old-fashioned definition of madness in the human being was a basis of consciousness so narrow and so small and restricted that it could not contain all these energies that were coming from the unconscious and that demanded to be expressed. And this is what our societies are doing. They've narrowed the values, the consciousness, the other awareness we need to contain these immense energies which human beings have. And this, I think, is what is blowing us apart.

NR: But the aim of science and technology has been to better people's lot, by removing some of the physical burdens from existence. Is our increased physical well-being reflected in our increased spiritual well-being in any way, do you think?

LvDP: Well, it's true that physically, men and women have never been more secure. We live twice as long as people did in Shakespeare's time. We live in greater comfort and in that regard we are singularly blessed. And yet inside ourselves we've never felt more insecure. People feel lost and people aren't happy. They rush about madly. So I think one must look at this very seriously.

Of course there are people who do look at this seriously; artists in particular are aware of this. But even art has been infected, it seems to me, by a sense of demoralization, because people increasingly try to present art as "idea." But it's much more than that. We're living in a sort of moment, I expect, where everybody's a little Descartes who says, "I think, therefore I am." And the Pascal side of people particularly, you see, has been thrown out of the window.

NR: What do you think has been the effect of this narrowed focusing of our consciousness on the spiritual lives of men and women?

LvdP: Well, one result is that all the transcendent values have vanished from life. There is no authoritative spiritual backup for what we are doing. The institutions which a century or more ago still gave us a sense of transcendent value—a value which corrected the hubris, which transcended the clash of the opposites—have lost their authority, have lost their world. The churches, for instance, no longer play the role in the lives of people that they did. Less and less do they stimulate our search for meaning, which is what religion is really about. It's about values. It's about ultimate values. There is no social help for us in our need of these things, and I think it's in this area that we must look for what you, in your question, called the sources of demoralization and spiritual bankruptcy, because we are singularly alone.

NR: Sir Laurens, are you saying that what we're experiencing in our culture is a collective loss of soul?

LvdP: Well yes, I think modern man, in a sense, has lost his soul or is losing his soul. But science and people don't want to talk about souls and things like that because they can't measure them, and they can't even define them. Yet there is a tendency for people to think that the only things that matter in life are the things that can be rationally expressed in words, that only what you are capable of articulating has meaning—which, of course, is nonsense because consciousness in the human being is not just rational. There's enormous non-rational input which comes from our feelings, from our senses, from our instincts. But we have become estranged from that.

NR: In an effort to make us more aware of what is needed to balance our over-rational, over-materialistic view of life, you have written about the importance of feminine consciousness in our lives. What do you mean by that?

LvdP: Well, this is the unacknowledged side of life, of ourselves, which is knocking on the door more and more urgently, asking to be let in. These are the feeling, the caring, the loving values of life which are all locked out.

What we want to do is bring up both sides—the spiritual side, the transcendent side we were talking about, and the feeling or feminine side—and contain them, in order to be whole. We have a sense of wholeness but we don't live in a way which will acknowledge it. We know how one-sided we are. What is depraved is not doing anything about it.

So we must discipline that part of ourselves, and recognize that what we're doing at the moment is not the whole story. It's at the most half of it; there's the other half—it has another partner. I think it's the feminine half in us which must be acknowledged and brought into the light of day.

NR: The Bushmen, among whom you grew up in South Africa, and who have been the subjects—and even the heroes—of so many of your books, seem to have had a great sense of what was meaningful in existence that we have lost—particularly the importance of feminine values. What can we learn from these people about how to reclaim our forsaken souls?

LvdP: Well, the Bushmen have their natural contacts with their souls intact. They have not got the power that we have over our environment—they haven't got *that* sort of power—but they have souls, and the soul has its communication with the consciousness of the human being through our instincts. Our instincts all taken, pulled together, are a vast storehouse of memory of all that life has been and what life means. And the Bushmen have a very close contact with their instincts. Perhaps their danger is that they project too much of the world within onto the world without. They haven't got enough sense of the validity of the world without in its own right—the extent to which the soul, the inner world, must acknowledge the validity of the outer. They may not have enough of that, but they don't lack meaning, ever. And the most serious thing for them would be to lose this once-upon-a-time thing which is the story, their own story, which comes in their dreams and in their instincts.

NR: Is there a Bushman story that would have particular meaning for contemporary people—a story which would illustrate our loss of soul today?

LvdP: Oh yes, well, there is one story; it's not really a pure Bushman story, but a story of the people who are very close to the Bushman. It's a Hottentot story, but the Bushmen know it as well.

> *There once was a man who had this wonderful herd of black and white cattle and lived in a clearing in a great forest, a very dark forest. And he cared a great deal for his cattle. And he looked after them very well. He always put them into a* kraal, *a corral, at night, and saw that they were well-guarded and protected.*
>
> *One morning he went to milk his cattle as usual, but they had no milk. And he was astounded. So he thought, "Well, I must see that they have proper grazing today." He thought something was wrong with the grazing. So he took them to the best grazing that he could possibly find, and saw that they were eating contentedly, and that they grazed happily all day long, and in the evening brought them home. He thought that now surely they would give a lot of milk the next day. And again the next day they were milked—but still they had no milk.*
>
> *Then, he thought, "There's something very strange going on; I know what I'll do." And he brought his cattle into the kraal where he sat up to watch by them all through the night.*
>
> *He waited and watched—and finally about midnight, to his amazement, he suddenly saw that a rope had come down from the stars and that a lot of rather lovely young girls were sliding down the rope. And the moment they got on the Earth they made for his cattle, carrying little milking containers under their arms.*
>
> *Then he knew what had happened and furiously he ran after the girls. They immediately scattered and shot up this rope into the sky, but he caught one of them by the ankle and pulled her down.*
>
> *The story says she was the most beautiful one of all the girls. And he*

took her and she became his wife and lived with him.

Now his wife had her container with her. But she had the lid firmly clapped on it.

And she said, "Look, I shall happily live with you. But you must promise me you will never take this lid off and look in the container. And that you will leave it standing right where I put it."

And he promised her. So it was kept in a corner of their hut and he never touched it.

But one day, in the heat of the day, while his wife was out working in the fields, he came back from the hunt, terribly thirsty, and he went into the hut to drink some water.

He saw the container standing there and he said to himself, "There's that silly container standing there. Really, this is nonsense, why should I not look into it?"

Towards evening his wife came back and she gave him one look and she said, "You've looked in the container."

And he said, "Yes, I have. But you silly woman, why have you always made such a fuss about the container when there is nothing in it?"

And she said: "Nothing?"

And he said: "No, nothing."

At that she gave him a very sad look, turned about, and walked away. She vanished into the sunset, and was never seen on the Earth again.

I said to my old Bushman nurse who told me this story when I was a little boy, "But this is a terrible thing for the man to do, why did he do a thing like that?"

"Well, men are curious," she said. "But the woman would have understood that; she didn't mind really about that so much. What she did mind was that, looking into the container, the man could not see in the container the things that the woman had brought from the stars with her. That's why she vanished."

Now this is really our plight. It's a story I tell because I say this is where we are. We have a container like that in us. It's the feminine side of the human spirit which is the link, certainly in men, with the soul, with the psyche. The psyche is always represented as feminine in the man. And we see nothing in it; we say it's only a dream. But a dream is a container of what comes from the stars, and we find nothing in it. So this is a great image, a great story of what's wrong. This is why we're in the plight that we're in. There's something in ourselves that we have, and that we must look at, and we'll find it full of exactly what we need.

So that is a story of the wisdom of life, of shared living, which was passed on from generation to generation among those early peoples.

NR: Sir Laurens, you yourself are a writer—a teller of stories. You have said that every person must find and live out his or her own "story" in order for the person's life to have meaning. Are you saying that we can find our souls in stories?

LvdP: Oh yes, I do say that. Every child knows the need for a story; every child is born with a feeling of once-upon-a-time. It's this once-upon-a-time emotion which is where the Source is; that's where we came from. It's that once-upon-a-time feeling, whether it's a fairy tale or not, which links us with all the feelings that we set out with on the journey, to the time in the here and now, to the time into the future. So the story maintains in us the once-upon-a-time reality that we need in order to do the journey in its entirety.

But there is a tremendous decline in modern literature. There are no real stories; at least I find I lack them. There is this terrible kind of realism that people throw at you instead of stories, but stories have a magic in them. A really good story is magical, and even in ordinary life a person can tell good stories about what happened in the day. He can see the story pattern all around him and every day he knows is full of stories.

This sense of the story in all of us links us up with the great story of the universe. We need stories all the time to give us a sense of direction in our lives. Primitive people knew this terribly well; their most important possession was the story.

NR: The Bushman stories were the first stories that you heard as a child growing up in South Africa. Why are their stories particularly important for you?

LvdP: Well, those stories are important for me because they are the oldest stories to which we have access. The Bushman is the oldest form of humanity still alive in our midst, so their stories are tremendously important. The surprising thing to me was the more I got to know about their stories, the more I saw the patterns of their stories reflected in the greatest artists and writers in the world, the greatest storytellers. So many of their stories had the same patterns, the same mythological patterns as the Greeks, for instance.

NR: Do the great stories of the world all give us similar psychological messages?

LvdP: Well yes, because they are outpourings of the human soul. They give pointers and directions. They're all part of the living reality of the soul, which is the sense of a tremendous story in which one is participating.

NR: "The tremendous story in which one is participating" is the psychologically aware journey that you have described as the journey which each man and woman must take in his or her lifetime. You mentioned earlier that people rush about a lot these days, and they travel so much that tourism is now the biggest industry in the world. Is this some sort of substitute for the real thing?

LvdP: Well, that again is the extroverted side of this projection. People travel so much these days because they take travel in a literal, externalized way, and they say travel broadens the mind. Well, the way we travel today doesn't broaden the mind. It narrows the mind, which is singularly sad. The real journey to be done is inside ourselves; it's turning towards what comes out of this other world within, the world of the psyche.

NR: Tell me more about the real kind of journey that people need to take.

LvdP: Well, I think that the real journey that people need to take is to know themselves totally and wholly, as fully as they can. It's a journey into their own natures, into their own beings, into their own spirits. That kind of journey—that's what we're talking about. Because if you look at the world, really *we* are the sources of good and evil today. Mankind has never been so singularly the source of evil, and it's because we don't know ourselves. It's because we truly don't know what we're doing that we do the harm that we do. And that, I think, is a sign of great danger.

NR: Is this what's at the bottom of our destruction of nature, do you think?

LvdP: Yes. We cannot see, any of us. We're blind to the damage we're doing to the Earth. Everybody knows about it and yet people behave as if it doesn't matter. It's almost what the New Testament calls, "When the eyes do not see, and the ears do not hear." This is decadence. It's imperviousness when we have the sources of correcting, and of coming back to our proportions within us, and we do not use them.

So we must search for the truth about ourselves and the truth about life. The point is that we are the only instruments for looking at the truth; finally, we are the instruments of our own truth. And if you don't know your own truth, you can't know the truth for anybody else; you don't know how to use your instrument properly and truly. But once one takes on this task, I think people not only find new energies coming into themselves, more power coming to them; at the same time they discover a sense of the "whole" which enables them to contain that power. People have been told this. But they've been told about this rationally, and somehow they must be made to *feel* it.

Above all, people must look for the meaning in their lives. We must see those values in the container in the Bushman story that I told you. That's what we don't see. And so we've been wrong, and we've lost that side of ourselves in sheer disaster and tragedy. That's the sort of thing, roughly, that I mean; I can only express it in images. But everybody, when they think, must realize what a one-sided society we are.

You know, one talks and talks. One doesn't really want to talk of this alone, but one has to express it in so many ways because this neglect infects everything. And one feels sort of limp when people say "Do something." Well, one does one's best in every dimension of life—it's never been more important. But there's an immense revolution demanded of ourselves in our thought and our feeling if we are not going to fail our task in the world.

Just the same, I think all over the world there are people who are

beginning to know themselves and are setting the example.
It takes a long time to come, though.

CHAPTER TWO

THE JOURNEY TO WHOLENESS

NANCY RYLEY: You have been talking, Sir Laurens, about how one-sided we have become in our society, and how you feel that it is desperately important—for the sake of our survival, and the planet's survival—to rectify this. Can you tell me about some of the sources for finding balance and wholeness in our lives?

LAURENS VAN DER POST: Immediately when one talks about these things, of course, one goes into the natural sciences that have dedicated themselves to try and answer the question of what is the psyche of man. And one immediately goes into psychology. I think an enormous amount has been done in this regard of directing man to the sources of his greatest transforming energies, his greatest values.

It started with Freud's discovery of the importance of the dream. The dream world opened a gateway and it was carried on, for me most convincingly, by Jung in his great hypothesis of the collective unconscious. This archetypal world, this ancient world, has at its disposal these immense patterns of behavior and energy in the human being. Above all, it has the pattern of the Self, this area of the human being where the "I" in the human being meets the "Thou" in life. And in this area if we search, and if we look, immense numbers of transforming energies are released.

For instance, I think that is why all our efforts at conservation fail—because we exhort people. We try to do it with an act of will, and we'll never do it that way because will and exhortation work very much on the surface. Our will, thrown at all these instincts that have gone wrong, is puny. It can't work. But once we turn to this master pattern inside ourselves, which is a pattern of metamorphosis, there is nothing that cannot be transformed. There is no darkness which can't be transformed ultimately into light. As the alchemists put it, there is no lead, there is no prime matter, which can't be ultimately transformed into gold.

So we've got a natural science now of psychology, which gives us an instrument of getting to know ourselves, and correcting ourselves, and taking up our proper obligations towards power. It started with Prometheus, who brought us the fire of consciousness. You see, consciousness is something new in the history of the world; it's certainly much younger than the unconscious. And when Prometheus gave humanity consciousness he gave us a certain power over these unconscious forces. But this power has been abused, and somehow it must be redirected to what I call the master pattern in the spirit of mankind where everything is transformed.

NR: The first book I ever read by Jung is called *Modern Man in Search of a Soul.* You mentioned how Jung has given us the concept of the Self, or master pattern, as an energy from the unconscious which can transform our consciousness. Since you knew him so well, would you say that Jung himself believed that his psychology would provide answers to our modern problem of finding meaning in our lives?

LvdP: Once, towards the end of his life, I went for a walk with Jung and I had quite a set-to with him because he was so singularly depressed. Nobody has done more in the history of mankind, I think, than Jung has done to direct us to what I call these great patterns of energies that human beings have inside themselves. Yet he was complaining and saying that he had done nothing, that he'd failed in his life, that he'd not done nearly what he should have done. And I suddenly realized that people who really have done the pioneering work in this area of the psyche—of getting people to go in search of their souls again, of starting on this journey again and taking it up as the great transforming journey of their lives—they *know,* and have shown us how to do it. It's there— it's *there*—and sooner or later it will break through. But I don't think Jung realized all that he had accomplished.

NR: I gather from what you've been saying that this "master pattern" within us has an insistent voice, and whether we listen to it or not, it demands a say in our lives. What happens to those energies when we refuse to honor their messages in some conscious way?

LvdP: Well, one looks at people in the street, you know, and each human being, on his way to his office with his little briefcase and with a collar and tie neatly pressed, looks like such an ordinary person. But nobody's ordinary. That person, you see, is full of the most extraordinary powers. I mean every human being is a potential atom bomb; yes, they are. That's why the atom is such a profoundly symbolic and mythological thing. Each person ultimately can blow up his or her own world. We see it happening all the time through the violence that breaks out. And this violence, to a great extent, breaks out because it comes from energy. Energy must go somewhere, and there are tremendous energies in the human spirit that are not employed. If they can't come out by fair means, conscious means, then they come by foul.

NR: Jung talked about the pairs of opposites which we experience in life—love and hate, revenge and forgiveness, and so forth. He said that when people live out one to the exclusion of the other, then we have to look for its opposite to come out unconsciously in a negative way. Does this mean that our greed, our lust for power, our brutality towards the planet, could be unconscious responses to our conscious attitude of joyless rationality as a culture? Are we, as a civilization, destroying ourselves from within by our unawareness of the unconscious energies that are driving us?

LvdP: Yes, that's what's happening, in a sense, in the world today. You see, there's this craving for drugs. It's an extraordinary thing, the way it's come into the world on a scale which we've never, never seen before, and it's all these forces stirring and coming out. Instead of coming out in a fair way, they're coming out illegitimately, because we will not let them come consciously and be part of our values and awareness.

NR: You said that whole civilizations in the past have disappeared because collectively they refused to recognize and contain their dark side.

LvdP: Well yes, certainly, because they couldn't renew themselves. They became repetitive and they became caught up in power struggles.

If you read Euripides' *Bacchae*—the coming of Bacchus in the ancient world—you see that there was a tremendous stirring of all the energies in a neglected area of the great civilization of Thebes at the time. Thebes was a tremendously powerful and great empire. Then there came this stirring of the underworld. But people thought that the thing that would save them was corrupting them, and so the king of Thebes did all that he could to stamp it out. The more the followers of Bacchus appeared in his midst, the more he said more law and order was needed. The whole thing—the coming of Bacchus in the underworld—is rather like a report from a narcotics bureau somewhere today. And in the end, by just stamping on these new energies, by dealing with them rationally and willfully, the Theban king destroyed himself. Actually, he was destroyed by the women in his own family. They tore him limb from limb.

NR: But how do people live out these things in themselves in a conscious way?

LvdP: By going and discovering and honestly confronting the dark side of themselves. People have what transforms these dark aspects inside themselves, because people, ultimately, in their deepest natures, have a pattern of metamorphosis, of becoming. The universe is a process of metamorphosis where you are continually involved in an act of becoming. And between what you are and what you are about to become, it's as if Creation moves in.

It's not merely a process of cause and effect; there's an element of Creation that comes into it, and one becomes more than one even plans to become. We have these things in ourselves and it's sheer neglect that we don't pay attention, because we know now how to do it.

NR: It seems to me that people today need guidance very badly in order to learn how to bring up those new energies which you say we have neglected, and that we need in order to become whole. Where does that kind of guidance come from?

LvdP: Well, it comes from the moment you start taking your dreams seriously. And from the moment you start saying: "Well, why do I *feel* this or that?" Physically, if we're hungry we go out and look for food and find it. But we've got this other, this great hunger of the human spirit. We must go and get food for that. That is what I'm suggesting.

So we must start to dream again. We do dream, but we ignore our dreams. Every human being dreams, but people think it's just a lot of rubbish and that dreams are sort of woolly little things. They think it's just a lot of nonsense—poor creatures who have not tried it. Actually, dreams are the hardest

O hidden Life, vibrant in every atom,
O hidden Light, shining in every creature,
O hidden Love, embracing all in oneness,
May all who feel themselves as one with thee,
Know they are therefore one with every other.
— Annie Besant

Please fill out this card and send it to us if you would like a complete catalog of Quest Books on Theosophy, world spirituality, alternative healing, creativity, yoga and Eastern philosophy, transpersonal psychology, and other information.

PLEASE PRINT

Book in which this card was found _____

Name _____

Address _____

City & State _____

Zip/Postal Code _____ Country_____
(if other than U.S.)

THEOSOPHICAL SOCIETY IN AMERICA
PO BOX 270
WHEATON IL 60189-0270

taskmasters in the world. If you start living by your dreams, you're in trouble with the world straight-away. But it's the only battle worth fighting.

NR: The dream is a voice of steel?

LvdP: I say that dreams are made of steel, yes, because they come again and again until they're heeded, and if you don't heed them you perish. You lose your meaning and your real life. A life that can be joyful and creative abandons you, unless there's an element of the dream in you. It's always there, always there.

NR: Following in the direction of one's dreams is a very challenging task, though.

LvdP: Well, yes, it is. Even the Bushman in the desert said to me, "It's really difficult, you see, because there's a dream dreaming us." They know it; all the great artists know it, you know.

NR: Edward Edinger, the Jungian analyst, echoed that when he said, "Perhaps the life dramas of the ego are the dreams of the Self."

LvdP: Yes. Shakespeare, for example—now *there* was a great journey—the whole of Shakespeare was a great journey. The journey from *A Midsummer Night's Dream* to *The Tempest* is one of the greatest journeys ever done on Earth. And Shakespeare ends up saying, "We are such stuff as dreams are made on." It's the end, and he says the rest is prayer, religion, God.

So there you are, there is a most profound journey. And where does it end up? Shakespeare says: "And my ending is despair/Unless I be relieved by prayer." What is prayer? It's *asking*, in the religious way of life.

NR: Is the dream God's response to our prayers? Is this where the dream comes from? From God?

LvdP: Yes. In the Bible, in the dream of Jacob's ladder, we're told quite plainly that through prayer man has a means of communicating with God; and God with man, through the dream. The dream explains to you what the dreaming is; it's a means of communicating with God. And the dream is God's language, the way God speaks to us.

NR: Do you think that all through our history there have been "great dreams" to guide us on our way?

LvdP: Yes. The world has always had great stories to tell. And many of the great stories begin with a dream. The great Homeric story of Greece begins with Agamemnon lying asleep, and the gods sending a dream down to him, which starts the *Iliad* and the *Odyssey* and all that great journey.

I've always used the statement that Jung made to me just before he died. He said: "I cannot define for human beings what God is, but what I can say is that my scientific work has proved that the *pattern of God* exists in every human being. And that this pattern has at its disposal the greatest transforming energies of which life is capable."

NR: Is "the pattern of God" that you speak of as being in the unconscious also the source for literature and for the arts?

LvdP: Yes. Art, in its nature, performs a religious function—not a dogmatic function but a religious function. Goethe said that unless art serves a religious function, it perishes and is merely repetitive and loses all creation. And the Greeks knew above all that art came from the Muses, who were part of the divine. Art was recognized to be divine.

Real art and the great stories of the world are profoundly religious in their meaning, so that everybody who goes into this area does a religious task. That's what Dante did in *The Divine Comedy*. Dante as an artist took the same journey as Jung did as a scientist. Art is always serving. That's why Blake could say: "Nations decay when the arts decay."

NR: But our arts today are flourishing, aren't they?

LvdP: That's true, but I'm saying there's a lot of art that isn't art. I see precious little real art in the world today; I would like to know where the great art is. People can't even produce Shakespeare properly. It's frightful. The early comedies are easy; they do it in the sensational way. But people can't do *Hamlet*. They don't understand it. I know the case of a sea captain who performed *Hamlet* in his ship with his sailors, but a modern sailor would think you were mad if you performed *Hamlet* for him in his ship. People don't know what it's about today.

The way that an artist works is by arousing the power of the imagination and communicating as many creative things as he can. But you can't do that without a sense of wonder, because the "now" is always insufficient—what we know is always insufficient. The mystery, the healing thing, is in what we *don't* know, joining in with what we know.

NR: Sir Laurens, you have said that as a civilization, we no longer have a myth to guide us and therefore our lives have no meaningful purpose. But you have also said that the story, or myth, which would have the greatest meaning and importance for men and women today—if we could live it—is the Quest for the Holy Grail. Why do you say that?

LvdP: Well, the great Quest for the Grail, which transformed the Middle Ages, was the discovery of the importance of the feminine. It was a quest for wholeness; it was a profoundly religious quest. But in our versions it was a quest which a knight did in service to his lady. It was the wakening up of the feminine which brought the medieval world out of its darkness. It's a very great quest and it's very relevant to this day.

NR: In the myth of the Quest for the Holy Grail, the hero Parsifal asks the wounded fisher king the crucial question: "What ails thee?" Do we need to look for the answer to this question in order to heal ourselves, and heal the planet?

LvdP: Of course, that's what we all must do. We must all do inside ourselves, with our own imagery and our own spirit, what is told in this great story of Arthur and his knights. We have to do a search for a Holy Grail.

But we have to do it in a contemporary way, not in an archaic way of knights riding through woods and rescuing people in distress. We've got to rescue our own people in our own parts of ourselves which are in distress and bring them into a common search, which is the search for wholeness.

Wholeness means holy; they come from the same word originally. To make whole was to heal, was to be whole, because in the beginning all sickness was spiritual sickness. We didn't say illness was caused by a germ; illness was a sickness of the spirit, even more, almost, than a sickness of the body. So this search for wholeness is a profound symbolic presentation.

All thought in human beings comes to us, first of all, in imagery. Then we transform it with words into what we call thought, and ideas, and concepts, and so on. The Grail story is the telling in imagery of what we have to do: to search for wholeness, to prevent the part from being taken as the whole.

It's the greatest legend that the English-speaking world has, because the Grail is a container. *Grail* is an old Provençal word for a great vessel which was put on the table at night and the whole family, the whole community, would partake—eat—out of the common bowl. So this is for mankind a whole container of spirit. It's like the milk of the Hottentot cows, the milk of human kindness. Compassion, love—it's all these things—and the Grail story tells that you must partake of these things.

NR: In the Grail legend, as I understand it, the sick king symbolizes sterility of spirit, which is so prevalent in our world today. Around the castle the kingdom—or king's lands—have become a wasteland, which would seem to mean that the king's spiritual state is being projected onto the natural world around him. Is the myth showing us that as long as our collective psychic wound remains untended the Earth itself cannot be made whole again?

LvdP: I think so, yes. In the symbolism of royalty, love plays a significant role. So we must start to discover our love of the Earth again. We have got that love in us but we've just trampled on it; we've exploited it for our own narrow egotistical needs, just for our comfort, purely for its sensation values. We don't realize that if you love something it's not really love unless you also serve it; you don't just exploit it. We don't give back to the Earth what we take from it. We think it's an endless source of taking, and of giving to us, instead of being a really loving partnership between two. It implies caring and feeling for the other as you do for yourself.

So this is what we've got to come back to. I think it's the most important thing in life. And once we start recovering the love for the Earth, we'll discover our love for one another.

NR: I wonder if people are unable to love the Earth enough because they haven't participated mystically in it; in other words, they haven't had a religious experience in nature where they felt the sacredness of every part of nature as the Bushman did. Most people today don't allow themselves that experience.

LvdP: I believe every human being starts with that reverence. It's astonishing that here in the city, one of the few good things that have come out about television are the nature programs. People in London lap them up; they've never known it but they immediately say, "My God, this is what we've been missing." These are the most popular things in television. The moment the human being sees them, he realizes this—because the pattern is there inside himself. And he says: "My God, how has this happened to us?"

So we've got it to start with as children—it's inside ourselves. But then we start exploiting it, and guilt and envy and greed move in. And if they rule the human spirit there's no room for love or reverence left in it.

Just look at what we do to the Earth every day. People have a feeling for nature but they push it away. They can't look, really, at the Earth with love because immediately they would have to change their ways, and they're so comfortable in what they're doing. So we're stuck exploiting the Earth for the moment, until the Earth turns and rounds on us, as She's about to do. And then we'll really sit up. I don't know what we'll do when that happens but it's coming near to that point.

NR: What do you think is going to happen?

LvdP: Well, I can't tell, but obviously we're going to run out of air to breathe and water to drink, because the air is already polluted, the water is poisoned, and the Earth is being washed away and won't grow things. I had some rain forest Indians here last year who said to me, "These storms that people get, don't they see that Nature's telling them what She shall do to them if they go on the way they do, cutting down our trees?" The evidence is so plain of our wrongdoing, and when you do wrong, you can't love. We do wrong to the Earth. You can't do the wrong without giving up some of the love.

NR: Sir Laurens, you've tried hard to save the Bushman of South Africa from extinction. Do you think that everything you're saying about our lack of love for the Earth applies to what we have done to our aboriginal peoples as well?

LvdP: Yes. Life in nature was far kinder to the Bushman, for instance, than civilization was. Our civilization has destroyed him. He did us no wrong; he's never done us any wrong, but we destroyed him. Why? It's as I said: we destroyed him because he's part of the Earth—instead of loving him too. He was part of that natural thing, and we just thought he had no right to be around. We thought he was wicked if he saw a sheep and killed it, because that was our property. Yet we were killing his animals all around him all the time.

It's plain as kindergarten stuff how wrong we are. We just make excuses all the time, but it's so plain that the fault is in ourselves. There are accidents and things of nature, one knows that. But the wrong, what's being done now and what is going to destroy us, is what's in ourselves. We can't blame it on God, we can't blame it on nature; it's in us and that's where the battle is, inside every human being.

NR: Are you pessimistic about the possibility of reversing what you see as wrong in our attitudes and values today?

LvdP: No, I'm not pessimistic. But one's got to acknowledge what the area is and what's wrong. You asked me what I feel, and I say we are the sources of evil, of our own evils. We *are*, and until we face up to that fact we won't get it right. But I think we are beginning to face up to it. I've heard that in Canada at this moment, they're cutting down trees, and all sorts of people are going and lying in front of the trees to try and protect them. Well, that's a good beginning, you know.

People know what's wrong. We don't need a wise man to tell us what's wrong. The rain forest Indians I told you about said, "But why do you do this? Can't you see that the Great Spirit is going to come and he'll take you all away as you've taken all his things away?"

NR: But we don't believe in the Great Spirit in our culture.

LvdP: Well, yes, there you are; that's what we've been talking about. As I've said to you, the problem is in the religious dimension. Our not believing in the Great Spirit doesn't mean that he's not there.

So that's what's gone wrong. This neglect of religion, the area of the master pattern as I call it, is completely excluded from the values of rational modern man.

I mean, the French Revolution officially declared that there was no God. The monasteries were not allowed to come back to France until de Gaulle's day, after the war. God was dethroned officially in Paris, and a Goddess of Reason was put in his place, so that tells you what's wrong.

In Russia you couldn't be a member of the Communist Party unless you were an atheist. Well, that's collapsing now, and all these godless things are beginning to crumble. Because what is wrong in Russia is a sickness of the soul, a mortal illness of eighty years of a denial of the soul. And the soul is beginning to rebel.

NR: It would seem that nothing less than a revolution in our consciousness about "what ails us" will help to heal our sick souls and re-connect us again to the Earth. But even if enough people are able to make the journey into wholeness that you've been talking about, will it be in time to save the planet, do you think?

LvdP: I think so, yes, in the end. Fortunately, the answer is not in the hands of human beings only, because Creation will have something to say about it. And when Creation pronounces judgment, that will be something which even the Book of Revelation may not have properly foretold. It's pretty grim, but it may be even grimmer than that if we don't heed. So there's a tremendous task in front of us.

Finally, the answer is that unless we turn to a full partnership with nature, we're in peril; we can be knocked for a six at any moment. It's simple; it's really very simple. I mean, one can't help sort of being in the role of the Old Testament prophets and so on. They were always warning the Israelites and the Jews about what was going to happen to them, and nobody listened. There's an immense amount of warning going on in the world at the moment. But I think, in the end, we'll win through.

NR: You really do believe that, do you?

LvdP: Yes, I do. If we can match our sense of obligation to life, if we can match our sense of obligation to what we know, then we could add enormously to what is going on in the cosmos. I think our role could be almost divine. That is the challenge—to match our sense of what we owe life, of what we owe the sources of our knowledge. If we match that, as I believe we must one day, the role of the human race would be absolutely priceless.

THREE MYTHS FOR OUR TIME

MY CONVERSATION with Laurens van der Post made me realize that my sense of having "lost my soul" came from my being cut off from the transformative energies in nature and in my own unconscious. Tragically, the same thing has happened to the culture. Laurens van der Post's belief in the great Quest for the Grail as the regenerative myth for our time is particularly relevant to our condition in that it directs our attention to our lack of wholeness—or holiness that the Grail represents—as the cause of both the planet's present distress and our own. In one of the greatest poems of this century, *The Wasteland*, T. S. Eliot projected the idea of our arid spiritual condition onto the image of a withered Earth. In the Grail legend also, the trees bear no fruit, the animals are in decline, and the waters have run dry. Today, neglect of the instinctive, caring values of the feminine principle is reflected in the clear-cutting of our trees, the extinction of our animals, and the poisoning of our oceans—and ourselves.

The loss of the Grail is equivalent to the loss of our souls' memory of our original home in the Garden of Eden. But when we sincerely search for answers to the question, "What ails us?" our crimes against both nature and our bodies cease. Our instinctive sense of direction is restored, our journeys are regenerated.

The Quest for the Grail carries within its imagery the search for the mystical *center* known to all cultures since our earliest beginnings. At the core of all Laurens van der Post's work lies his belief that our greatest task is to consciously re-create ourselves through that journey to the center where each person's uniqueness lies. Early tribal peoples spoke of the hub of the universe as the place where everything was created, and believed that whenever we are in tune with the harmonies of Creation we become that center. Artists think of the core of the individual as the place where our creative fire is ignited into activity by the powers of our imagination. In either case, to journey to the center is to unite with the Source of our holiness, or wholeness—the ensouled body—the Mecca or Jerusalem or Promised Land within ourselves.

Although he thought that the medieval legend of the Grail was the myth that spoke the most clearly to our present spiritual condition, Laurens van der Post also believed that the 4,000-year-old Promethean myth of the theft of fire from the gods addressed itself to a particular aspect of that condition—namely our hubris. Stealing fire, or consciousness, from the gods conferred on us not only a divine gift but a divine obligation as well—that of sharing in the stewardship of Creation. If we were to survive, we would have to become worthy of the gift of consciousness and act responsibly—with love and not with power—towards our fellow creatures. Otherwise, Prometheus's action becomes hubris and we begin to act like gods, just the way we are now behaving towards the planet.

In Laurens van der Post's interpretation of the myth, it was for this knowledge that Prometheus suffered the eternal punishment of being chained to a rock where every day an eagle—the bird which most symbolizes the spirit of Western consciousness—tore at his liver; and where every night his liver, his life essence, was healed up again. In psychological terms, the winning of consciousness through the daily effort to integrate the unconscious messages that are released in dreams at night is a Promethean task. But Laurens van der Post believed that—painful though it may be—it was this never-ending struggle which gave meaning to our lives. Prometheus, in his view, was a Christ-like figure who also paid the price of trying to bring us out of our unconscious state—a task in which we must all engage if we are to become whole.

Near the end of his life, Laurens van der Post undertook to further broaden our understanding of the relevance of classical mythology for our time through an exploration of the myth of Chiron as the successor to Prometheus. Chiron, the wisest of all the centaurs of Greek mythology, was famous for his knowledge of health and medicine. It was he who taught the art of healing to Asclepius, the Greek god of medicine; and it was he who eventually became an inner healer for me.

In Laurens van der Post's view, the collective unconscious of our present age has shifted, so that the Promethean myth of the suffering god undergoing endless torture in order to hold consciousness is no longer a complete image of how we are evolving. In his book *About Blady* he tells us that Chiron—half man, half horse—symbolizes our culture's rejected instinctual feminine side and is rising as a healing energy from the unconscious to rescue our inner Prometheus. If Prometheus, like Christ, suffered to make us conscious, Chiron, through "the instinct and the intuition, the feeling and the heart of the animal in man," is restoring the balance in our lives. Within that balance lies the feminine awareness we particularly need today for the healing of the planet.

The inner journey to wholeness that Laurens van der Post urges each of us to take is fraught with peril as the traveler confronts the demons and angels in his or her own unconscious and slowly integrates them into the conscious personality. Once we are committed to it, however, all the powers of Creation conspire to help us, for the universe acts as One Mind, striving for balance and wholeness in each of its parts. Engaged in the act of re-creating ourselves, we find that the possibilities are infinite and often surprising in the novelty and subtlety of their inventiveness. On the other hand, if we hold back from allowing the new life within us to be born, little by little our souls atrophy. It's a lonely task, however, because the world we live in is not comfortable with the introversion required for the job. Nevertheless, to strive to be fully self-aware is the greatest contribution we can make to life.

> I think the whole of one's life is a search, a matter of reunion as Dante sought it, with God, a reunion with one's origins. I always feel that origin and destination are one; they are the same thing in the human spirit, and that the whole of life consists of making your way back to where you came from and becoming reunited with it in a greater awareness than when you left it. Then by adding it to your own awareness, you become part of cosmic awareness.[9]

In his books and films, Laurens van der Post anticipated the birth of ecopsychology, which in our day has fostered an understanding of the connection between our own psychological health and the well-being of the natural world. Recognizing that conserving nature is essential to the preservation of our souls, he became an advocate and practitioner through the World Wilderness Foundation of what is now known as "wilderness therapy." Using solitude in nature to help people rediscover a sense of their place in the natural world, he hoped to make them aware that there was much more to conservation than simply a political or scientific approach. Over and over, Laurens van der Post pointed out that even the most entrenched urban dweller becomes a committed defender of the Earth after a week, or a month, spent close to nature. It was for this reason that he wrote:

> Every bit of unspoilt nature which is left, every bit of park, every bit of Earth still spare, should be declared a wilderness area as a blueprint of what life was originally intended to be, to remind us. When we do see that, it is like having a religious experience—we are changed by it . . . . For man without nature is unthinkable, and known or unknown, his spirit needs it: needs it for his survival, sanity and increase, as his body does.[10]

In 1991, Laurens van der Post recalled his own *participation mystique* with nature in the South African desert, where he had gone to heal after the difficult years spent as a prisoner of war in a Japanese concentration camp during the Second World War:

> When after many days the cloud subdued the heat at last and the rains came down, the transformation was magical, because the sands of the Kalahari are fertile. . . . Everything, from the flowers to the sudden leaf on the skeleton-white thorn, the birds singing and building nests, and every living and growing thing filled with excitement of re-creation, was so vivid and unmistakable that a similar process was released in myself. I had no doubt that in a sense, everything I saw was a natural priest and acolyte, and I had what, in this age of reason and from a great height of contemporary intellect, is referred to as some sort of "religious experience." My own reaction was so intense. . . .[11]

In his writing and lectures, Laurens van der Post always emphasized his essential concern for individual consciousness because without it, an ecologically sound and reverential approach to the planet becomes impossible, and the wasteland is never redeemed. For him the greatest threat to our survival would be our failure to achieve a sense of spiritual communion with nature—the realization of which, he believed, would end both our "loss of soul," and our devastation of the planet.

Many of us would have to testify with agonizing regret that despite the examples of dedicated men devoted to their theological vocation, they have failed to give modern man a living experience of religion such as I and others have found in the desert and bush. That is why what is left of the natural world matters more to life now than it has ever done before. It is the last temple on Earth which is capable of restoring man to an objective self wherein his ego is transfigured and given life and meaning without end.[12]

What wilderness does is present us with a blueprint, as it were, of what Creation was about in the beginning, when all the plants and trees and animals were magnetic, fresh from the hands of whatever created them. This blueprint is still there, and those of us who see it find an incredible nostalgia rising in us, an impulse to return and discover it again. It is as if we were obeying that one great voice which resounds and resounds through the *Upanishads* of India: "Oh man, remember." Through wilderness we remember, and are brought home again.[13]

NOTES

[1] Laurens van der Post, *The Heart of the Hunter*, London: Penguin Books, 1965, pp. 131-2.

[2] Laurens van der Post, *A Way of Truth* in *A Testament To The Wilderness*, ed. by C. A. Meier. Zürich: Damion Verlag Press, & Venice: Lapis Press, 1985, p. 50.

[3] Laurens van der Post, *The Heart of the Hunter*, p. 126.

[4] Laurens van der Post, *A Way of Truth*, p. 49-50.

[5] Laurens van der Post, *The Heart of the Hunter*, p. 129.

[6] Laurens van der Post, *The Story of C. G. Jung*, (film) BBC, 1971, Part II, *67,000 Dreams*.

[7] Laurens van der Post, & Jean-Marc Pottiez, *A Walk with a White Bushman*, London: Chatto & Windus, 1986, p. 145.

[8] Laurens van der Post, *The Dark Eye in Africa*, New York: William Morrow & Co., 1955, p. 163.

[9] Laurens van der Post, and Jean-Marc Pottiez, *A Walk with a White Bushman*, p. 146.

[10] Ibid., pp. 140-1.

[11] Laurens van der Post, *About Blady*, London: Chatto & Windus, 1991, pp. 9-10.

[12] Laurens van der Post, *Testament to the Bushman*, New York: Penguin Books, 1985, p. 162.

[13] Laurens van der Post, *A Way of Truth* , p. 48.

PART TWO

ABANDONED SOULS, ABANDONED PLANET

"So long as the sacred feminine is not honored in ourselves, we will be driven to rape Mother Earth."

MARION WOODMAN

THE ARCHETYPES AND THE EARTH

AFTER MY initial exposure to the ideas of Laurens van der Post, a deep longing came over me to find someone with whom I could share my story and further explore both my soul's journey and the collective consciousness of my culture. That person, as it turned out, was Marion Woodman, a Jungian analyst who in 1980 had opened a practice in Toronto. As an avid reader of her books, I was drawn to passages like these which so perfectly described my gnawing sense of soul abandonment:

> What a person needs is a bigger framework than the smaller personal framework, because a personal framework can become too humdrum. We need to ask ourselves about the meaning of life. What is the purpose of life, why should we keep going? The images in our dreams give us that meaning, and at the deepest level they are connected to myths. . . .
>
> It doesn't matter whether we go to church or a synagogue or a temple—what matters is that we have an archetypal framework which gives our life a universal meaning, so that we are part of humanity, part of some bigger plan. Otherwise we are isolated and alienated.[1]

My search for answers to my own and to the environment's illness meant that I needed to learn first-hand about the neglected feminine archetypal principle that Laurens van der Post had so clearly emphasized. Marion Woodman believes that our rejection of the feminine has caused it to compensate by forcing itself into the lives of many individuals through a growing number of eating disorders. Eating disorders are among the most serious symptoms of environmental illness, and one of my most persistent ailments. Such disturbances, Marion told me, signal an unconscious distress over the missing acceptance and nourishing by the Great Mother which is so absent in our patriarchal society. Environmental illness is one of the body's responses to the assault we are making on the Earth because of our failure to recognize and honor the positive feminine principle in nature and in ourselves. As I talked to Marion Woodman, I knew I needed to learn more about the world of the archetypes if I was to gain a deeper understanding of my own and the Earth's illness.

Our psychological and biological inheritance links us back two billion years to the very beginnings of life in the universe. It is an inheritance which encompasses the archetypes of the collective unconscious that manifest in universally recognized forms and images found in all the religions and mythologies of the world. According to Jung, these built-in patterns of psychic and physical energy—which are carried through generations to us genetically—are the equivalent of chromosomes in their ability to influence our behavior. They are like magnetic fields that inherently shape both our bodies and our psyches, and draw or repel our energy no matter how oblivious we may be to their presence. Common to the entire human race, they affect both how we look and how we act. They are our heritage, our birthright.

In *Conscious Femininity*, Marion Woodman goes on to say, "We cannot see the archetype, but we can see the archetypal image. The eternal world is revealed through personal images, the timeless through time." Archetypes, then, are visible in the world of dreams and of the imagination from which our greatest works of art, poetry, and music have sprung. Their roots go deep into the timeless realm of the symbolic images which make up the language of the unconscious. They are also visible in the countless forms of nature, including our bodies. In their positive manifestations they convey the unifying energies we need to heal both ourselves and the Earth; in their negative manifestations they carry the dispersing energies that can destroy our bodies and our environment—microcosm and macrocosm.

As we become preoccupied with making our way in the world, we gradually lose touch with the urgings and promptings, the dreams and messages from what Jung called the archetype of the Self—the image of God and Goddess within. The Self is an archetype that embraces both our transcendent yearnings and our material existence as bodies living on this Earth. Perhaps when life goes awry, and certain moods or physical symptoms overcome us, we try to delve a little below the surface to fathom the Self's intentions. Otherwise we seldom think about its existence as the Source of our being, to which we can and should return for sustenance and wise counsel. Finally, most of us lose contact with its reality altogether.

Jung believed that children, like aboriginal people, have an innate identity with the world of myth and archetypes which is often revealed in their art. Our culture, in molding us to its extroverted values, neglects or rejects the importance of this connection. The natural link that we had as children to the Source of our being is then so damaged that we spend the rest of our lives trying to regain entry into that wondrous inner realm. In a remark he once made while looking at an exhibition of children's artwork, Picasso expressed his longing for a reconnection to the kind of wholeness that their art reveals. "We spend our whole lives re-learning how to paint like that," he said.

The archetype of wholeness, or the Self, being unapprehended inwardly can only be projected outwardly into the world. Edward Edinger, a Jungian analyst, attributes the present state of our personal and cultural disintegration to our loss of connection to any kind of consciously recognized transpersonal, or greater, meaning. He writes:

> When the archetypes have no adequate container such as an established religious structure, they have to go somewhere else because the archetypes are facts of psychic life. One possibility is that they will be projected onto banal or secular matters. The transpersonal value can then become how high one's standard of living is, or personal power, or some social reform movement, or any one of a number of political activities. . . . Personal, secular, or political actions become charged with unconscious religious meaning.[2]

As the archetype of wholeness seeks an outlet, its numinosity exerts a magnetic influence on our behavior. If we do not handle that energy positively, it can surface in obsessions and complexes, disrupting our lives with painful neurotic symptoms. The sense of alienation and soul loss which follows often manifests dramatically in the violence and addictions of all kinds so prevalent in our society today. It is also expressed in our assaults on the planet, for the Earth has become the dumping ground for our lack of connection to an inner centering principle—its resources depleted, its body poisoned—as we heedlessly continue to feed our addictions at its expense. Our inability to relate to the numinous symbols of Christianity which once embraced our souls has brought us face-to-face with the problem of having to find, as individuals, our own religious archetype, both within and without. Without embarking on that symbolic quest, our lives become a meaningless round of secular distractions, and our yearning for "something more" is projected into the everyday world as we try to fill our emptiness with more consumerism and more diversions.

Jung distinguished between a left-brained approach to God and Goddess which demanded proof of his/her existence, and a right-brained predisposition towards the God and Goddess archetype. Not being concerned with the former, which was impossible to prove, he nevertheless showed empirically that we are biologically programmed towards an instinctive apprehension of the numinous. We have, in other words, what Laurens van der Post has called "the pattern of God" within us.

Two fundamental energies which have dominated the life of our species from its inception are the masculine and the feminine principles. Characterized by the ancient Chinese as the yin and yang principles in nature, their harmonious interaction is believed to maintain equilibrium in the individual. It was Jung's belief that through the union or Inner Marriage of these two complementary energies, the archetype of wholeness, or the Self, unfolds in the individual. The God and Goddess archetypes, when consciously understood, then become inner guides that direct the soul in its life in the world. Attending to their messages, which come to us as symbols, is not some disembodied experience, however. The Self's messages are conveyed to us through our bodies, both in symptoms and in dreams. This is the essence of Marion Woodman's bodysoul workshops. The body, through its expressive language—its movements, its sensuality, its illness—is a primary route to the soul.

Unfortunately, the masculine and feminine archetypal energies that together comprise our wholeness have become severely distorted in our culture. Instead of being focused positively on creativity (masculine) and relatedness and feeling-value (feminine), they have degenerated into power and materialism. Cut off from our feminine instincts that would connect the Self to the archetype of the Earth Mother, we abuse both our bodies and the body of the planet. It is that severing from the larger world of our psychic and physical environment which is at the bottom of our feeling of alienation and "loss of soul."

As the nurturing soul of the world (*anima mundi*), the Great Mother, or Goddess, has become part of our collective unconscious. She has been celebrated in human rituals from the time of early tribal cultures to the spiritual practices of today's ecofeminists. In his book, *The Voice of the Earth*, Theodore Roszak explains the power of that feminine archetype, embodied in nature and in the history of human consciousness:

> In the case of the *anima mundi*, we may be dealing with one of the oldest experiences of mankind, the spontaneous sense of dread and wonder primitive humans once felt in the presence of the Earth's majestic power. When they were no more than the first few representatives of a timid, scurrying new species in the world, these early humans must have greeted the immense creativity of nature with an awe that has since been lost to all but the poetic minority among us in the modern world. The Earth does go so powerfully and competently about her work, bringing forth the crops, ushering in the seasons, nurturing the many species that find their home in her vast body. She can, of course, be a menacing giant; that too is remembered in myth and folklore. Many of the oldest rituals are acts of propitiation offered to a sometimes fierce and punishing divinity, an Earth who can be an angry mother as well as a bountiful one.[3]

Denied conscious recognition, the feminine deity can make her presence known through her destructive mode. This is happening today through the increased disturbances of the Earth's equilibrium, experienced as hurricanes and storms, extreme temperature changes, and Earthquakes. I don't believe that Mother Earth, striking back at us for our neglect, is literally an angry female deity breathing vengeful fire and brimstone onto her children for their rape of the planet. Rather, I'm referring to the Earth's pain, which I see as a fundamental energy disturbance, both psychic and physical, which arises as the inevitable result of our distorted values. These values exclude the feminine principle when they allow such destructive practices as nuclear bomb tests, ozone layer depletion, and global warming to continue. For a society to negate a huge part of its psychic heritage in this way is to invite disaster.

In Jungian thought, the *shadow* that each of us carries within us is that neglected part of ourselves that we cannot see and that we therefore often fail to incorporate as part of our conscious lives. In our patriarchal society, the collective shadow we carry as a culture is the repressed feminine archetype.

While abuse of the feminine principle is rife in our society, it is also very apparent in our bullying contempt for Mother Earth. With reports continuing to accumulate about our wanton extermination of wildlife, as well as our assault on the Earth's resources, it is appropriate to ask if we are now scapegoating the whole of the natural world. Are we projecting our own denied feminine onto the flora and fauna of the planet, destroying them because they are the carriers of that unitive natural world that we deny exists in ourselves? The feminine archetype as a container for instincts, irrationality, chaos, destruction, and death is a principle of nature that we don't wish to acknowledge because it is too painful for us to do so. But as a part of nature, these aspects of life are a part of us, too. Following our feminine instincts will disrupt the placidness of our lives, but they are not only our reality, they are also our primal life-force. Dissociating from them only breeds self-destruction; we destroy the habitats of our bodies just as we destroy the habitats of our precious wildlife.

The rape of the feminine in our time is a primary concern of the four people whom I have interviewed, and a central theme of this book. In the conversation which follows, Marion Woodman shares her view of what happens both to us and to the Earth when our souls are abandoned and consciousness of feminine values is excluded from our lives.

CHAPTER ONE

BROUGHT UP TO BE GODS

NANCY RYLEY: Marion, my first question is about the collective loss of soul in our society. What do you think has happened to our souls in this culture?

MARION WOODMAN: There is certainly a loss of soul in the collective. Our souls have been raped by the culture's values. There is a listlessness, a passivity, a machine-like weariness palpable in so many groups and individuals. It manifests as the trance-like quality of an abused child.

In the nineteenth century, the projection came off the white-bearded father God. Nietzsche saw the cultural shift and said: "God is dead." For centuries the church had been able to contain a collective soul. That container held in one way or another into our century. Now more and more people have no relationship to a church. They think the Mass is hocus-pocus. They think ritual has no value. They think Christmas is about Santa Claus, and Easter is about the Easter bunny. Basically, we're a culture of Christian illiterates. (Our sacred holidays can hardly be called sacred.)

Some people have other religions; that's fine. But as a culture we do not have a collective belief system; we do not have one spiritual myth to hold us together. Now that's not such a terrible thing. If individuals were mature enough to find their own souls, then the collective would be a collection of empowered individuals working from their own soul values.

NR: What religious values are left to us after losing the church as the center of our spiritual life?

MW: The way it's going in our culture, as I see it, addictions are taking over as perverted religions. People are worshipping whatever concrete god or goddess happens to be at the center of their addiction. As a result, they are dropping into unconsciousness.

NR: Can you spell out what you mean by addictive behavior? Is addictive behavior connected to the loss of soul?

MW: I think it is connected to the loss of soul, because soul in religion connects to God. There is a reflection of the god in the soul. People who are *consciously* worshipping know when they are entering sacred space. Christians, for example, cross themselves with holy water. This is a symbol of crossing the threshold between the sacred and the profane. In the Mass they recognize that they are identifying with the god in sacred space. They go through the death of the god, the three days in Hell, and then the resurrection (that's usually the pattern of the Mass), so that they are consciously moving through a ritual, consciously connecting with the eternal.

And when they step out of that sacred space—on a Sunday morning or whenever—if they have been present in the Mass, they have been in the presence of the god. Their ego is slightly expanded, and they can walk out of that sacred space knowing that they were in the presence of transpersonal energy. And they can take that with them for the week, *consciously* take it with them.

Now what happens in an addiction is that the yearning for that transcendent space comes up. Individuals who have no spiritual god or goddess to identify with in that space put the spiritual projection onto something material like food, alcohol, cocaine, or sex. And they put the same kind of intensity into their binge, or fix, or orgasm—whatever they call their addictive behavior. They spiral into unconsciousness until they pass out. Then there is no consciousness to relate to whatever experience they may have had. The unconscious has forced them into the addiction, which means that the ego no longer has control. No addict is the master of his or her ship; the unconscious has become master. They have a stone god or goddess at the center, and that stone energy eventually manifests in their body. We become what we worship.

Some people take drugs in order to enter that space. We say they are "stoned." They may have numinous experiences, but if there's no conscious container in which to integrate what happened while they were on the drugs, there's no ego expansion. There is nothing new being taken back into conscious reality.

NR: Can you give examples of what you have called in your books this "concretization of spirit into matter," of specific situations where this happens?

MW: We certainly find concretization in eating disorders, where a girl who tries to relate to her mother—consciously or unconsciously—sees the lack of womanhood there, and decides she doesn't want to be like her mother. She doesn't know anything about the female god. Her mother probably doesn't, either. So there's no feeling in either one of the sacredness of matter, or of love for the feminine essence. Even if a mother is doing the very best she can to love her children, to nourish them, to cherish them, if she has never learned to love her own body, if she does not love her own sexuality, if she isn't in touch with her own body in relation to the moon and in relation to the Earth, then she cannot give to her daughter (or to her son, but particularly to her daughter) a love of her own body, a love of her own femininity. And that daughter will grow up without a positive sense of mothering, although she may love—and be loved by—her personal mother.

She may decide that if her mother's way of life is what femininity is, she's not going to participate in it. She rejects nourishment, sweetness, sustenance. She holds light, spirit, and air as everything that is desirable. The more she starves, the more light she receives. The more she runs, or dances, the more euphoric she becomes and therefore the more light she craves, until everything associated with the body is filthy, heavy, dark, and all she wants is that euphoric escape. So the anorexic tries to escape from her humanity into disembodied spirit. This cutoff from her own matter is the concretization of her rejection of femininity.

Now the opposite to that would be the binger who goes heart and soul into food, because she craves the positive mother who gives food and cherishing. The lack of any connection to the feminine essence often creates a hole in the psyche, a yearning, an emptiness in the psyche that manifests as a compulsive drive for sweetness, or fullness, or nourishing of any kind.

The binger misunderstands the signals and imagines that she needs sweet food to fill her up. This can manifest with such energy that she is compelled to eat. What, in part, is happening is that she is misreading the yearning for the positive mother, changing it into physical yearning, not understanding that it is spiritual yearning. Then the Goddess (the positive side of the spiritual mother) for that woman will become concrete, not symbolic, food. A false communion will take place where she eats food in an effort to incorporate the Goddess.

In these situations there is no spiritual essence. There is no spiritual sense of security, no spiritual sense of fullness. If she could take a walk in nature, if she could feel her feet firmly planted on the ground, and if she could experience that grounding, then she might take in the cherishing she seeks in nature. She might feel her soul expanding into the soul of everything around her. She might belong to an ensouled community of birds, plants, animals, people.

NR: What has happened in our culture as the result of our lack of connection to a feminine deity?

MW: The feminine is very abused, often annihilated, in our culture. What I call "the positive mother" is consciously not present for most people. She is, of course, present in the food we eat, the water we drink, the air we breathe—but we do not recognize her.

The spiritual mother, as I see it, Nancy, provides the loving container that looks at the child and recognizes the essence of the child and does everything in her power to mirror that essence. So then the child knows that it's loved; it doesn't feel that it has to justify its existence. The energy of that love is so real that the child's soul blossoms in that love. It's this loving container that's so lacking in our culture.

I want to make it quite clear that I am not talking about the personal mother here. I'm talking about the sacred feminine as it has been understood and honored for centuries in the Chinese yin and the Hindu Shakti. In dreams, that spiritual mother might appear as larger than life and be quite glowing in golden, beautiful high energy. And her name might be Mary, Sophia, Isis, White Buffalo Woman—maybe Ann or Hannah.

Culturally, I'm talking about an archetypal energy that has become polarized in matter. You see, an archetypal energy is a magnetic field. An archetype cannot be seen; it is an inner magnetic field which forces an individual to move towards whatever the field is picking up.

It's the confusion of the concrete and the spiritual that we're concerned with when we're talking about addictions. If the inner magnet is yearning for spirit, and the individual is trapped in matter, then alcohol is spirit.

NR: Do you feel that our whole Western society is into addictions of one kind or another?

MW: Yes. Instead of worshipping a feminine deity, I think our society worships concrete matter as "mother." That is our collective addiction. I would call it the "negative mother" complex. Where the spiritual mother is no longer recognized, then the society worships a materialistic mother; because we are a consumer society, we worship matter (*mater* is the Latin word for mother). We want more and more; the drive is insatiable because it is unconscious and disconnected from its natural instinct. Natural instincts find their own satiation point.

NR: In other words, the child's *need* for that lost feminine essence becomes the adult's *greed* for more and more things in order to fill up that spiritual gap?

MW: Yes, we try to find our security in more money, more possessions, better houses. What we have at our center is matter without spirit. Greed. And if we lose our matter, chaos breaks loose. People are terrified of losing their possessions because who are they without them? There's where the huge fear comes in. There's where you see abandoned adult children dependent on matter. Then, of course, when possessions are endangered, huge problems of power and powerlessness develop. We see this in response to a recession, and to divorce.

NR: Isn't this where doing immeasurable harm to the planet comes into the picture, as we use up more and more of the world's resources in an attempt to fill the void left by the lack of a real spiritual connection to *mater?*

MW: So long as the sacred feminine is not honored in ourselves, we will be driven to rape Mother Earth. Someday, hopefully before it's too late, something horrendous will tear the scales from our eyes and we'll see what we're doing.

NR: In this matter-obsessed culture you're describing, are we any more positively connected to masculine archetypal energy?

MW: We call ourselves a patriarchy, and we are a patriarchy so far as the power principle is concerned—basically aggressive, thrusting towards a goal, competitive. But patriarchy and masculinity are not synonymous. Indeed, patriarchy has wounded masculinity as much as it has wounded femininity.

What I mean by masculinity is the assertive energy, the energy of discretion, discernment, clarity, the clarity that moves toward a goal. And it exists in women as well as in men. Some women call it the "feminine yang." I don't care what the words are.

But for me, the masculine principle is parodied in the patriarchy as we have it now. It has become a despicable power principle. Our society functions through power—controlling other people, our bodies, nature—for the sake of controlling. I don't call that masculinity.

The tragedy is that people who are really into that kind of control are essentially very insecure little boys and little girls. They have very childish attitudes, and therefore they are very dependent on mother, on matter, and on the worship of the goddess archetype, the Great Mother, in her materialistic, concrete aspect. In the Great Goddess religions, men who were the priests of Cybele or Astarte cut off their testicles and put them on her altar. I think that many men in our society are doing that in marriage because their masculinity is crippled by the power principle in their mothers and wives.

The Nazis are a perfect example of what I'm talking about. If you look at the leaders of the Nazi Party, most of them were mothers' boys, and very sentimental. Sentimentality is false feeling—Göering, for example, crying over his canary and at the same time ordering mass murders. Genuine feeling says: "I know this is of value to me. I have worked through to this knowing." Those Nazi leaders, when they were brought to trial, said, "We were doing what we were told to do." They had no sense of knowing their own values and therefore no guilt because they had perfectly obeyed. That's all they understood—baby boys obeying. From their point of view they had done exactly what was right. That's the negative mother complex. And that's the kind of addiction our society is falling into—gobbling massive doses of undigested values and ideals.

NR: If, instead of a connection to a positive masculine energy, we have authoritarianism and power, what happens to the soul of a child growing up in this culture?

MW: If parents "know" what the child should be, then they—consciously or unconsciously—control the child. They want a "perfect" little scholar or a "perfect" little athlete. They have an image which they expect the child to fulfill. That's power.

NR: So the child learns power right at its parent's knee, and loses its soul right there?

MW: Yes, to the first question. In part, to the second. "Loss of soul" is a phrase that means the ego loses touch with soul, but I wonder if soul is ever totally "lost." If the child comes running in covered with mud because he's had such a wonderful time down at the river, and the parent cannot mirror the child's joy in mud and calls him "a bad boy," then the child very quickly concludes, "I am not lovable. Who I am is not lovable. Therefore I will cease to be who I am. Instead, I will please my parents and be lovable." That's where the soul is outcast, right there.

If a child decides to drive instinctual hope and desire and interest and energy underground, then she puts on a mask and performs for the parents—that's the point where the soul goes into the cellar. That's where the abandoned child is in most people's dreams. And I think that's where the collective soul is today. Think of the energy repressed in our society, how it festers and destroys. This is the very energy that should be transformative in a creative way, constantly blooming and maturing into something new.

NR: Do you think that most people feel that they have an abandoned child in them?

MW: I do. The orphan is a very popular archetype in our culture. And I think that most people feel they did what their parents wanted them to do, with the "shoulds, oughts, and have-tos." But the tragedy is that as adults they're still doing it; there's still somebody whom they have to try to please, whether it's their wife, or their boss, or their corporation, or their kids, or their grandkids.

Most people are crippled in this way. They don't know any other reality. So they have no alternative but to listen to the voices of their mothers and fathers that they have introjected since they were born. They please, collude, or rebel. They are living their lives in terms of an authoritarian figure inside and outside.

NR: What other things would the parents say, or do, to a child that would make it feel abandoned, make it feel that it had to wear a mask, that it had to pretend and perform—and so experience a sense of having lost its soul?

MW: If, for example, a child cries over a tree that's been cut down, or a father ties the new kittens onto the exhaust pipe of the car in a sack and the child experiences that from the point of view of nature, and cries, and becomes hysterical. I hear these stories in the office all the time. Or the child has a tremendous passion to do something—to give lunch to some little kid she found on the street. The parent says, "You're not going to do that." Or, "I'm not raising any crybaby; the kittens had to be killed." Or the dog simply disappears, or the cat, because the parents decide that they're not having that creature around any more. But the child has a soul identification with the animal. Very quickly she learns not to trust the parents. And the soul gradually pulls back, and pulls back so that it won't be struck again.

Also, the soul can be struck in school if a teacher rips up a child's painting. Or the singing teacher says, "You just keep your lips moving, but don't utter a sound because you can't keep pitch. You can be in the choir, but don't sing." How many people do you know who are not singing?

Their soul is smitten. If the person finds the soul child in dreams, that soul child looks out and says, "If I'd come out, you would have killed me." Simple as that—the child is terrorized, not only by the external authority figures of childhood, but by the ego itself that has learned to be its enemy.

NR: So we have a patriarchal, mother- or matter-dependent culture that bludgeons our souls as we struggle to express them while we are growing up. One of your books is entitled *Addiction to Perfection*. Is this what the child develops?

MW: Yes. You see, there is a huge compensation that happens. Without the attitudes of natural mother (nature loves imperfection) there is a compensatory swing to perfection. The child feels it has to live up to the unnatural perfectionist standards that the parents set. And the parents set these standards because the culture sets them, and the culture is riddled with tyrants. So the standards are coming from authority figures at one end of the social scale or the other.

But the soul is not "perfect." The soul is living in the human body, accepting the natural human limitations and human instincts. And perfection has nothing to do with being human. So there's a huge conflict there for the child, and later on for the adult as well, because if we aren't living from our own humanity, our own bodysoul, we have no ground of our own to live from.

NR: You said that, "having been brought up to please in every way, the tragedy is that as adults we're still pleasing." Are you saying that performing to be perfect causes you to internalize the tyrant-victim you've been exposed to growing up, and act it out with other people?

MW: Yes, you end up with that combination. Somebody tyrannized you and therefore you've got that tyrant in yourself, so you play victim to your own tyrant. Moreover, you've got to know that although you pretend to be victim, somewhere in you unconsciously there is a tyrant voice that bullies other people, making other people victims. They may want to be victims, because they too have a tyrant in them that says, "You're not good enough; you never will be good enough; you really don't deserve to live." And so it goes on and on unless it's brought to consciousness, and worked on, and changed.

NR: How does one combat this terribly damaging inner voice, or drive?

MW: The only way to work with it is to recognize that tyrant voice speaking. You have to be strong enough to say, "I don't have to listen to you. You are the voice of so-and-so in my life; you are not me. I know what you're saying, but you're not going to bully me." It takes years to eradicate that voice. I don't know if you ever completely eradicate it. There's where you get the negative inflation: "I'm the poorest me in all the world." Negative inflation can take you into an addiction, trying to escape from self-loathing.

NR: Could you be more specific about how negative inflation takes you into an addiction?

MW: Because we have these high standards that are going to make us into perfect creatures, we—creatures of spirit—want to be gods, rather than human beings—creatures of nature. Then the inflation of the perfection creates the negative inflation: "I'm the worst slug that ever lived. The worst things happen to me."

Negative inflation is the opposite of inflation. If you think of a pendulum, it swings up as far on one side as it swings on the other. Think of inflation swinging the pendulum high on the right into perfection, then swinging back as high on the left into imperfection. The higher the swings, the deeper the pits of despair. "All or nothing." Patriarchal thinking! Either/or—nothing in between.

That kind of thinking leads to negative inflation. "I am so terrible I pollute the world." That self-abuse is what leads into addiction. Because it's so painful, you can't stand it. You've got to get out. You do that through an addiction. Most people escape into gambling, or food, or compulsive relationship, or work. Anything to escape the lies of that negative voice. The tragedy is that so many people don't realize that they're driven by that negative voice. They don't realize they can bring it to consciousness and shut it up, and be free.

Now we're into another level of addiction here: people slowly commit suicide, unconsciously, when they cannot face truth. In any full-blown addiction there is self-destruction at the center of it. For me, self-destruction is soul destruction.

NR: Considering how our loss of soul is manifested in how we treat the planet, is it possible that the person who was victimized with power as a child is going to try to victimize or bully the planet by plundering and destroying it for profit (which, of course, is the ultimate form of self-destruction)? There is such a rapacious attitude towards the wilderness among the people who are running corporations, for example, that I wonder if at the bottom of it is this victim-tyrant psychology which says: "If I don't deserve to live, neither does anything else." All of this would be unconscious, of course.

MW: The tyrant-bully is destructive unconsciously, and not so unconsciously. We *know* we are poisoning our planetary water system. We *know* we are destroying the ozone layer. We *know* how many species are becoming extinct each day. We *know* the Earth will not sustain our growing population by the year 2150. We *know* rich tyrants are destroying national economies by moving factories to Third World countries where labor is cheap. So it is not all unconscious, what we are doing. We are *consciously* blinding ourselves to our children's future, which is self-destruction in the broadest possible sense. We *choose* not to look at our greed.

NR: You made an interesting comment when you said, "I am so terrible that I pollute the world." If we as a society have the kind of victim psychology you describe, could this account for why so few people are willing to stand up and fight for cleaner air and water, and try to put an end to planetary destruction in general? In other words, are we as a society playing victim to the tyrannizers in our society—the "bully" corporations and the seductive advertisers? By pleasing them just as we pleased our parents; by consuming more and more; and by going along with corporate rape-the-planet policies, are we not, in fact, abandoning our souls, and abandoning the planet at the same time?

MW: Yes, it's true that our culture is not coming from its own desire. It's undermined by an addiction to be victim; culturally, we are trying to hold on to the patriarchal values that are destroying us. We don't want to give up our standard of living, so we elect leaders who promise to keep it for us. Politicians want to please moneyed tycoons, so they jump to do their bidding whatever the irretrievable cost may be to ourselves and to the environment. Victims do not take responsibility, or cannot take responsibility, for what is happening to them. What are we doing about all these horrors? Victimizing ourselves further. Putting more locks on our doors, more scales on our eyes, trying to forget possible destruction. We ordinary people have got to stand on our own ground and care enough *to do* something—to reconnect to our souls that would roar "STOP."

NR: In order to relate to our souls that would roar "STOP" to the direction that the culture is going, you have emphasized our need for reconnection to our feminine roots. How would that reconnection change the way we are behaving towards the planet?

MW: The feminine is connected to feeling. It says, "This is what is of value to me." One of the ways we hear the messages from our souls is through a gut response in the body. But most people don't have a gut response any more, because they are cut off and don't feel the reaction in their cells. (The kids' word is "cool" or "numbed out.") The muscles are so chronically locked that there's no feeling going through the musculature of the body that says, "That's what I feel. I'm angry, I'm happy, I'm . . . whatever." This would include being connected enough to our anger about what's happening to the planet to rise up *en masse* and force politicians and business people to put the planet's interests *first*.

NR: There's an example of exactly what you're talking about going on right now in the town near where David and I live in the winter. In the past five years, the local town council has issued permits to developers for the construction of so many hotels, golf courses, and houses that our current population of 5,000 will reach at least 25,000 in ten more years! This is happening right at the gate of Canada's oldest and most beloved Banff National Park (which is also a United Nations World Heritage Site) and very little is being done to stop it.

MW: What you're telling me just makes me so angry. The people who are responsible for this have no feeling-value whatsoever for the land, for our own quality of life, for our children. All they can think about is the money. Negative mother in her *really* negative form is out to *concretize* the Earth—literally. These people literalize everything, so that if you want "plenty," you want more "mater," more "mother." But more "mother" in the concretized form will destroy itself. It's death.

NR: What developers want here is a concrete city all right—right up to the Park gate. And if the gate didn't stop them, they'd march right in and pave over the land in the Park.

MW: But how long is the government going to hold the law on the gate? There's no moral law anymore. It's a terrible situation we're in. We're being eaten up by the negative mother complex. If we don't wake up soon we'll lose everything we value. Unconscious people don't fight for what is of value to them, Nancy.

NR: As well as including our feeling-values, Marion, what else defines the feminine principle? How do you know when it's animating your life?

MW: I would say that the feminine principle (not female—we're not associating this with gender, but with the feminine energy in men and women), can be associated with certain words: *process, presence, being here now, paradox, resonating, receiving, surrendering, listening.*

If you look at those words, you can see that our culture isn't particularly interested in any of them, as a culture. There are people who are interested, but as a culture *product* is what matters, not *process*. As for *presence*, very few people have the capacity to be "in the now." They're addicts, always ahead of themselves or behind themselves—living in the glorious future that's going to be, or in the great past that once was. Of course, both are fantasies. There's another big addiction: fantasy addiction.

To spell out further what I mean by some of these words as part of the feminine principle: *paradox* is the capacity to accept "both-and" instead of living an "either-or," black-and-white life, which is patriarchal life. As for *resonating*, most people haven't got the resonators in their bodies open at all. They've got a few resonators in their heads, but the big resonators in the belly they don't know exist. Therefore, they have no way of tuning into their own Reality, their own souls, because they don't *feel* the body vibrating with "yes" or "no." They *think* their feelings.

As for *receiving*, I think people are terrified of what might come in and blast their rigid values to smithereens. The same goes for *listening*. People are so interested in what they're going to say themselves that they don't hear what's coming at them from outside. They've got their filter systems too highly developed—not for differentiating things, but simply for shutting off anything that isn't them. We're a very narcissistic society.

NR: Then how do people see the feminine in this culture?

MW: The feminine in our society is considered stupid, illogical, naive, childish. If you try to live it you are told, "You're being histrionic, you're being melodramatic, you're being hysterical." I tell you, Nancy, the feminine in our culture is hated. It is horrifying to realize how some women hate the feminine as much as many men do. If they're unconscious, they'll go as fast as they can. They'll beat their body into submission. They'll starve it. They'll laugh at feminine values and mock them. Words like "presence," "surrender," "yield," "paradox," are mocked by women just as much as by men.

NR: Does the fact that many men are not living their feminine side either enter into wife-beating in some way?

MW: Of course. A man who beats his wife is beating his own feminine, projected onto her. In dreams he will probably throw his femininity into a bag and connect it to the exhaust pipe of his car, or throw it into a ditch. And a woman who stays with an abusing man is colluding in the destruction of her own femininity because her own masculinity is a patriarchal tyrant.

NR: Apparently violence towards women has become the most common violation in the world today. Is there a connection between abusing women and abusing the planet?

MW: Yes. And abusing boys and men. All are abusing sacred matter.

NR: Why is this abuse much more prevalent today than ever before?

MW: Because the feminine is coming to consciousness. These feminine figures are appearing in their dreams and they are forced to recognize them.

The sobs that broke out through so many people's bodies at the time of Princess Diana's death makes it clear how anguished our own unconscious feminine is. Diana's death released the unconscious projections that had been sitting in there, unrecognized for years. Now, suddenly, we're able to see the yearning that is in us for the feminine that she represented.

NR: What aspects of the feminine does Diana carry for us?

MW: Diana carries mother, abandoned child, abandoned wife, adulteress, humanitarian, and a woman who has the courage to stand up for her own beliefs. She represents all of these, and her death instantly threw this into consciousness. People who didn't like Diana particularly at all cried when she died, and millions around the world mourned. What were they mourning? They were mourning the loss of their own hope.

Now it's up to us to live our own truth. We are no longer unconscious. We have seen what we're carrying in our unconscious, so we can no longer blind ourselves to our own inner Reality. Since Diana's death that new image of femininity is there for us to see.

NR: Nonetheless, for people to live new images of the feminine, as Diana did, is very difficult, isn't it?

MW: It seems that some people, like Diana, are being *chosen* to live this energy. It's not a pleasant thing to be chosen, though, because there's huge suffering involved in trying to live your femininity. Even so, some people are being chosen to discover it, to integrate it, to bring it into the culture. And to try to manifest it in terms of living it every day.

NR: Why is living out the feminine so painful?

MW: Because it is very threatening to the patriarchal ego, very threatening to social status, very threatening to life as we know it in this society.

To live those images that embody true feminine value is, I think, even more painful for men than for women because men are mocked more perhaps by their own gender if they try to live it. The pain comes from trying to pull themselves out from the mother complex, and at the same time find security within themselves. I think that many men confuse femininity with mother, and think that mother is the only aspect of the feminine. For them, mother means security—holding onto material possessions, holding onto a woman who represents mother. But when that archetypal energy turns negative, it becomes the devouring side of the mother that can emasculate them. Remember though, we're not talking about the personal mother here; we're talking about the energy of the archetype.

To be able to cut yourself off from that destructive energy and step into your own shoes and live your own life is to mature.

NR: You say that a few men in our culture are trying to bring their feminine to consciousness. Do these individuals understand the feminine in the same way that you do?

MW: I don't know. I know that when I did read Thomas Berry's *Dream of the Earth*, I was so excited I could not put the book down. Here at last was a man who understood process, paradox, receptivity, surrender, the glory of diversity in the unity of the Earth. Although he doesn't use the word *femininity* his perception is feminine.

Similarly, when I read Laurens van der Post's *The Seed and the Sower*, *A Mantis Carol*, and most of all, *About Blady*, each of these books was an opening for me. I saw the feminine at work in a male consciousness.

My husband, Ross, has worked throughout our married life to integrate the feminine and masculine. I have been his grounding female in that process. That has often been painful for both of us.

Part of what is painful for me is my realization that, despite the obvious understanding that men like these have of the feminine, it is seldom named. At a recent conference about chaos theory that I attended in Toronto the panel was all male. Much of the discussion focused on words like *acausal, irrational, paradox, synchronicity*—all words describing the timeless-spaceless world of quantum mechanics. All of these phrases and words are feminine attributes, recognized as words related to feminine energy. However, when I gently pointed out to the male panel that they were talking about the feminine principle, one panelist referred me to the prehistorical, matriarchal world before patriarchy as a possible illumination of my point. The gentleman could not understand that I was talking *present* tense.

Even though quantum physics in its understanding of the universe and our place in it balances the two energies, until feminine energy is *named* it will not be recognized as complementary to masculine energy. There is no possibility of an Inner Marriage of the two as long as there's no recognized Bride. We have to start pulling in the words of quantum physics because our whole world runs on the Inner Marriage—on that day-and-night principle where there's obviously a time of opening and receiving (the feminine), and where there's an alternate time of thrusting and permeating (the masculine). The two energies work together. They are complementary. If we can put that all together in our minds, then women will become equal to men, and the put-down that patriarchy associates with the feminine will no longer be possible.

NR: Do the two energies have to be in balance?

MW: Yes, and we're totally out of balance. That's the whole problem. Without being balanced by the feminine, the masculine becomes either passive-aggressive or brutal. It moves into that patriarchal rejection of the feminine.

NR: How would trying to live this feminine archetypal energy—which is such a totally different way of "being" from the patriarchal/negative mother complex which has such a grip on our society—relate to how we might better live with nature?

MW: Abuse of the planet is the ultimate form of abuse against the feminine. The feminine principle is grounded in the rocks and trees, in all living nature. When we brutally tear down forests, when we allow magnificent animals to be murdered, to become extinct, we are abusing sacred matter. Somehow in all this we've got to learn and live the fact that all nature, all matter is sacred. We have to know what *sacred* means. Someday humankind will know, not simply believe, that in our diversity we are *one*.

The feminine loves to "be," and our task is to bring that "being" into consciousness. We wouldn't be able to breathe if the feminine weren't here. She's all around us in nature; all we have to do is open our eyes and see Her. But we don't see Her, we don't honor Her.

However, I don't believe for one minute that in trying to bring the feminine deity to consciousness we're alone. Destiny or God/Sophia are working on the other side, and She will be manifest. I believe that Sophia, the Goddess, the Shekinah—whatever we call Her—is determined to be consciously seen, determined to restore the balance so life can continue on the planet.

NR: Would you say then that our living-out of this Goddess energy is crucial for our survival?

MW: I would. Otherwise we're left with a two-dimensional, logical, goal-oriented, perfectionist, either-or world which will eventually cause our body to say, "If this is all there is, I'm not interested. I'm not interested in my own life, and I'm not interested in the planet's life."

Without feminine energy, the red vitality in the blood, real life energy isn't there. Life becomes a drag. People try to reach some kind of Reality that either takes them out of this mundane materialism, or takes them more deeply into it. Ultimately, at the heart of this materialism is the eye of death. It reduces life to dense matter, disconnected from both instinct and spirit.

NR: People go into perfectionism and self-destruction. As you said, we're brought up to be perfect.

MW: Perfect gods or perfect devils. We are brought up to be perfect at both ends of the pendulum. Gods in heaven or hell!

CHAPTER TWO

No Song to Sing

NANCY RYLEY: Marion, we've been talking about how our failure as a society to disengage from patriarchy and materialism has resulted in the rape of our souls, which in turn has led to our rape of the planet. What do you think is the state of most people's souls in today's culture?

MARION WOODMAN: For most people, I think the soul is like a little nut that's hidden somewhere down in the gut. In dreams that little soul appears as a small Biafran child that's buried in a pile of garbage. And it knows it's going to be struck, so it pulls all its power in, takes the strike, and does its best to protect itself. It may open up again. Generally it spends its life trying not to be hit.

If we can hear our own soul, we know how often it's struck in its encounters with the world. And how often our own power complex strikes it by saying, "You shouldn't be listening to music; you should be working; you ought to be making money." And the soul says, "But I just wanted to play, to imagine, to create my own world for a little while." Well, certainly there's no time for playing with that power complex in control.

Or we have dreams of this little starving bird up in the attic and the dreamer is told to go up there and get that little thing in that black box. The dreamer goes up, takes it out, and it's a living skeleton. But it's still able to whisper, "I only wanted to sing my song."

Most people don't even know they ever had a song to sing, let alone try to sing it.

NR: We have no song to sing because we're rejecting a vital part of ourselves?

MW: Yes, namely our soul. We are colluding with the original authoritarian figures in our lives by rejecting our Reality. But the soul knows that it wants to live, and knows that it has a birthright to life. And we can't talk to the soul part of ourselves and say, "You're no good." The soul knows that it is real and that it has a right to live. If we're going around under a false mask, we know we're phonies.

NR: How far back does this devastating authoritarian pattern go? I don't want to go back too far, but obviously there's been something at work in our society for a long time to cause this self-destructive pattern. Is it possible that our parents had the same thing done to them that they've passed on to us, so that blaming our parents is irrelevant when it's really the culture that's to blame?

MW: A child that's brought up with power is going to raise children the same way. Unless consciousness intervenes, it gets worse from one generation to the next. Patriarchy has been handed down from generation to generation. In each generation a little bit more power is constellated.

Looking back we see that gradually the masculine principle in our society has moved further and further away from what it started out to be. I think that originally, in classical Greece, for example, the masculine was trying to free itself from the power of the unconscious archetypal nature mother. This was a very important step—ego consciousness separating itself out from nature. But if we go too far, if we alienate ourselves from nature, then we kill nature, including our own nature. That's what we're doing now.

NR: As a part of nature, in this patriarchal culture are we killing ourselves physically as well as psychically?

MW: I think so. The rhythms that we're trying to keep up are far too fast for our bodies because of the speed that is demanded in the patriarchal value system, and the perfection. They're not only too fast, but they are also too exacting.

NR: Marion, you've spoken about the addiction to over-work in our society. It's so prevalent in Japan that the Japanese even have a special word for it— *karoushi*—a word which means "dying of over-work, due to stress, strain, and illness." Is it technology that is causing this addiction?

MW: Technology is part of the conspiracy. We have to remember, though, that we do have conscious choice. We do not have to lose ourselves in technology.

NR: What happens to one's sensual enjoyment of life if one is always in a hurry?

MW: Well, then there's no soul time. Soul matures through our senses. Soul loves to play. Now, of course, it's true that there are lots of people who say they play with technology. But for me, play has to do with the imagination, and with the whole excitement of creativity, and with the constant re-creating of oneself through inner images. That's play. To be tied to a machine that doesn't give you freedom to explore your own metaphors is soul-destroying. It can't grow, it can't open, it can't blossom.

I can hear someone argue that you can be very creative in the way that you handle a computer. But there's a difference in working with a machine in a highly creative way and working, for instance, with a garden in a highly creative way. With a garden you are working with the natural responses of the organs of your body. Your body flourishes when it is in nature. The images that come out of our body are absolutely essential to our psychic health.

NR: The body moves at one rate; you say its natural rhythm is slow. But then we've got these incredible machines that accelerate our nervous systems beyond their capacity to cope. What does this do to us psychologically?

MW: I find it splits, or polarizes, the personality. I'm not masterful at technology, but I do know that if my body doesn't have time to operate at its own speed in nature it becomes sick.

I also know that the organs of my body receive messages, and they respond with feelings, and they simply have to have time to allow those feelings to grow and expand. That's soul, just meandering; the soul has to meander in order to play. And it cannot do that in an obsessive technological milieu.

NR: Do the values that our culture has adopted pose a grave problem for the child who grows up and tries to find a soul connection to the world?

MW: Many children have worked hard on their masks, but they have not had the opportunity to work hard on their soul values because those have been derided. The child brought up to be perfect is saddled with guilt because it cannot be what the parents expected it to be. So it carries guilt and resentment, probably becomes depressed or just outrageously rebellious. And I think that's part of what's going on in our culture that's breaking up the relationship between generations. Children are rebelling.

NR: If they believe they have something creative to contribute but what they find out there is power and consumerism, then many of them must be left in spiritual isolation, don't you think?

MW: Yes. Unfortunately, many young people today aren't interested in finishing university, or even high school. They're opting out, because they see that the values that they're holding for themselves and for the planet are being mugged. They're numb with alienation from society. They're numb with rage, and they're numb with grief.

They're doing odd jobs, being taxi drivers, trying to put in time until they can figure out what they can do. Many are brilliant people, and beautiful souls—sensitive and highly imaginative. But—big but—the society has no room for these people. You look into their eyes and you see health. You see integrity. You see their bodies moving with intention. They refuse to betray their values: I respect that. They're saying "No" to it all. Well, if the society has no room for these people it will destroy itself. The underbelly of unlived life is vicious.

NR: Then you look into the eyes of those who have sold out for money and you see the opposite, right?

MW: Soul betrayal.

NR: Nearly everybody's addicted in this patriarchal society, it seems.

MW: Certainly that's the cultural treadmill.

NR: We seem to be finding everything wrong with the world. . . .

MW: I really think the society has gone down tremendously in the last year.

NR: In the last year? To what do you attribute that?

MW: I think people have less and less faith in the values that are driving the society. They have less faith in the leaders and they are more and more interested in things that have to do with soul. Look at the best seller list: books about the soul are the books that are selling.

But it is also true, unfortunately, that many people are treating the soul as an addictive object. They want a quick fix. And they don't want to do the hard work and they don't want to hear about the hard work. So they try to find a book that will give them a quick fix for the soul.

That is just another perversion of the whole thing. It's like being a Jesus freak. A lot of people get out of one addiction by becoming Jesus freaks. Then they go so fast in the direction of religion that the religion becomes another addiction. Their attitudes and ways of thinking are not changed.

NR: When I think of addictions I also think of food addiction. When I look around at people in restaurants and I see the everyday things they eat and drink—the junk food—I can hardly believe my eyes. What shocks me is the lack of real care that people give to their bodies.

MW: The trouble is that we lack basic respect for our bodies. There's a complete denial of the sacredness of matter. And that is very much connected to any addiction. That's certainly true of eating in our culture. It's true of workaholics too because they don't pay any attention to what they're doing to their bodies so long as they can keep working eighteen, nineteen, twenty hours a day.

NR: In order to live up to those early parental standards?

MW: Yes. Or to escape. I think many people are escaping from situations. Many of us cannot face the pain of our lives. So work is an escape, or compulsive relationship is an escape, or eating is an escape, until we weep when we look into a mirror.

NR: You say that this sort of behavior is "a complete denial of the sacredness of matter." What do you mean by the sacredness of matter in this case?

MW: The body can either be a hunk of flesh—totally undisciplined, unloved, and abused—or it can be a temple for the holy spirit. If, unconsciously, you think of the body as something to be abused, then you will feed it garbage. You will go to bed with anybody who comes along for a one-night stand. You don't care what comes into it, and you don't care how you mistreat it.

But if you think of your body as the temple in which your soul lives, which one day the holy spirit might visit, then you treat it with awe.

NR: In order to do the "hard work" of rectifying this, you don't mean that everyone ought to go to a Jungian analyst, do you?

MW: No. I mean that there are spiritual disciplines that one can do: meditation (listening to the inner world), working with imagery (any creative work), working every day on self-discipline. A bad word in our society—self-discipline—because it suggests taking away freedom. But people have little freedom in our society now; I mean they're bound by their own license. They think that freedom is doing anything they like. That is not what freedom is. Freedom is living your essence to its absolute fullness. And you can't do that without discipline—daily, hourly discipline.

NR: Freedom, in other words, isn't just vegetating in front of the TV. . . .

MW: No. If you are going to be a great athlete, or even a good athlete, you are going to discipline your body every day. It's only through that discipline that you learn what your body is capable of doing. Then, when you put it to the real test, it has the muscles ready to move with the spirit that flies in. If you honor your matter, you don't drive it beyond its own capacity. Without discipline, you cannot hear your own body.

NR: So it's discipline in ordinary daily things?

MW: Everything. It's physical discipline, emotional discipline, spiritual discipline. The three of them.

If you're going to enjoy doing a sport, enjoy your body walking, or running, or blade skating, or whatever—if you're going to experience the miracle that your human body is—you're going to have to eat proper food, exercise, and listen to the messages it conveys. Only if you dialogue with your body, can it be the free, graceful, beautiful participant it is meant to be.

What's lacking in our culture is the feminine voice that naturally knows that the body is sacred. To the contrary, a voice in our society says: "The body is evil. It is related to Eve, and to the snake. It is to be despised because it is the source of evil."

NR: The body seems to have become a sort of sexy machine in TV-land: everybody's gorgeous. I just don't have the feeling that anything's animating them, really.

MW: That is true for those people who have lost their soul. You can call them gorgeous, but they're like Barbie dolls. Nothing inside, nothing animating them—the eyes dead, the voice coming from the top of the throat, not from the full-bodied, rich beauty of an embodied soul. Walking cadavers, on one level—they really are. If you start looking at television with the eyes of soul, you do see many walking cadavers. The makeup's all there, but the light is out inside.

Sometimes as I listen to TV I weep for people in our culture with their dead voices. The sad part is that they can't hear themselves. The voice is not connected to the root; there's no passion in it. What's taken over in our society is mob psychology, which is unconscious. Many people have to remain unconscious in order to keep their job, so they don't let the passion out. That's what it comes down to.

NR: It's interesting that we both feel so deeply about the crucial importance of keeping passion alive in our lives. I'm amazed, for example, at how people these days bounce in and out of relationships, and bounce in and out of jobs, as though they were all of equal value and therefore all interchangeable.

MW: They do that for the same reason that they bounce in and out of an alcohol bottle. There's no passion in the situation in the first place. You and I are close enough to our own Reality that we're still in touch with the passion that can move a life. But many people don't understand this; they label it "hysteria."

NR: What happens to that light, to that passion? In our addicted society where our bodies have become numb to soul messages, what happens to the soul that has gone underground?

MW: Oh, the soul will stay fairly quiet up to a certain point. Then for most of us there is a moment when the soul starts to scream out, either because we're sick, or because our job is intolerable, or because our marriage is smothering us. In other words, the part that is who we really are is refusing to be killed. And that's the wonderful thing about the psyche—it does want to be whole. So the soul will cause so much trouble that eventually we have to face up to why we are either so sick or so unhappy—psychically or physically or both.

NR: How do you help people out of their addictive behaviors so that they can reclaim and regain their souls again?

MW: I work through bodywork in trying to let people inhabit their own selves. Whether it's Feldenkrais, or T'ai Chi, or Yoga, or whatever the body-work is, the purpose is to live in the cells of the body so that we can hear what the cells are saying. There is a wisdom in the body, but if we don't bring that wisdom to consciousness, it cannot be transformative.

Consciousness often comes through the dreams that come after a bodywork session. Dreams are connectors between body and soul. They are pictures of our spiritual connection.

I also think it's very important with soul work to paint, dance, sing, design, write poetry, verbalize. The soul lives on metaphor because metaphor connects the eternal and the temporal worlds. The bridge between the eternal and the temporal is metaphor in art and in dreams. Therefore we have to bring the embodied soul into a place where it can be seen through art, or heard through music, or articulated through poetry.

NR: Could you be more specific about how you help people reclaim their souls through working with metaphor?

MW: Soul work is incarnation, the process of soul incarnating in the body. By soul I mean the eternal part of ourselves that lives in this body for a few years, the timeless part of ourselves that wants to create timeless objects like art, painting, and architecture. One aspect of soul work is working with the imagi-nation: it's working with the metaphor, which comes from the Greek word for "transformer." That's exactly what a metaphor does: it transforms one kind of energy into another.

The metaphor in dreams gives us a picture of our psychic condition and how to change it. In working with metaphor, I focus on an image, or symbol, from a dream and have the dreamer concentrate on it. If we allow the imagination to play with the metaphor in the body, the energy in the image is released. Particularly with psychosomatic problems, metaphor can be a powerful healer—matter and spirit cooperate in the healing process. For instance, if the image of a rose should surface from the unconscious, and you work with both your instinctive love of the color, smell, and form of that rose—as well as your imaginative idea of the rose which could symbolize love—that process can be transformative.

If people give themselves half an hour a day with the imagery in their dreams or with their music (whatever their creative process is) the soul becomes very quiet. They're located in their body, and they feel nourished by the activity. Addiction, in contrast, thrives on frenzy. The faster people go, the greater the frenzy, whereas becoming quiet and living with these metaphors takes them back into their own creativity.

The creative process for me is extremely important. Whenever the ego surrenders to the archetypal images of the unconscious, time meets the timeless. A human being has a divine, creative intelligence. One way or another, that creative intelligence is going to find an outlet. If it can't find an outlet through the imagination, which is its natural route, it will find it in a concretized way.

NR: What is it about body movement—movement itself—that connects to soul?

MW: If the body remains still all the time it's usually holding in anger and depression. Instead of expressing, it is either repressing or suppressing. The body that is truly expressing soul is a healthy body. And it loves to move, and life is movement.

I have this image of a hard little nut that's got all the possibility of life in it and wants to grow into a great tree but it just can't grow. Of course, there is such a thing as meditation that is quiet, that is still. And the still body, under those circumstances, can flower in meditation, psychically and spiritually. But there's got to be a balance with movement. The soul moves the body. The soul is life itself.

NR: There's a lot of body awareness in our culture, including aerobics and body-building; we seem almost obsessed with the body in our society. But is that what you're talking about?

MW: Our culture is into fitness (not that I have anything against fitness) but that's not the same as being *in* the body, being *embodied,* so that soul is living in the body. So that soul is responding to life through our eyes, ears, noses, all the orifices of our body, including sexuality. So that soul is living the imaginative life in this body that it lives in for eighty years, or however long we're on this Earth.

NR: When you're doing bodysoul work, you're working with what Jung calls the *shadow;* in other words, with those parts of the soul that got buried as a child, such as creativity or sexuality. Do many of the emotions that accompany the loss of those aspects of oneself—grief, anger, jealousy—come up during bodywork?

MW: Yes, to be in the body also means to suffer. You see, Nancy, the grief that the soul experiences when it's laughed at, or when its values are not recognized, goes into the musculature of the body. But underneath that grief is rage. "I am not living my life. I am pushed down here. And I am not going to stay down here." So there's a volcano in the belly. And the soul has huge energy when it starts to move in rage.

Many people are having heart attacks nowadays because the soul finally says, "I am feeling something and, by heaven, you're going to feel something too in the muscle in your chest." Or the part that is hidden in the bowel suddenly says, "Well, I'm going to live." And there may be the beginning of bowel cancer. The cells suddenly take on a life of their own and live it the best way they can. That way is not in harmony with the body if the ego has made the soul the enemy.

If we don't hear the wisdom in the body, eventually the body says, "OK, you'll hear it this time." And then we're dis-eased, physically and psychically. It's in the suppression of the passion that we break the immune system down. That's when people go into an auto-immune breakdown.

NR: By that time illness is the only way the soul can get us to pay attention. But what happens if we acknowledge our own darkness, our own wound?

MW: Acknowledging with the mind is one thing; acknowledging through experience in the body is quite another. If rage is buried in the body it may take five, six years to touch into it, or longer. And there's a terror of fragmentation. What happens is that people will say, "If I actually let this out, I will kill somebody. Or I will destroy everything in my surroundings. I will go crazy. I will fragment."

Indeed, when they do hit the core of that rage they do fragment. And there's a huge fear that they'll never get it back together again. So they're dependent on whoever is with them to psychically contain them. When they come out of it, they realize they can go through that place without dying or going crazy. And that's the place of the original trauma when the soul was driven under.

NR: But in order to release the rage or grief buried in the original trauma, it's not simply a question of painting, or writing poetry, or doing T'ai Chi. It's a question of much more than that, isn't it?

MW: The way to ease and wholeness is through reconnection with soul as friend, listening to what it has to say in our body. It's a question of *consciousness*—without consciousness nothing changes. If you work consciously, after you do the drumming, or painting, or dancing, you become a witness who can detach and look at what you did. Then you can see the shadow—the energy that's been repressed. Then you can see the anger or the grief, the twisted, perverted thing that has happened in your life. You get a taste of it in each drawing or each dance or each poem. Sometimes there's no big revelation. Sometimes you incorporate it, integrate it, tiny bit by tiny bit.

NR: That's the insight?

MW: Yes, that's the insight.

NR: Jung claimed that we cannot relate to our feminine side until we know our shadow. Does that make getting to know our shadow the first step in healing ourselves?

MW: It's very important. But the shadow comes out in many different ways. As Jung uses the term, it's the side of us that we have not recognized. It is genuinely unconscious. That means it's not known to our conscious ego.

And although it's very painful to release and incorporate that shadow energy, it's very important to recognize that that energy isn't necessarily negative. For most people who have been trained until the life energy is almost knocked out of them, the best part of themselves is in the shadow. That's where the life-force is, and that's where our wholeness lies, if we give it a place in our conscious lives. That's certainly true with women who have been brought up to think that their sexuality, or their menstrual cycle, or their whole feminine body is sinful. Then their best energy in their dreams will appear in a whore figure, or a Mary Magdalene, or some kind of lady in a bright red satin dress. In bodywork we try to connect with that energy.

NR: Surely you don't encourage women in therapy to go out and become whores?

MW: No, blindly living out whore energy will never integrate it. I think this happens to many people in our culture. They allow their body to be a machine, but they are not connected to that machine by their feelings. So they can sleep with anybody, feel no guilt, feel no betrayal of their sacred temple.

You see it also in a woman who is unhappy in her marriage. The marriage is culturally successful, but there's no lust in the marriage bed, so the life-force that should go with the sexuality is not present. Therefore, she finds a man who is in the same situation. There's no lust in his marriage bed, either. So the lust is lived out secretly. But if it is not brought to consciousness, it is still not part of the personality. It is not experienced as part of the life-force. So, many men have to keep finding younger women, and many women have to keep playing little girl in their sexual games. Their personalities are split; they are not maturing through the experience because there is no consciousness present.

Let's shift our perspective. Let's consider the prostitute who can betray her body repeatedly because she is committed to a pimp. She doesn't claim her own soul value, either.

NR: What if she were connected to her feelings through recognition of those feelings in her body?

MW: Then she would be connected to her soul. It would not be possible to do what she is doing in the betrayal of her body, because it would be soul-killing every time she did it.

You see, at the same time that she's doing that—earning her money by selling her body—she could, on the other side of her personality, be quite religiously connected to some kind of a cult. So she would live out one side, and then change her clothes and live out the other side. But the two would not be integrated. Integration happens when you bring the two together: you live the sexuality in the spirituality and the spirituality in the sexuality.

NR: Is this splitting apart of sexuality and spirituality a fairly common affliction in our society?

MW: I think it's very common. The Judeo-Christian church says that matter is sinful, and spirituality is the God-given gift that we're supposed to develop. As far as I can see, the culture's been schizophrenically split by this.

NR: In your workshops and intensives, how do you bring an awareness of the shadow into the participants' consciousness?

MW: A weekend workshop is very different, of course, from a week-long intensive. In the longer workshop, we have time to gradually open the resonators in the body and allow the dream work to open the psyche. As the energy permeates the body, the participants begin to feel what has been numbed for years. They all work at their own pace with total concentration. On the fourth and fifth days of the work, many containers are tested to their limits as the anger and despair of a lifetime are released.

NR: How do they deal with their despair at this point?

MW: After the session they inevitably go running outside for healing. Once we did a workshop on the third floor of the Royal York Hotel in Toronto. After it was over, people were so intense that they instinctively looked for nature outside the room we'd been working in. What they found instead were the pillars in the foyer, so they unconsciously used these pillars as tree trunks. The foyer was full of people lying on the ground, or leaning against the pillars. It looked for all the world as it does in other workshops when people are out among the real trees and lying in the grass.

In other words, the body had to have nature at that point in whatever form it could find it. This is why we try to find a place in nature for workshops—because nature is the natural healer for the body.

NR: That's an astonishing story in its revelation of how desperately we need the natural world, and of how the body instinctively knows this and tries to re-connect to it even in the most unlikely of places. Does working with all these repressed emotions locked into the shadow—including the love and acceptance by the therapist of ourselves *as we are*—also change how one feels about oneself and about other people?

MW: By working with the repressed emotion in the body—anger, for example—we realize that we are human, and that there is no such thing as a perfect human being. In fact, the better we think we are and the more perfect we imagine we are, the darker our shadow is, and the darker the material that we have to release. When we know how much rage and grief and jealousy and greed and lust are in us, we have to forgive ourselves for being human.

To forgive is to transform what we otherwise reject. Some people find that very hard because they've been brought up to be perfect. But once we know that we can love ourselves with all our human warts then we can love others from that same place. Or, as W. H. Auden said, we can learn to love each other with our own "crooked heart."

What a relief! No longer having to be a God or Goddess! No longer having to be perfect!

CHAPTER THREE

SURRENDERING TO THE MYSTERY

NANCY RYLEY: It is my assumption that without restoring our souls to health we can never restore the planet to health. With this in mind, Marion, I want to ask you about dreams. What is the nature of the dream in helping us reconnect to our souls?

MARION WOODMAN: The dream is part of the metaphorical body—instincts, if you like. To be in touch with your own metaphors which are rising out of your own bones you have to be in touch with your own imagery. That's where your sense of Reality comes from. "These are my images and nobody can take them from me; these are the truths of myself, just as my body is the truth of myself." There's no way of having self-confidence without those images, and without a connection to the body from which they arise.

NR: Who sends the images? Where do they come from?

MW: Well, if you believe in a Dream Maker, that's where they come from. The Dream Maker is what I would call God—God and Goddess; for me "God" is both feminine and masculine. And I believe that we are guided through our dreams. There's nothing unusual about that; that's centuries old.

NR: Do dream images from the God or Goddess come from within, or are those deities external to us?

MW: The dream images come from within, but I do believe that the microcosm within mirrors the macrocosm without. For me God and Goddess together—like Shiva and Shakti in the Hindu world—are always in divine embrace. That is an image that mirrors my own soul.

NR: Tell me more about this God and Goddess imagery for you. What are those energies and who are these divinities?

MW: For me, God is a mystery. I have no idea what God is. But I recognize that there is some divine order in the universe, and that everything moves in perfect order, and I assume there is some kind of intelligence and love behind that. For me that is God.

In your garden, that love is manifested in those trees and those delphiniums and those marigolds and those cabbages. And it's manifested too in your face, and in the faces of those people walking in the street.

And the manifestation of God in matter is the Goddess. She is *Sophia*, or the feminine side of God. The two are one. Spirit manifests in matter.

NR: Is this the "divine embrace" that you're talking about?

MW: Yes. To continue the metaphor, the creation that is bountiful in your garden requires the sun to bring it to life. Creation opens itself to the consciousness of spirit. The sun, of course, is the symbol of spirit.

NR: Is this what happens in our souls: spiritual energy, which is masculine, penetrates the soul, which is feminine?

MW: For me, yes. The feminine soul, which is embodied in the Divine Marriage, surrenders to the masculine spirit. God and Goddess are in divine embrace, and my soul—or your soul—mirrors this divine activity, which is the microcosm of the macrocosm.

Soul to me means "embodied essence." It is part spirit and part matter. So long as we are on this Earth, body and soul are inextricably bound together. Mozart can feed the soul; so can homemade bread and strawberry jam.

Traditionally soul is thought of as feminine, as matter is thought of as feminine. When we talk about the "conscious feminine" we're talking about an awareness of our subtle body in our material body. That "embodied essence" is the container strong enough to take the penetration of light, of spirit. That's how I imagine the androgyne, as the Inner Marriage, the feminine soul receiving the masculine spirit, which is where real creativity happens. True creativity, true soul-making comes from that deep intercourse with what Jung calls the archetypal world. Georgia O'Keefe, Emily Carr, and the French Impressionists, for example, had the containers to see that energy in motion and to paint it on their canvases. Their canvases are alive. They resonate in our bodies.

It's very dangerous, however, if we try to fly into spirit before we're grounded in the body. Too much light too fast, and we're blown away. This Earthly dimension has to be strong enough to magnify the God. It's one thing to vege out in nature; it's another to consciously open ourselves to the divine light manifesting in nature.

NR: In discussing dream images then, where they come from and who sends them, is that divine combination the internal guide?

MW: I would see it that way, yes.

NR: But messages from the God and Goddess within aren't always pleasant, are they? Reclaiming your soul by following your dreams can be extraordinarily challenging.

MW: Yes, if you follow your dreams you'll certainly go through some dark waters. Dreams are not the least bit sentimental; they want you to mature into your wholeness. If you believe that God is the Dream Maker, you know He doesn't provide a daycare for infants. You've got to grow up.

It's very painful, because you are going to have to use a very decisive cutting process to cut away what is false in your life. You are going to be required to say, "These are illusions which are no longer of any value; they cripple me. These are lies." And name the enemy. That is really painful because it feels as if you're losing your whole life when you start really working at it.

NR: If the "enemy" is whatever you're doing, or have become, that is crushing your soul, do you have to give up a great deal of your present way of being in order to rectify this?

MW: Yes, you have to make sacrifices for soul growth. But I have to stress that all the time that you're giving up things, the soul is coming into conscious-ness. That's the other side of this. So you are enjoying music, or you are enjoy-ing whatever your particular world is: poetry, dance, painting. You go back to nature, you take your walks on the Earth, you go back to the lake, to the stars. There is a double thing going on. The psyche isn't out to destroy us; the psyche is essentially very kind. It will test us to the very limit of letting death take away the old—symbolically or literally. But then it will bring new life in on the other side. That process is very well-balanced by the psyche. And the dreams guide us in that process.

NR: You say that going back to nature helps bring the damaged soul back into consciousness. How does the experience of nature help reconnect us to our souls?

MW: Nature's beauty of forms and colors—the innumerable ways they move and relate! We are so used to multiplicity on Earth, we don't value it. Anyone who takes time to walk in nature every day knows the resonances in the body when the purple finch sings, when the white roses shine in the moonlight, when the herb garden perfumes the night air. Anyone who loves nature knows its cruel side, knows and accepts its rhythms of death and rebirth. Soul recog-nizes itself in that beauty and order. It sings us into connection with our eter-nal roots.

NR: Can you give me specific examples of the chaos that a person can go through when he or she tries to live life by listening to the soul's messages, rather than by what the ego dictates?

MW: Chaos turns our value system upside down. You may have thought it was "you" to be a good wife, a good mother, to be faithful to your husband, to obey all the standards that you were brought up with. Then you suddenly fall in love with someone who brings immense happiness into your life—joy, vi-tality that you never knew before, and you say, "This can't be me. It's not possible that I would fall in love with somebody else."

Yet the dreams give you these wonderful images of this person whom you are in love with. And suddenly you see that the structure that you thought was "you" is going to collapse. Do you cut off one side or the other? Or do you try to live with both? And if you do try to live with both, will your partner agree to live with both?

So you've got two value systems all turned into one great mush in the middle. And there's chaos.

NR: Sounds like a crucifixion to me.

MW: It is a crucifixion because you're trying to hold two different value systems without collapsing in the middle. So you're stretched out on a cross.

NR: Is this the meaning of crucifixion?

MW: In part; taking responsibility for your own life and staying with the pain of the conflict until you find out who you are.

NR: What does it mean symbolically to hold both arms on the cross?

MW: In the example we are using, to hold both arms on the cross would be to say, "I do love my husband. I have a huge investment in this marriage. I do love these children. But I also love this other person, because this other person has connected me to my soul in a way that I have not been connected before. And this must be why I've fallen helplessly in love. Still, it doesn't change my love for my husband. I do, in fact, love the two men." (Tell that to your husband!!)

Where the abandoned soul is not connected to the husband, it will find somebody outside the marriage whom it can connect to. You have got to pay attention here because it feels like death to cut off that projection. It feels like death to cut off your own soul value.

NR: Is this what it means, then, to be confronted by the shadow—by an unlived part of ourselves projected onto another person? Is there any soul value in this experience which pulls us apart, yet is such a common one?

MW: That sense of being pulled apart happens in many situations. Take compulsive relationship, for example. The compulsion happens because we unconsciously project part of ourselves, or even all of ourselves, onto someone else. Then we are in love with our own projected image. But projection is also valuable and necessary because once we recognize what we are doing, we can claim parts of ourselves that we were not conscious of before. Then, instead of yearning for that part, we can break the compulsion by working at integrating into ourselves what we projected onto someone else. The key is to recognize what we are doing *consciously*. This is painful work and lonely. The most lonely I know.

NR: So while you're doing this you can't really lower one arm or the other?

MW: You can. You may even cut one arm off. But if it's a soul connection, you can't lower one arm or the other without willfully rejecting, even murdering, a precious part of yourself.

NR: So what happens?

MW: What usually happens, if you stay with the two arms nailed, is that a third possibility will come through that you could never have anticipated. So long as you cannot figure out the solution, you trust that the Dream Maker has a solution. Now there's where you have to learn patience, where you have to learn to surrender. I think you have no alternative. It's like being an alcoholic and saying, "I recognize that I cannot conquer this addiction and I surrender to a power greater than myself." So that—and this is the feminine principle—you surrender to that unknown, that mystery that is greater than yourself. Then something new happens.

It's a similar process for any artist who is blocked creatively. The conflict in "I want to write, I can't write" has to be held consciously, until the unconscious crashes through with new awareness. Similarly with a blocked relationship or blocked marriage.

Everybody is different. There is no one solution for all of us, so it will be different for every individual. Surrender means something different to each of us. That's what's so incredible about dreams; I've never seen two dreams exactly alike.

NR: If you're consciously surrendering to the Divine Will—to the archetypal mystery in the unconscious—for the sake of your soul's growth, are you always prepared for the suffering and pain that follows, do you think? I mean, what keeps you on track?

MW: Once you have surrendered to the mystery that operates in life there's no going back. It takes hold of you. You may try to forget it periodically but it picks you up by the scruff of the neck and says, "This is where you belong, not there."

I'm not saying that there's an authoritarian, cruel God, but rather a God that puts us into the places where we can live our destiny in its fullness. And we have to realize this, or we go back to our old ways—the old addiction, the old marriage, the old job. Death to a vibrant life.

NR: So something that happens to us—like an illness, or the loss of someone we love—which seems like a cruelty, is really a kindness?

MW: From the perspective of "the divine comedy," it simply *is*. It can appear very authoritarian and dogmatic. Still, if you have your eyes sufficiently wide open, you can see that this is divine love.

Burning is one image. In the Sufi tradition, for example, they talk about burning the heart empty so that it can love. In other words, you burn the heart empty of the ego desires so that the heart is open to become an instrument for the love that transcends it.

NR: Suffering can have a positive transformative effect?

MW: If suffering is the letting go of the ego desires, then it becomes totally transformative because as you let go of the ego desires, the soul grows. And the soul begins to say: "This is what I desire and this is who I am." The "I" of the soul is the soul that is in harmony with the Divine Will, and the more you recognize the love in the Divine Will, the more you surrender.

NR: Many people don't think about divine love when they're going through a desperate illness, or experiencing some terrible loss in their lives. Instead, like Job, they say, "Why me?"

MW: Why me? Well, you can get into "why me." And you can get into self-pity. It's natural in the face of crisis. But you're only going to diminish yourself if you stay in that place. You can become bitter and say, "God has done this to me," and again you diminish yourself and become a little prune instead of a sweet, fat plum.

NR: Marion, you recently had an operation for cancer. Was it the feminine in you surrendering to a Higher Power that made it possible for you to get through an experience like that without becoming bitter? Because you give me the impression of someone who has been enriched by having had cancer. Do you feel that way?

MW: I do. Yes, I feel enriched. I think the cancer may well have saved my life.

NR: How do you mean cancer "saved your life"?

MW: Well, it certainly stopped all the speed in my life. I still believe that I was doing the things that I was being called to do, in order to allow my soul to blossom. I don't think that I was going against that. I tried daily, through meditation and journaling and dance, to open to the Divine Will. But I was also being called to do something else, and I didn't make the transition soon enough.

NR: What do you think you were being called to do?

MW: To let go of much of the old way of life which I had been in for fifteen years. I had enjoyed it so much and lived it so fully that I didn't want to let it go, though my unconscious knew it was going, and was preparing for the shift. All my photographs the summer before the diagnosis were focused on shadows. And I literally began giving things away—books, shoes, precious personal objects. I was constantly sorting, so that my drawers are now almost empty and my cupboards almost bare. And I'm glad. I loved those things, cherished them while I needed them. Now I have let them go. It delights me to see them charged with new energy from their new owners.

NR: Are you saying that ultimately this experience has been a gift?

MW: It has been a gift. I don't deny the suffering for me and my dear ones, but it has opened deeper levels of love, and new dimensions of trust in the divine purpose.

NR: It must be terribly hard to consciously give up control, though, to abandon the idea that the ego alone knows best, to completely trust the Unknown.

MW: *Surrender* is often considered a wimp word. Feminists hate the word. They think it has to do with weakness and giving in to the male. But you have to have a very strong container to surrender. For me, it has taken huge strength to surrender, to trust myself to the Unknown. It feels like death because survival for me has always depended on willpower. But personal strength alone is not sufficient.

People say: "How could anybody with your kind of strength go down the way you did?" It's simply because the blow from God—from the divine energy in the unconscious—was harder. And to break our rigidity and bring out the unlived life—which is, of course, the surrender and the capacity to love—takes that kind of a blow.

NR: That's truly the only thing that opens us up to God, is it?

MW: Yes. Soul surrenders to a Higher Power in order to receive the energy that can magnify the Divine. Anything genuine is charged with that energy. Facing death strips away all that is not sterling. Once you've looked death straight in the eye, your vision is radically changed.

NR: How is it radically changed?

MW: All I can say to answer you, Nancy, is to repeat what Jung said when they asked him if he believed in God: "I don't believe. I know." Having cancer took me from "believing" to "knowing." I lie in bed at night and I wonder what it's going to be like to be dead, and something comes through in my cells. It's the mystery of the eternal in the ordinary.

Suddenly the ordinary becomes sacred, like my husband bringing in a flat of raspberries. Or the garden becomes just too beautiful to be endured. It's seeing "a World in a Grain of Sand/And a Heaven in a Wild Flower," to quote Blake. Everything becomes more intense.

But in order to make room for that intensity you've got to make the clearing.

NR: The clearing?

MW: Yes. I've let so much of the ego-world go: efficiency, leadership, expectations, politeness. I have no time for conversation now where I have no

interest. I have neither time nor energy to be bothered with it. With the cancer, what has burned off in me is unbelievable. I feel as though a powerful
purifying system is at work in me. Life is being simplified as a result. Simpli-
fying for me is a bosom friend of concentration. Both are sacred values.

NR: Along with simplicity and concentration, what role does discipline play
in your life?

MW: My life is very disciplined now. Discipline is such a beautiful word; it
comes from the same root as "disciple." You know Christ's saying: "My yoke is
easy, and my burden light"? You, the pupil, look into the eyes of the teacher
whom you love, and because the teacher loves you as you are, you want to be
like the teacher. So it's not a forced discipline—it's a discipline of love.

NR: The teacher in this case being the feminine?

MW: Yes, the fiercely loving Great Mother. There's another law operating
through her which is totally different from what we experience as the wishes
of our egos.

NR: In my own situation with environmental illness it's still a mystery to me
how I've been able to apply the required discipline to my life. As you know,
this illness has forced me to live a very careful existence, restricted by what I
can eat, where I can go, and so forth. Much to my surprise, out of all the chaos
and feeling of loss of control which was my initial reaction to this illness, has
come a loving discipline—although it took ten years for me to get to the
"loving" stage.

   People think that kind of change, in which you give up many addictive habits and accept a more natural way of being, happens overnight. It
doesn't.

MW: No, it does not. What you've been going through may have seemed like
chaos at times but underneath the chaos there is the order of the feminine
principle. The order of the unconscious has its own morality that takes you to
a much deeper level of Reality.

NR: It felt like a rebirth. One day something just turned around inside me, and from then on I was able to apply the discipline to my life that I needed to get well. Before then I had been living on willpower, resenting all the changes that I didn't want to make. When I let go and just *accepted*, and tried to live a day at a time—that's when I began to feel the beginnings of healing.

This turning around certainly wasn't anything that came from my head; I didn't talk myself into it. I had already tried that and it hadn't worked.

MW: Illness puts many things in place. What happens is that once the body remembers its archetypal pattern it will not go back to the neurotic one. During your illness, you discovered there are laws from the unconscious to be obeyed, and that when you learn that discipline you become a different person.

I can see a profound change in you, Nancy; I can see the turn around in you as much as you see the turn around in me. I can hear the clarity in your voice now. I can hear the hope; I can hear the passion, the vitality. You're interested in life again; the instinct is supporting the thinking. The vitality has taken you over and you are *in it*. Ross says that you're no longer the passive person you were when he first met you. You're fierce!

NR: Fierce?

MW: Yes, you have a fierce pursuit of understanding, of the life-force. That's exactly the way I saw you when I first knew you, but then you lost that. By the time Ross met you several years later your physical strength was down, the concentration wasn't there, the focus wasn't there. Then the physical energy became less and less, and gradually you became a victim.

NR: Seeking through this book for an understanding of my soul's health and for the planet's health has been a huge pull up for me, Marion. Both have strengthened me; I no longer feel like a victim. I now see that environmental illness is patriarchy's gift to our society. It is a bully which moves into bodies already made vulnerable by a lack of consciousness. Not too many people are going to want to be turned around like we were, though.

MW: Well they're either going to turn around or they're going to die early. The world of the unconscious tends to be shockingly lawful. The Sufi poet Rumi said:

Since you are properly a clod
You will not break as dust.
If you do not break as dust,
Then He who molded you will break you.

That's tough!

NR: Destiny has its way of dealing with us, hasn't it?

MW: Oh, indeed it does. People say that there is no law in the feminine, but you build levees along the Mississippi River and you'll find out whether there's a law concerning that river or not. And you drive yourself as fast as you can for twenty years, and you'll find out whether there is a law within your body that says whether you need rest or not.

NR: Do you think that drivenness had anything to do with your cancer?

MW: No, I wouldn't say so. When I was a school teacher I was driven—I was a perfectionist of the first order. As an anorexic I was driving myself to death.

NR: You wrote that wonderful book *Addiction to Perfection* right out of your own gut experience then, didn't you?

MW: Yes, I did. But then I had five years of analysis and I certainly gave up my perfectionism after that. My speeches since then have not been perfect, and the books certainly aren't perfect. So I wouldn't put that accusation on myself. My analysis did a lot for me.

NR: Do you feel that you're more in tune with the Divine Will now?

MW: I try to be. That's the meaning of *kairos:* that you are where the universe wants you to be at any given moment. Kairos operates in a spiral which is the way the feminine thinks, as opposed to the patriarchy which sees everything in terms of *chronos,* chronologically, in linear fashion. In kairos you as an individual are in harmony with the wishes of the universe. There's a moment when everything lines up and you can feel it lining up, and you know "this is it." It's a different kind of time.

NR: You're out of yourself at that point, are you?

MW: There's the paradox: you are both out of yourself, and you are one hundred percent in yourself. You and the other energy are one. For that moment that little spark of the God and Goddess that is in you is totally in sync with the total God and Goddess of the universe. That's surrender. Here again is the paradox: we think of that word *surrender* as weakness, but in fact by surrendering we step into our Reality.

It's important to remember in all that I'm saying, Nancy, that I have been concentrating on my spiritual journey for most of my life. Surrender doesn't arrive once and for all. Surrender has become a way of life that takes me ever deeper into Reality. It costs us everything that we are.

NR: How do you know when it's a Higher Power that is directing you, and not your ego?

MW: Ego direction is driven; soul direction has its own rhythm in harmony with the One. With soul surrender you find purpose, illumination, transcendence (all those bad, New Age words!)—whatever you call touching into that soul place. When you're dancing, for example, and you are taken over by the music, "you are danced." Or you are painting and you find your arm is being moved and you are filled with a life energy that you, in your ego, don't possess. Then you know you've *surrendered* to a Higher Power.

NR: How would learning to surrender to a Higher Power affect how we treat the planet?

MW: Once we're in connection with that Love coming through our own cells, then we can feel the suffering in the cells of the tree, in other people, in the planet. We recognize Oneness. Then we simply cannot violate the Earth.

Here's where I think the feminine archetypal energy is trying to reach us: in order to reconnect to nature we have to turn the destructive, patriarchal energy of our addictive drives around. We have to open ourselves to that feminine energy—to *process, presence, paradox, receptivity.*

Here's where we have to learn to *surrender* and hear the messages from our abandoned souls before it's too late.

CHAPTER FOUR

ENSOULED ON THE PLANET

NANCY RYLEY: Marion, you have said that we have to confront our addictions first, before we can connect to nature. Does our refusal to confront our addictions lead indirectly to our destruction of Mother Earth?

MARION WOODMAN: I think so, yes. As children many of us feel a deep connection to Her. But our culture warps our natural instincts. That warping leads to addictions. But there's a suicidal drive in the addicted individual and in the addicted society. Our planet is coming up against the wall. There's famine over much of the Earth, problems with the rain forests and the ozone layer and over-population, and garbage that we put into ships and set afloat because we don't know what to do with it.

Yet, despite these horrors, we are still doing precisely what we know will be ultimately destructive. Denial! Denial! We are still accepting a cultural value that annihilates the Earth. If we don't change, we are going to our own extinction. This is precisely what addicts do. Addicts—in other words most of our society—pretend there's nothing wrong. As they laugh and talk and plan, they deny their dying souls. That's what we're doing to the planet. We fight about things that won't matter if we are extinct.

NR: You mean addicts have lost touch with the instinct for survival?

MW: That's right. We have a consumer society where there's no hope for a satiation point, because we're cut off from our instinctive roots that would know when to stop eating, or drinking, or consuming, or whatever.

NR: And what's the result of that on the planet?

MW: To destroy it. An addict is destroying himself. Or herself. And if we have no respect for our own matter we will certainly have no respect for the planet's matter. We'll just go on plundering it.

I saw a film this morning that was horrendous. It was about Yosemite and Yellowstone Parks and what was happening to destroy the habitat of the grizzly bear, and all the glorious animals who live in those areas. It was sad, sad, sad—the great bull moose were letting out their great shrieks, and the narrator said that soon these sounds would not be heard again.

NR: How can we stop all this, Marion?

MW: The only way to stop it is to reconnect with the roots.

NR: When Jung said that we had "lifted ourselves up from our roots and were about to lose our connection to the Earth,"[4] is that what he meant?

MW: Yes. He meant that we've lost touch with our archetypal instincts, with the feminine, with matter. In the physical dimension the archetype is a natural pattern. The pigeon follows a natural courting pattern; the mourning dove has a slightly different one. Every creature has its own inner antenna that says hibernate, or fly south, or whatever. Everything in nature has an archetype within it that directs its growth and its behavior. One day someone is going to say, "Of course, the archetype contains the DNA." The DNA is the pattern that makes you what you are, physically.

In our society, we don't relate to our instincts in our bodies any more than we relate to the spiritual side of the archetype. Jung pictured the normal rhythmic flow of energy between the two as a spectrum with red at one end of the spectrum representing our instincts, and blue at the other representing the spiritual dimension. He saw this as an image of the energy of the *psychoid archetype,* because it has two sides. And he considered the physical end of the spectrum just as important as the spiritual dimension of the archetype. In other words, our relationship to the patterns of our bodies was as important as our relationship to the patterns in our psyches. That's where the totality lay.

NR: And you're saying that if we lose touch with our instinctive knowledge of those natural patterns we no longer know how to function and respond in a normal way?

MW: I would suggest that when we pollute the Earth because of our various addictions—when we destroy the natural unity in nature—that physical human responses, and plant and animal responses, are disturbed and in some cases destroyed.

There was a tragic film made years ago called *Mondo Cane* which showed the devastation wreaked by the 1945 atomic bomb on the Pacific. Great sea turtles, instead of following their natural archetypal patterns to the sea, turned and went inland to find water. They died there in the sand.

NR: Is that because they no longer knew where the sea was?

MW: Exactly. It was the saddest thing; I just sat in the theater and cried. Here were these 400-year-old turtles, and the darling things had done what they had always done: they'd laid their eggs. Then they turned in the wrong direction. They turned away from the sea and they climbed the sand dune, and turned upside-down as soon as they got to the top. They tried to go over the dune but their bodies had upset and they died stranded like that. They had lost touch with the instinctive side of the correct thing to do. An addict is like that great turtle turning around to the sand dune instead of to the sea.

NR: And as addicts we too have lost our proper orientation to the planet?

MW: I think so. If the Earth isn't functioning the way it was meant to, we have no guide, no compass to steer by. More than that, we've lost the North Pole. So it's a double tragedy because the compass is no longer true and the North Pole is no longer there.

NR: Because of us, the Earth has never before been in such a diminished state.

MW: That's exactly my point. Why is the universal sperm count so diminished? Why doesn't the body remember how to get well? This is a very important point because of your interest in the mystery of why the body turns against itself when the auto-immune system breaks down. Why does this happen? Why does the body become its own enemy?

My point is that it has disassociated from the physical energetic field of the archetype. It has done so because the Earth is so full of unnatural pollutants that it no longer carries the pure archetypal energy for us to relate to.

Now even our food is in danger of genetically engineered tampering—which, incidentally, we may be oblivious to as we eat our tinkered-with tomato.

NR: I just read a paper documenting recent studies in Poland showing that urban smog there is damaging the DNA of their children. And that the cancer-causing particles in this smog can be found—to a greater or lesser degree—in all urban industrialized areas in the world. And we, the people of the globe, aren't massively protesting this and changing our lifestyles in order to do something about it!

MW: I know. When I walk down my street and find myself reeling after receiving a huge dose of diesel exhaust from a passing truck, I ask myself, "What are my human rights?" Surely we and our children and our grandchildren have the right to walk on the sidewalk without being poisoned.

NR: You know, we talk and talk about these things, Marion, but very few people seem to be registering.

MW: People, as you say, aren't registering—but we aren't just talking words, Nancy. That's where people like you and me come in: I am one of millions of people with cancer, and you are one of millions with environmental illness. What will wake people up if their own death sentence doesn't?

NR: I don't even know that cancer will do it, or environmental illness, because we humans seem able to adapt ourselves to anything. If the tap water is contaminated, we buy bottled water. If the air is giving us problems, we buy an air filter. But the poor can't afford vitamin pills to make up for denatured food, or filters for the air and the water.

What worries me is that by adapting and then hunkering down to look after ourselves, we better-off people are forgetting the bigger picture. I did that myself—I went right off into that self-protective space. Psychologically, I couldn't get beyond the four walls where I knew I was physically safe from the contaminated world. Then my life became a prison.

MW: I know; I have had people in my practice who went from sickness to sickness. It became a neurosis, and all their energy got tied up in nourishing the neurosis because they couldn't look at the larger picture. This is not only annihilation of the individual, it's annihilation of the planet. *It's all one.* That's the point, Nancy. It is a *uni*-verse. If we don't relate our individual illness to the planet's illness, life becomes purposeless.

NR: How do you make people understand that as long as we're "addicted" to patriarchal/materialistic values we run the risk of destroying ourselves?

MW: I don't try anymore. I did for a while, but I think people have to come to a place where they're against the wall and on their knees before they turn around. If we haven't been on our own knees in front of our own wall, to the point where we want to do something about the plain fact that we can't get up, we won't do anything for anybody else. Certainly we won't do anything for a tree. Not to mention the Earth. So long as we're trapped in our arrogance, we know nothing about compassion.

I know from my own experience, and from my experience with my analysands, that until we're against the wall we don't really do anything to change. It's terrible that we have to learn this way, but it seems that extremity is necessary to open people's hearts. I think that it's that striking down that opens the heart. And the opening of the heart is where the forgiveness comes in.

NR: Is it only out of the world's awareness of its collective pain that soul awakening will come?

MW: Yes. I think we have to open our hearts and feel our collective wound. That's where we learn love. Through our own suffering, our hearts are broken open in love for one another.

But *love* in our culture is such a sentimental chocolate-syrup word. So often it means need, compulsive need. But *love is an energy.* It moves through our bodies; it moves between people, a force that holds atoms together. That's how I understand love.

NR: Do you think that the pain many of us are now enduring is being given to us so that we may reconnect with God?

MW: If you think of God as an energy coming from inside, and God as both masculine and feminine (I insist on that because for most people God tends to have only masculine connotations)—if you think of that energy as God and

Goddess, then yes, I believe ours is a journey to the realization, the *making real*, of the god and goddess within each individual. "The Kingdom of God is within you." It is also without.

But I think that to mature into the society where we are now moving, we first have to be free of the old father and his patriarchal laws that protect the old mother and her deadly security, because they cripple us. We have to be free of the archaic images of God and Goddess.

God and Goddess are manifesting in new imagery. Our task, I believe, is to connect with those images that are now the new perceptions, the new experiences of love within us.

NR: Can you elaborate on these new perceptions of God and Goddess imagery?

MW: I have talked about God and Goddess as archetypal energies, and the fact that we cannot see those magnetic fields with our eyes. But artists have always created images of them. Dreams are images of those archetypal dimensions, and how their energies are relating to each other. We look at a medieval painting and we see the old God, God the Father, whirling fishes about in the sea. We may admire the artistic energy without being able to connect to the image. Or we may look at a nineteenth-century sentimental Christ and not be able to connect to that either. Different periods of history have different images that they put onto the archetype of this huge energetic field called God, or this other huge field called the Goddess.

The images that were once so popular in the church, images that satisfied the imaginations of people who believed in them (transubstantiation as metaphor, for example) are no longer satisfying for many people. In part because technology has made such inroads on the imagination, people can't imagine the mystery. For us there's got to be new imagery.

So the Dream Maker, or whatever you want to call the energy that creates these dreams, gives us these miracles—these images—every night. Sometimes we're struck down by the uniqueness and originality of the images that appear. We've no idea where they come from: we call them bizarre. Yet, if you pick up a book on quantum physics, you may see the image that appeared in your dream; you may see the energy moving in the electrons and photons as it manifested in your dream. There is a profound connection between quantum physics, the body, and the spiritual mysteries. The new imagery is connected to that relationship between matter and energy.

Many artists today are painting energy; many healers "see" energy fields in the body and attempt to reconnect them into a harmonic whole. It's in our unconscious and it's been this way from the beginning of time.

NR: Can most people relate to these images?

MW: Most people? No, they can't relate. They think they're bizarre. The imagery's way ahead of them. But, you know, it's the magnet that's trying to pull us toward this new vision. And you know, "where no vision is, the people perish."

But people who are culturally secure, within the confines of the cultural paradigm, don't want to know what's in their unconscious. It is too dangerous. So they disown their own inner violence and project it into movies and television. But would they spend hour after hour watching a television trial if their own soul weren't on trial? No way!

Many of the greatest artists, like William Blake and Mozart, died and were thrown into paupers' graves because nobody believed they were sane: their images were too far out. And these were the men who were blessed with incredible vision. Now, of course, we recognize it. But how long has it taken? Two hundred years. And the same thing is going on right now. Some people are blessed with incredible vision. Of course, it's very hard to tell the real vision from the insane one. Genius and madness are two sides of one coin. Blake was considered mad and so was Mozart at the end.

NR: Do you think that the new imagery will connect us to the higher energies we need to evolve, even if we don't understand it right now?

MW: Yes, I think we're going into a totally new ethos, one that is beyond our imagination, where there's a new masculine and a new feminine. But we still have no idea where it is that we're going. Still, the images in our dreams each night take us a little closer. I think that by keeping in touch with our dreams we will very slowly move towards a different Reality.

Cultural patterns are being shifted through individual dreams. For example, a person who is locked in matter (a negative mother complex) in a body that is dense, without consciousness—if that person works daily with dream imagery, body consciousness, and sound in the body, then the metabolism of the body changes and the cells vibrate with new, light energy. The sensibilities and sensitivities are transformed. Perception is opened to other levels.

So all we can do is stay on our paths and move with the imagery that is taking us. That's the feminine principle: enjoy the process. Trust the process. We may never see the product, but that's all right.

NR: The imagery that's coming into your life now, are you able to work with it and have it help you?

MW: The imagery that's coming into my life now is brand-new imagery. It has to do with vibrations. That's why I'm so interested in quantum physics, and in the power of images in dreams to change the chemistry of the body. The images that we eat, psychically, are able to change the chemistry of our body. Do you know that, Nancy? It's the science of psychoneuroimmunology.

For example, we can choose whether we're going to watch the television news every night at eleven o'clock. We can choose whether to eat those horrendous images and take them to bed and try to digest them all night. We need to be conscious of the connection between those images and the fact that we can barely crawl to work the next morning and that our immune system is gradually breaking down.

Just as we have the power to choose to eat junk food physically, so we have the power to choose to feed ourselves murderous imagery psychically. Then we create a murderous interior. And that is partly what's going on with our whole technological world.

NR: Which I guess is one reason why we're raping and plundering everything—we pick it up on the tube every night.

MW: That's right. And that's where the masculine sword has to be used, where we say, "I will turn those images off at this time of night." This is where a lot of people haven't got the masculine strength to protect the feminine. The sword is important, Nancy. I'm not talking about blinding ourselves to reality. I'm talking about making space for our soul to communicate with us.

NR: Tell me about the sword.

MW: Well, the sword I'm talking about is the sword of discretion, with which

I say, "Is this program of value to me? Is this the right time to watch it? Is it sapping my energy?" Questions such as these have to be asked about ideas, relationships, possessions, anything that may be becoming destructive to the soul's growth. What is destructive has to be, first of all, recognized; and, secondly, cut. That takes courage.

Time is huge now. We have to ask ourselves, "Is there *time* for this in my own individual life? Have I got *time* to spend on this, or do I have to work on the new imagery? Where is the value here?" That's what I mean by using the masculine sword in one's life.

NR: Are these the questions that everybody should be asking themselves?

MW: Yes. But it's easier to sleep in the past than to open our eyes to a future we don't know.

NR: This is a lot for most people to take on, you know, Marion. Most people will say, "I'm going along all right in my life; why do I need to do all this soul-searching? Why do I need to go through all that pain?"

MW: I think that the people who are doing the soul-searching have no alternative. It is very painful, and it gets them into painful situations. But I think some people are, either by destiny or by their own nature, called to do it, and they have no alternative.

I don't think anybody chooses to do this work. On the other hand, I don't really think anyone escapes either. Some people die rather than do it. Things happen to all of us. Jung tells us that what is not brought to consciousness comes to us as fate.

NR: What do you think life would be like without doing this work?

MW: Well, it would be unconscious—vege-ing out; it would be living the life of what I call a happy carrot. And if you're a happy carrot you just say, "Well, that's fate, this was meant to happen. I accept what comes along, and I get on with it. I don't ask a whole lot of questions and I don't pretend to be God with a whole lot of answers. I can't see the point of philosophizing and intellectualizing everything until there's no joy left. And all this business of writing down dreams—it's all fantasy. Mystical crap."

That's what they say. And I'll tell you, I honestly envy them sometimes. I would love to be a happy carrot. But I can't be. I have to keep asking questions. And I can't be bothered living if there's no purpose; that's the truth. I cannot be bothered living if there is no purpose.

NR: What is your purpose?

MW: I believe there is a higher purpose. I believe that my soul has work to do while I'm here on this Earth, that there is a karma, that I have to burn off a certain amount of darkness, unconsciousness, garbage from my soul in the few years that I'm here, in order to go on to the next life.

Because I don't believe the soul can die, Nancy. That's the agony of it. You can see the abandoned soul looking out of the eyes and saying, "See me. Don't let me die in here." The soul can be abandoned and left in a dark hole in the attic, a dark hole in the cellar. But it doesn't die. That is the agony that manifests in dreams.

In India they say that the soul repeats, and comes back again. And the process goes on and on and on. That's what is meant by burning off our karma.

Addicts tend to abandon their souls. They go screaming and roaring off in whatever direction, but if they're drinking themselves into eternal sleep they're not living the soul. In dreams it shrieks and screams and begs for attention.

Finally there is a moment in life when they're thrown against a wall and have to decide: "Do I want to live or do I want to die?" And that means, "Am I going to let my soul live or am I going to abandon it and hold onto my addiction until I die?" Which is it? And they choose.

Many people go to sleep and never ask themselves the question. They just quietly go on sleepwalking. But the soul is no less abandoned.

Now, once you make the soul choice you're in different territory— totally different territory because you allow the transcendent to manifest through your body-instrument. It's like being a dancer, or a cello, or a paint brush. You are the instrument that's being used to animate the love that's coming through.

NR: Experiencing life through the inner eye of the soul, and through the life of the imagination, is everything to you, then, isn't it, Marion?

MW: If soul and imagination are surrendered to God and Goddess, then it is everything. It's the real purpose of being alive. For me the creative masculine is the surrendered imagination. My conscious feminine container surrenders to that creative masculine. Then life is intercourse with the Divine. Out of that union comes the Divine Child, the new consciousness.

Without the imagination . . . why, I can't even imagine what life would be without the imagination. There would be no culture, no painting, no books, no science. Nothing! Why, we'd be back in caves.

NR: About the tie of the imagination to the Divine, is there "a glory to be expressed," as you once put it?

MW: Yes, there's a glory to be expressed! But it depends on how you see that. I'm not going off the Earth in saying that. For me the glory to be expressed is the glory of the violet with a raindrop on it, or the glory of the pink on that cloud out there. Or the clouds of glory surrounding a newborn baby. Or the fact that I can move my finger and know what it takes to move that finger. All these are miracles. Matter is sacred: the human and the Divine interwoven.

This is why I have such faith that the planet will survive. I don't think that we are the ultimate boss. I think that there is an evolution going on now from within the psyche that is pushing consciousness towards a recognition of the conscious feminine. And it's never been on this planet before. Human beings have never before had to perceive the sacredness of matter in order to survive.

Whether we like it or not, we are being forced, right now, to recognize that. It's not in the future. Right now if we look right there, we can see the manifestation of the Divine on Earth. If we can't see it, then we're either blind or stupid; our eyes aren't open to the miracle that is happening every minute in nature.

NR: You do see hope for "the Forsaken Garden" then, do you, Marion?

MW: You know, Nancy, maybe this is the period in which we are *returning* to the Garden. Adam and Eve, when they were thrust out of the Garden, had to then walk all the way around it, experiencing the other three gates until they understood the meaning of the *whole* Garden. Then they could re-enter it at the gate from which they were turned out. Maybe Eve, who originally introduced Adam to the Tree of Experience, is now taking him back and introducing him to the Tree of Life.

NR: What do you think that Garden would be like?

MW: If we ever did return to the Garden it would be a very different place from the innocent paradise of our childhood because it would have within it our awareness of a balance of nature, humanity, and divinity.

NR: Was there ever such a place?

MW: No, but we do have a dream of wholeness inside us. It would be a Garden where human beings would treat each other in a very different manner than we do now, a place where there was a natural moral law that could be depended on.

I grew up in my father's garden, and I took everything for granted. If I wanted a carrot I went over and pulled one and ate it. I was innocent. But there's a greater innocence than childhood innocence. It's the wisdom of someone who has gone through life and realizes the price that is paid for consciousness, and who can then value the Garden. Older people can come to that simplicity, that higher innocence.

NR: We can never go back to that original Garden, to our original innocence, though, can we?

MW: No, there's no way to go back. The return to the Garden is about coming full circle. It's about returning to a place with *knowing,* bringing to it a consciousness that was not there before. It's a new vision of the Garden because *we* have changed. Understanding the meaning of the Garden makes us a part of the whole of life. Blake talks about the child's world of innocence. Then we go out into "generation," as he calls it, or the world of experience. We live in that world until we return to the Garden, bringing to it our knowledge of experience and consciousness so that we see it as if for the first time. That conscious seeing is the higher innocence, Blake's Jerusalem. Now we can see, and we can hear, and we can smell, and we can touch—with a *totally* different perception.

That's where my illness has taken me. I thought it was all being taken from me; then suddenly I was able to see in a totally different way because I valued what I was looking at.

NR: The ordinary things?

MW: The very ordinary extraordinary things. Ever since I've had cancer the whole world has become the sacredness of matter. That's the Garden that we return to. I feel that I've done the full circle.

NR: As you said earlier, your illness took you there. Do you feel that one of the reasons that you are still here is so that you can convey the meaning of your experience to the rest of us?

MW: Well, I can describe it, but I really feel that we human beings have to go through some near-death experience in order to value the Garden. Everyone has to go through that in some way. Once you realize that life could end tomorrow, you see trees, you see the sky, you see everything differently. I'm very aware that this could all end in a flash, literally. One heart attack and it's all over.

A fundamental principle of the feminine is that it's a transformation process based on death as part of life. That's nature. In winter we're into the death cycle, in spring it's a rebirth. That's the important thing about the feminine: you always look to the birth. When I'm lying in bed at night, Sophia very gently whispers and reassures me that Her cycle is life, death, and rebirth. Accepting that principle makes death possible.

NR: Do you feel that most people try to avoid the pain of consciousness—the pain of the life-death-rebirth experience—in our culture?

MW: Yes, I do; that's where the addiction comes in. When it comes to pain, we don't want it; so we avoid it in any possible way we can.

As you know, Nancy, I see this culture in terms of addictions. An addict can be blind to the death wish that is killing him, or he can open his eyes and choose life. As people on this planet we can do the same thing—we can choose to live in the Garden or we can destroy it. We can either stupidly proclaim that we are all-powerful; there is no miracle out there; there is no life-force that we have to bow to. Or we can humbly acknowledge that there is an incredible mystery creating all those different life forms.

NR: Including us. Are we each a spark of some Greater Soul, do you think?

MW: That's how I see it. If we believe in a divine order, then everything, everything on the Earth, is part of that divine order. We're all little sparks of One Soul. We are "ensouled" on this planet. And once that comes through to consciousness, we understand what love is. The atoms are held together by love; love is the glue that holds it all together.

Maybe that's what the new millennium will be about, realizing that we are all ensouled in One Soul. I do believe in Divine Providence. I don't think that the globe could have evolved this far only to be annihilated. My sense is that this chaos that we're going through could go on for a long time yet—that maybe we're only at the beginning of the real chaos. But when we finally come to our knees, something else will happen.

NR: What do you think will happen?

MW: We might realize that we are one people inhabiting one country—that we are all part of One Soul. That we do belong. That we are all part of one cosmos.

And that the life-force is in the willow, the daisy, the chickadee, in every animated thing. And that we are part of that totality, part of that love.

THE DEEP MEANING OF ENVIRONMENTAL ILLNESS

THE CHANGES that have come about in me as a result of the time I spent with Marion Woodman have been many and varied. As I grow older, I continue to struggle to integrate all that I have learned, and I know that this is something that I shall do for the rest of my life.

Marion and I have bonded at a very deep level through our illnesses—not as victims, but as survivors. It is, as Albert Einstein once said, "a fellowship of those who have been marked by pain." Ours is a very sick society, it's true; but it goes far beyond that. These environmentally related diseases, such as cancer and allergies, are like sores on the face of a very sick planet. Marion and I have also bonded in our mutual compassion for the pain of the Earth.

Our failure to recognize the validity of the feminine as an energy that everyone must live out in a positive way means that some people inadvertently live out its dark, destructive side. Cancer patients and the environmentally ill are among these, because these illnesses tend to surface in people who have been overwhelmed by the culture's anti-feminine bias.

A dream which I had in the early 1980s shows how a patriarchal culture can kill the feminine in individuals, and in the collective.

Dec 14, 1983
It was very dark, but I could see a man's head coming towards me. I knew he had a knife, which he was holding low down. Then everything became completely dark and I couldn't see him any more, but I knew the knife was there. It was flashing with light, and it was about level with my abdomen. I started to scream and scream.

I woke up from this dream terrified. The abdomen is at the center of much of the feminine world, including the ability to conceive and bring forth new life. If considered psychically, as well as physically, this birthing of a more feminine acceptance of life is about to be murdered by my own culturally approved, over-intellectualized attitude, imaged as "a man's head." The man in this dream is my assertive creative spirit, who is trying to relate to me but doesn't know how, since he cannot reach past my intellect to communicate with me through the feminine feelings in my gut. So he uses a knife.

When our bodies are dissociated from our heads, the emotions in our bodies are no longer available to us, leaving us lonely and isolated. Our inability to act out of our feminine feeling-values becomes a familiar story, in many cases caused by the attitudes of our patriarchal culture. Patriarchy demands perfection from us, and in the ensuing struggle to *achieve* at all costs, it forces us into our "heads," which is death for the feminine soul.

The effect of adopting patriarchal thinking on the health of the body is illustrated by another dream.

June 13, 1981
I dream of a boring, conventional woman (me) who is trying to get past a guard at the door of a doctor's waiting room. He is a traditional MD, and I have a long list in my hand showing all my health problems. Once inside the waiting room, I see a snake there which really frightens me, although it's not very big. A woman with dark hair picks it up and tosses it into a lower area (a pit) at the back of the room by way of getting rid of it.

This dream is seventeen years old, but worth repeating because this is the energy I've been working with since then, trying to transform it. The snake represents our life-force. As a symbol of healing, it entwines itself around the staff of Asclepius, the ancient Greek god of medicine, and is doubly present on the caduceus of today's physicians. But the life-force not only emerges in our instinct for survival. It also bursts forth as our whole joy of life, where it expresses itself in the spontaneity of song, dance, and play, and in everything else that makes us glad to be alive.

In Jungian psychology, the snake is a major symbol of psychic energy, and is aligned to the feminine through its associations with the Earth and the underworld. Who was the unknown woman in my dream who was tossing out all that beautiful energy? I suspect that she was my repressed feminine feeling-value which, because I was not living out her energy at the time, was cutting me off from the life-force in my body.

Seventeen years ago the "pit" (gut) of my body was the site of many repressed emotions, "tossed" in there since childhood. If expressed, they would no doubt have been considered unacceptable by the "conventional" society in which I was brought up. Later, by making my vulnerable gut its target, the "pit" became the focus of my environmental illness. Meanwhile, since my own life-force (which would have healed me) was tossed aside into an out-of-the-way "back" area of my life, I "waited" for the doctor to cure me of my long "list" of complaints, including my chronic "back" aches.

From an archetypal perspective, this dream shows how repression of feminine feeling is linked to illness. In my case it is environmental illness, but it could just as easily have been cancer of the colon or the reproductive system. This dream also shows that an unadventurous ("boring") approach to medical treatment for these problems isn't going to work because most of today's conventional medicine isn't in touch with the healing snake-energy in the body. Just to be sure I got the message, there was even a "guard" against my entry into the doctor's waiting room, where my own deep healing energy (the tossed-out snake) might not be included as part of the treatment.

Marion Woodman has been a model for me of how to live with disease, not by medicating it in order to mask the symptoms, but by trying to learn from it about the state of our psyches as expressed in our bodies. When I look back at the kind of person I was before my illness, I can see that only a deep trauma could have forced a change in the controlling, perfectionist kind of person I had become. Environmental illness had become my fate because, like so many contemporary women, I had become a driven daughter of the patriarchy in my thoughtless acceptance of its demanding pace. For us it was fight or flight all the way—our adrenals wrecked, our immune systems broken by that inner voice that whipped us on. What the society through its addictions was doing to the planet, we were projecting onto our bodies.

Here is another dream which illustrates the damage that patriarchal thinking can do to our souls.

June 17, 1982
I went down into a garden where there were two snakes in a bas-

ket. They were raised up on top of some kind of letter-box or platform arrangement. One snake was white, the other was pale green. They both glistened as though covered with diamonds, and they seemed to be playing with one another. Then a man from my office—who, in actuality, always made me feel that I was neither good enough at my job, nor as good as the men who were doing the same job as I was—said to me, "Quick, run! One of the snakes is coming out and will come after you." So I ran.

I woke up brokenhearted from this dream. I associated diamonds with precious treasures of great worth, both physical and spiritual. The two snakes, "glistening as though covered with diamonds," are luminous beings whose playful energy—had I been able to follow it—would have led me to the mystical center of my body and soul, to my Self. Instead, the "mind-forg'd manacles," which William Blake claimed the patriarchal culture had used to fetter our souls, enter my consciousness in the form of a disapproving male colleague. His bullying attitude triggers my own internal bully, which colludes with his disapproval, and—in the end—victimizes me. Since I am unable to stand up for my own true feelings against a perfectionist patriarchal attitude which tells me that my best efforts are never good enough, the "profoundly religious quest" that had begun in the "garden" of my dream (which Laurens van der Post calls the quest for the feminine) is lost to me. Instead "I run," and the garden that held forth such promise becomes "the forsaken garden."

These dreams, while personal, are also archetypal because my psychology is typical of many of those brought up in this society. Without bringing what Marion Woodman calls our "bully/victim psychology" to consciousness in our individual lives, we will victimize ourselves and scapegoat others—and the planet—for what is our personal responsibility. Unless we, as a society, start relating to these deep psychological scars within us, we will not survive, because eventually Mother Nature will find a way of bringing us face-to-face with our transgressions.

Eventually I realized that my survival depended on my ability to silence the judgmental voice of that demanding patriarchal world that I had unconsciously absorbed. Taking my cues from Marion's example, I discovered that this illness had much to tell me about how to do that. In order to restore my connection to the feelings locked in my poisoned gut, I had to learn to work with my body, honoring its messages and giving it the love and discipline that it needed to heal. Equally important, I had to learn to become more flexible, more trusting, for the message that this disease was sending me was that nothing is predictable, nothing is controllable. The only way to live with it was to surrender, to accept what was happening to me, to bow my head to a greater wisdom being sent to me in my dreams, and say, "Thy will be done."

Throughout my entire experience of environmental illness, the thing that has most kept me in touch with my healing feminine side has been bodysoul work. Working to discover the transformative power of the dream symbol placed in my body was a life-changing experience for me. Using bodywork and dance to express the love and the anguish contained in the imagery, I was gradually able to get in touch with the life-force that was acting through my illness to make me whole. Long walks and cross-country skiing grounded me and reinforced an integration of body and soul. Through the insights which followed, I knew that a healing process had begun which I hoped would eventually enable me to experience my own wholeness. It was out of the intimate connection that I was then able to feel between my sick body and the bodysoul of our ill planet that the writing of this book evolved. I am now convinced that through such afflictions as cancer and environmental illness, the conscious feminine is trying to come into the world as one way to help turn things around on the planet. For me, sharing that experience is currently where the work of transformation lies.

As a Jungian analyst and daughter of a United Church minister, Marion Woodman has always had a deep personal and professional interest in the way the soul's life is given positive expression in our spiritual and artistic lives, and a desperate voice in our addictions. Well-known as an international lecturer and workshop leader, she has pioneered bodysoul work, exploring symptoms and dreams as bridges that can connect inner and outer worlds. In this way both a new feminine consciousness and a new masculine consciousness can be released into the planet. Inherent in all her work is her conviction that the evolution of masculine and feminine energies, as they relate to each other, is of central importance in the development of consciousness, and that the marriage of these two archetypal energies will give birth to the authentic personality that recognizes itself as belonging to the unity of the Earth.

Marion Woodman is the author of several books and tapes which focus on eating disorders and the recognition of feminine consciousness as the healing power in addictive behavior: *Addiction to Perfection, The Pregnant Vir-*

gin, The Ravaged Bridegroom, and *Conscious Femininity*. Her work with poet Robert Bly—which incorporates story-telling with poetry, commentary, and bodysoul work—has been extensive. In 1994, their six-hour video series *Bly and Woodman on Men and Women* was aired on the CBC. Recently, Marion Woodman and Robert Bly have co-authored *The Maiden King*, a book about the relationship of masculinity and femininity, within and without. The result has been an increasing demand in universities, churches, and learning circles throughout Canada, Europe, and the United States for Marion Woodman's lectures and workshops.

Marion Woodman is the recipient of three honorary doctorates from the University of Western Ontario, Pacifica Graduate Institute in California, and the Institute of Transpersonal Psychology. She lives with her husband, Ross Woodman, in London, Ontario.

NOTES

[1] Marion Woodman, *Conscious Femininity*, Toronto: Inner City Books, 1993, p. 125.

[2] Edward Edinger, *Ego and Archetype*, New York: Penguin-Viking Books, 1973, p. 65.

[3] Theodore Roszak, *The Voice of the Earth*, New York: Simon & Schuster, 1992, p. 137.

[4] C. G. Jung, *Psychology and Religion*, New Haven: Yale University Press, 1938, p. 95.

PART THREE

BUILDING JERUSALEM

"The work of saving the planet, which is clearly the work that most engages us, must, I think, be grounded in our relationship to God."

ROSS WOODMAN

JERUSALEM:
THE VISION OF WILLIAM BLAKE
AND THE ROMANTIC POETS

I FIRST heard Marion Woodman's husband, Ross Woodman, speak on a tape which I borrowed from a friend who had studied with him in the 1960s while a student at the University of Western Ontario. A professor of English there, his lectures on William Blake and the other Romantic poets still resonated for her many years later. For me, hearing Ross Woodman lecture on this same subject a few years ago offered me a new perspective on my environmental illness, my own descent into what Blake called "the dark Satanic Mills." And his observations about the emergence of the conscious feminine principle as a bodysoul in the imagination of William Blake greatly enhanced my own soul journey.

My interest in the English Romantic poets stemmed from my fascination with their acceptance of nature not as a fallen world but as our natural home, our own larger body, which we must learn to love and care for. This view of nature is very different from our culture's brutally exploitative one. Faced with my own illness, I have experienced first-hand the close connection between my body and the nature we are raping. I know that the healing of my body is intimately bound to the healing of the planet. But most people do not understand this connection between their own bodily health and the health of the planet. "Trying to get them involved in saving the planet is like trying to talk wine merchants into embracing prohibition," Ross Woodman said to me when I approached him about his involvement with this book. What he said on that occasion echoed my own beliefs about our extraordinary resistance to change when it comes to the environment.

What did the Romantic poets, and William Blake in particular, have to do with our planetary crisis? Why did I approach a professor of English to help me with my problem of environmental illness?

It is Ross Woodman's belief that the mind-body split which had taken the soul out of the natural world, and that Blake had experienced and tried to rectify, was now allowing us to bombard the planet with the chemicals that were making so many of us ill. Where had the soul that would protest this pillage gone to? My conversations with Ross Woodman amounted to an inquiry into the extent of the injury to the modern soul which had occurred since the onset of the scientific era. My main interest in talking to him, however, was to gain some understanding of the work of the Romantic poets in which they had explored the important connection between psyche and soma, soul and body.

The soul's re-emergence as the metaphorical bodysoul in the work of the Romantic poets was a concept that I had become familiar with through Marion Woodman's workshops. It was a reality voiced by Blake himself when he declared as early as 1790 what we are now only beginning to grasp. "Man," he wrote, "has no Body distinct from his Soul; for that call'd Body is a portion of the Soul discern'd by the five Senses, the chief inlets of Soul in this age." The question I ultimately addressed to Ross Woodman was: "Did the Romantic poets, by envisioning the marriage of soul to body, masculine to feminine, and mind to nature, start a change in our consciousness which would eventually evolve to become a new concept of the sacred suitable to our twenty-first century global culture? If so, how did this come about?"

By the end of the seventeenth century, any remnants of the symbolic imagery that had once supported an Earth Mother as the vitalizing principle in nature had been replaced by a new metaphor—that of a mechanical universe. Along with her disappearance in the natural world went any hope for continuing development of a bodysoul consciousness in the human world. For the next three centuries, the subjugation of nature was accompanied by a devaluation of feminine values in a rationalistic and scientifically oriented culture dedicated to patriarchal values.

In the early nineteenth century, William Blake and the Romantic poets clearly saw that an earlier unitary view of the soul, which had included both a feminine Eros consciousness and a masculine Logos principle, had been irrevocably altered. Calvinist Protestantism, which preached a separation of mind and body, and mechanistic science and the industrial revolution which reinforced the split between them, had completely changed the environment where the soul could flourish. How did these poets view the loss of soul which resulted and which has continued unabated into our own day?

The Romantic poets saw a parallel between the expansion into the rational, outward control of nature, and a violation of their own inner world. For them soul was embodied in the physical—in the imaginative life and sensuality of their own bodies, and in nature. Madness would ensue from an estrangement from nature. It would also result from the restriction—by a repressive rationalism—of the redeeming powers of the imagination.

What William Blake construed as soul destruction in his time was reflected in the devastation that he saw all around him as a result of the new industrial technology's impact on the landscape. He saw the threat to both our sanity and our souls in the presence of those "dark Satanic Mills" which were beginning to sully the landscape in early nineteenth-century industrialized England.

Another Romantic poet, Percy Bysshe Shelley, saw the advancement of science and its control over the external world as the greater threat to our internal worlds. The more science advanced, the more the internal world was circumscribed. Far from being hostile to science, however, Shelley celebrated the increased knowledge it provided. He just wanted the two worlds to be in balance. If people would only turn their attention to the internal world and get as much knowledge of it as they had of the external world, they'd be in paradise. In Shelley's view, people needed the *imagination* in order to see what science had really accomplished. Poetry, by defining the world imaginatively, would counter science's narrowly focused one-sidedness. In this way the external and internal worlds would be mirrored in each other; not only would they be in balance, they would be one and the same.

What concerned the Romantics was how to build a new concept of the soul out of the spiritual wasteland of an urbanized/industrialized world that had buried older beliefs about its nature. In his poem *Jerusalem*, Blake espoused the life of the soul as the Kingdom of God Within. His epic vision of the world of psychic reality pertained to the whole of humanity, but it was a vision which, in the name of material progress, was to be stifled and nullified by the same deadening forces which afflict our own time. For the Romantics, gaining entry into the world of the unconscious mind—to the repressed instinctual feminine roots of our own being as the repository of healing energies—was the only way to counteract this aggressive violation of the human spirit. Romantic poetry would be the gateway into that rich world—a world where the energies of the fettered psyche could be released, and besieged nature could be defended.

The masculine principle was the other soul energy at work that the Romantics addressed in their poetry, which William Blake notably did in his poem *Milton*. To Blake, whose work anticipated Jung, the clarity and discernment of the masculine principle had nowhere been more distorted by patriarchal thinking than in what he considered the morally bankrupt tenets of Judeo-Christianity. The distortion of the masculine principle by the patriarchy that would inflict irreparable damage on our natures—as well as on external nature—was a palpable threat for him and for the other Romantic poets. Jehovah morality was a tyrannical, judgmental outer and inner voice that dictated behavior in the repressive society of their day, just as it has in ours.

For Blake and the Romantics, the Puritan repression of sensuality and instinct was the slamming of the gate on both freedom of individual expression, and the celebration of nature, art, and the ecstasies of sexual love. Traditional morality spouting ideals without any grasp of psychological reality was blind to its own true motives; power was the shadow behind Jehovah's severity. The sought-for perfection in an age of science and enlightenment, when the feminine had been enthroned as a Goddess of Reason and the masculine had been bound to implacable laws and mechanistic science, would have to include in its reaching for the light what also lay in the darkness of the unconscious body.

If the Romantics experienced enormous difficulty in integrating feminine soul values, they also struggled to find a new paradigm of masculine energy that would release it from oppressive identification with a destructive patriarchy. For this new paradigm to emerge, the feminine had to be released from its largely unconscious state so that as the *conscious* feminine it could enter into a new and creative partnership with the *conscious* masculine. For the Romantics, the *androgyne* was one paradigm of this union. This union of masculine and feminine energies would then become the building blocks of a new "bodysoul" for a society which was devastating human and external nature because it had lost its spiritual rudder.

C. G. Jung was part of that Romantic initiation. He saw the feminine principle as an energy which ideally balanced its opposite—the masculine principle—in the psyche. The soul was a union of these energies which needed to be understood in the totality of both their positive and negative aspects if were are to truly become ourselves. For Jung, the uniting of masculine and feminine energies—the divine Inner Marriage—was the *sine qua non* of psychological wholeness. It is because our society today lacks that whole vision that we are exhausting the soil, over-fishing the oceans, and spilling chemicals into our food and water.

The estrangement from nature which was so evident in Blake's time has resulted in a serious collective pathology in our own. We in modern urbanized society increasingly manifest it as a diseased state that author and historian Theodore Roszak describes as follows:

> Industrialism, with its rapacious use of the environment as either raw material or dumping ground, has further entrenched the city's alienation from nature. It has more solidly institutionalized and rationalized urban culture's psychotic habits. Wilhelm Reich coined the phrase "body armor" for the neurotic defense mechanism that cuts us off from spontaneous vitality and sensuous intimacy. The industrial city might be seen as the collective "body armor" of our culture, a pathological effort to distance us from close contact with the natural continuum from which we evolve.[1]

If the donning of "body armor" is the price to be paid for survival in industrial society, we have certainly paid it in the widespread mental and physical disturbances experienced by many today as a result of disconnection from both our instincts and from nature. Only a deranged species would foul its own nest.

What remains unredeemed in "the darkness of the unconscious body" of industrial society's attitudes and behavior is one aspect of our soul life that Ross Woodman explores in the interview which follows. The social value of the Romantic poets today lies in their understanding of the negative impact their Puritan inheritance had on their culture; through their eyes we can see the effect that this same inheritance has had on ours. In his interpretation of John Milton's *Paradise Lost*—as seen through the extraordinary unitive vision of William Blake—Ross Woodman has shown us how our society has been traumatized by that legacy. In our obsessions with security, conformity, and efficiency we are failing as a society to integrate and live out the feminine instinctual energy that is our human heritage, shoving it into a prison of un-conscious activity until it is forced to seek an outlet in what Laurens van der Post called the "stirring of the underworld."

Today we are largely unaware that it is the managerial elites in corpo-rations, government, and the media who are the controlling mechanics who would rob us of our souls and our humanity. Ross Woodman's fear is that the power that annihilates both the feminine soul and the masculine spirit in a patriarchal world will lead us into planetary self-destruction. His concern re-ally comes home when we read a passage such as the following:

> There is no question that the way the world shapes the minds of its male children lies somewhere close to the root of our environmen-tal dilemma. As long as the men who run the media keep feeding the minds of the boys they seem to think are their only audience on a steady diet of *Terminators* and *Liquidators* and *Annihilators* and *Die Hards* and *Top Guns*, we cannot expect to free ourselves from the morals of extermination. We are tied to it by the psyches of the twelve-year-old boys who will grow up to become thirty-year-old corporation executives and forty-year-old colonels and fifty-year-old politicians. Consider for a moment the *Robocop* mov-ies that have enjoyed such popularity among males between the ages of ten and twenty-five. What do we have here as an example of male prowess? The corpse of a cop reanimated by science, equipped with an indestructible metal physique and an electronic brain, sent into the streets with an armory of hair-trigger phallic weaponry to perpetrate instantaneous mass annihilation. The bodies fly, the buildings explode, the vehicles collide, the blood gushes. All the kindest appeals and gentlest gestures on the part of ecofeminism and Feminist Spirituality pale before the virulent power of images like these that tempt but do not assuage the most violent appetites of the death instinct.[2]

In this scenario it is clear that the English Romantic poets are seminal figures for those of us struggling to become more conscious 150 years later. As a way of perceiving soul loss in our culture, the work of these poets has enor-mous psychological significance. As studies of the human drama in both its archetypal and mythological dimensions, their poetry is essential to us.

CHAPTER ONE

MAKING LOVE TO YOUR MUSE

NANCY RYLEY: Ross, you are a Blake scholar and an authority on Milton, Shelley, and the Romantic poets. What is the soul value of these poets to us today?

ROSS WOODMAN: "Poets," says Shelley, "are the unacknowledged legislators of the world." They are the prophet figures in the sense that they gave birth to the consciousness within which we live, even if we don't know it. It's a consciousness which we are still struggling to absorb. Shelley described this process of absorption as copying the creation of the poets into the book of common life.

NR: You say that theirs is "a consciousness which we are still struggling to absorb." To start with, weren't the Romantics reacting against a huge area of the thought of their time, which we too are trying to deal with?

RW: Yes. Romanticism may be superficially defined as a reaction against the triumph of Rationalism—of the Enlightenment in the eighteenth century. Above all, it is a reaction against the one-sided triumph of science and the scientific mind. In his *Defence of Poetry*, Shelley put it this way:

> The cultivation of those sciences which have enlarged the limits of the empire of man over the external world, has, for want of the poetical faculty, proportionally circumscribed those of the internal world; and man, having enslaved the elements, remains himself a slave.

Science affirmed the reality of matter, of the body; yet in discovering

135

the laws that governed it, it basically treated the body as a cadaver. Put another way, it treated the physical universe, including the physical body, as a machine. The scientific mind is horrified by the unruly human body subject to blind instinct. Until the senses are controlled by technology, turned into machines—the eye as microscope or telescope, the ear as radio waves, instinct as radar, et cetera—the senses are not to be trusted. The result is not a human being but a monster. When mind is imprisoned in this kind of materialism, the result is a nightmare. Mary Shelley enacts science as this kind of nightmare in her novel *Frankenstein*. Life is shooting an electric bolt into a cadaver and setting it in motion as if it were running on a battery.

The body as machine, humanity as a technological construct, a robot, a terminator which in the end self-destructs, has become a figure perfectly suited to science fiction and, above all, to the advanced technology of film. Our children really now do, from an early age, imagine themselves as monsters. And the monsters they imagine, we have largely become. We really are, or almost are, Mary Shelley's Doctor Frankenstein; I mean we have almost fully absorbed what her prophetic imagination created in 1818.

NR: In what way has Mary Shelley's monster become *us?*

RW: The monster in *Frankenstein* talks continually in the book about his alienation and loneliness because, as an artificial construct, his soul has been cut off from its roots in the natural world. It's because of this that he goes on the rampage and destroys everything in his path, just as we're doing with the planet. Science and technology make the same mistake that Victor Frankenstein did every time they build a dam, or clear-cut a forest, without noticing that they're destroying the souls of the people and the creatures that live on that land. In the case of indigenous peoples, they're destroying their culture, their collective soul.

By constructing the monster, Victor Frankenstein is trying to realize science's dream of conquering death and founding a race of immortal beings. In *Frankenstein,* which has the subtitle, *The Modern Prometheus,* Mary Shelley shows herself to be totally opposed to science's perception of its own omnipotence. Because she was aware of the implications of the Promethean act of stealing power from the gods, she considered the construction of the monster to be blasphemous.

NR: William Blake was another artist who envisioned our future in a patriarchal, industrial society. How did he express this fear of the machine age and of the machine body?

RW: Well, Blake spoke of "the dark Satanic Mills" of the industrial age, where we become simply cogs in a vast machine, where our feelings and thinking are taken over by a collective consciousness and a collective common-sensical attitude towards life. And where we've cut ourselves off from the unconscious so that all we've got left is technology.

From this perspective, the whole notion of nature is seen as a fixed order, governed by immutable laws, an order of nature to which we all must ultimately submit. And what doesn't belong to that order is considered to be simply either demonic or chaotic. But what Blake and the Romantics were concerned with was everything that doesn't belong to this view of nature as a fixed order of things, in other words; with feeling, with the whole realm of sensual life and the body, with the irrational world.

NR: Weren't the Romantic poets also concerned with a return to nature?

RW: Yes, but by a return to nature they mean a return to the dynamism of nature, the creative operations of nature. In our day we would say they were concerned with the indeterminate sub-atomic world that confronts the new physics. Shelley called it "the One Spirit's plastic stress" that sweeps through "the dull, dense world." He stressed the energy of nature—the life-force—and the importance of getting in touch with and giving new shapes to it.

NR: Is it possible that the images in external nature that were once a source of soul enrichment for a pre-industrial age dropped into the unconscious once science denied their existence? And were the Romantics concerned with reconnecting us to those energies?

RW: Yes. I would say that Romanticism is very much involved with the modern rediscovery of the unconscious; that is, with the journey into what the poet John Keats called "some untravelled region of my mind." Using a perennial plant as a metaphor of the soul, I would say that the Romantic poet is interested in the roots, what goes on *under* the Earth as the source of what happens above it.

Keats described the process of discovering what's going on in the un-conscious as "soul-making." For example, in his poem *Lamia*, he describes the transformation of a serpent into a beautiful woman who, as the poet Lycius's anima or feminine soul, becomes his bride. In the poem, the old philosopher, Apollonius, rejects this transformation as a delusion. He sees in her a threat to the established patriarchal order. When Lycius brings his bride, Lamia, before the court to celebrate their marriage, Apollonius cries out, "Begone, foul dream!" But the poet does not have sufficient faith in his own creative power to reject the condemnation of his anima muse by his old teacher. The result is the loss of his soul, which is his death as a poet. Here is how Keats concludes his poem:

> "A serpent!" echoed he [Apollonius]; no sooner said,
> Than with a frightful scream she vanishèd:
> And Lycius' arms were empty of delight,
> As were his limbs of life, from that same night.
> On the high couch he lay!—his friends came round—
> Supported him—no pulse, or breath they found,
> And in its marriage robe, the heavy body wound.

NR: It's fascinating that nearly two hundred years ago Keats expressed in his poetry the problem we now have of loss of soul at the hands of the established patriarchy, which is given voice by the old philosopher Apollonius. Can a soul really vanish permanently, in this case causing the death of the creative life of the poet?

RW: Well, to carry on with my metaphor of the soul as a "perennial plant," it can survive even the coldest winter; in other words, the most materialistic and patriarchal of cultures. But it can (and does) descend into "Hell," rise into "Heaven," suffer and grow in "Purgatory."

The epic poem is the soul of a people. But, like the soul of an indi-vidual, it's not static. It grows and changes, and retreats and collapses, and grows again.

NR: Even though the soul is perennially there, does the perception of it change over time? And if so, are these changing perceptions reflected in the poetry of each period?

RW: Yes, they are. The medieval imaging of the soul which Dante constructed in all its rich complexity—moving as Dante himself through these three worlds of Hell, Purgatory, and Heaven in his *Divine Comedy*—is very different from the Puritan soul which Milton showed us in *Paradise Lost*. And Blake's vastly complex structuring of the agonized Romantic and Modern soul in his epic, *Jerusalem*, is very different again. Though the soul in itself remains the same, our experience of it changes from age to age. The soul in each age has its own distinct character.

NR: What is the "distinct character" of the soul in our age, do you think?

RW: Like Lamia in Keats' poem, the soul in this century has for most people virtually ceased to exist except as a fiction. In psychology, for example—which purports to be the science of the soul—one of the goals appears to be to demonstrate that the soul does not exist except as an illusion or delusion. Freud identified the soul with delusional systems, with crippling fictions, and opposed it to the reality principle. So that never, I suggest, has the soul found itself so threatened by what feels like extinction as in the Romantic and Modern periods.

For Dante and Milton, extinction was not even a possibility. The soul burning in Hell was very much alive. It could never be extinguished, however much a soul in Hell might long for extinction.

In contrast to Lamia, who vanishes the moment she is exposed to public view, Dante's soul inhabited a hugely public world. The soul was out there in the vast cosmos, identified with its every movement. Dante's soul was Reality itself. Without soul there would be nothing at all. The extinction to which Keats subjects the soul was unthinkable for Dante, because a universe without God, a Creation without a Creator, was unthinkable.

NR: Marion describes the modern soul as having shrunk in most people to the size of "a little nut that's hidden somewhere down in the gut" because it has been so struck by the inner and outer power complex. Besides this fear of extinction, what else is distinctively modern about the Romantic soul?

RW: The Romantic soul, like the modern soul, is a soul in hiding, afraid to reveal itself lest it be, like Keats' Lamia, annihilated. The more the soul is threatened with extinction the more it retreats back into its own hidden origins, like a tortoise into its shell.

You can see this by contrasting Dante and Blake. In the older medieval sense Heaven was up and out, and Hell was down and in. But in Blake particularly, the directions are reversed: Heaven is down and in, and Hell is up and out. Heaven is the roots. Hell is the up-rooted. What is up and out is a world which has been objectified in a mathematically fixed space/time order of things which the Enlightenment thought of as Heaven but which Blake considered Hell.

Heaven for Blake was the internal dynamic soul-world which we're always in the process of making. Hell was the energy we repressed in order to live conventionally. By identifying soul-making with "Hell," with rejected or outlawed or forbidden energy, Blake knows he is dealing with the soul as hidden, as withdrawn from the world, as a frightened onlooker that does not interfere with the workings of the omnipotent motions of matter. That is why his epic, *Jerusalem*, appears to be so obscure, so unreadable, so "modern." Blake, like James Joyce after him, is exploring a forgotten or abandoned or rejected reality. What he unveils is something that almost two hundred years later still appears to be radically new.

In this sense, Romanticism is a prefiguration of depth psychology, which is a new understanding of the soul. I think of Jung as the last Romantic. What Jung provides is, among other things, a theoretical framework for Romanticism.

NR: The Romantics, then, were concerned with reconnecting to the soul that had been abandoned by mechanistic science. In order to do this, they saw nature as a life-force, and felt it was important to get in touch with that energy. Jung also worked to connect us to what he called "archetypal energy" for the same reason. How do the Romantics treat this archetypal energy or life-force?

RW: The Romantics say that this life-force—this energy of nature—is perpetually creating a second nature, what I would refer to as a metaphorical body. Basically, what the Romantics are building is a new anatomy, a new body, a metaphorical body. It's very much like the Christian notion of a spiritual body, or a resurrected body.

NR: What do the Romantic poets mean by a metaphorical body? How does it connect to soul in a way that the machine body does not?

RW: What characterizes Romanticism is the body as psyche—as incarnated soul or soul in the process of its making—the body *as* psyche rather than body *opposed* to psyche. In Romanticism the distinction between body and soul completely breaks down. The *body* of a poem *is* a soul, a metaphorical body related to the resurrected spiritual body, a body that is celebrated, for example, in the Anglican funeral service. All the Romantics wrote elegies celebrating the risen body, one archetype of which is the resurrected Christ.

It's basically a body of the imagination, an embodiment of that vast realm of images that Jung would call the collective unconscious which the poet reshapes over and over again into metaphorical patterns. This is what I think the Romantics think of as the *body* of literature.

NR: Did they not refer also to the human body?

RW: Oh yes, they certainly referred to the human body, but the human body as it is imaginatively perceived. The time is fast approaching—and for the Romantics it had already arrived—when we will no longer think of the body, human or otherwise, as other than soul. The body as a purely physical thing will completely disappear. Matter is congealed energy. Energy is waves or particles, at once neither and both. When the Romantic writes a poem with a shifting shape, a pattern of sounds, a pattern of images, a continuously shifting meaning, do you think he is making a body? Or is he, as Keats says, making a soul? You see the question is wrong. Body *or* soul is wrong. There is no "or." The body *is* soul. The soul *is* body.

NR: Yet even today there is this conflict of matter resisting its soul form. There is this resistance to the integration of traditional feminine soul values which are so badly needed to balance out the patriarchal belief system that dominates our lives in this culture, and threatens to devastate the entire Earth. What about this resistance, which we still normally view as a body-soul conflict?

RW: Let's look at it in relation to Blake and Milton. Milton, shortly after the Restoration in the 1660s, wrote *Paradise Lost*, a major English epic in twelve books. And he wrote this epic to "justify the ways of God to men" and to assert "Eternal Providence." He referred to this as his "great argument." After he completed his poem it very quickly became a kind of dogma, a statement of Puritan belief. And the poem was treated almost as a religious artifact, a creed.

At the same time, in the act of writing it, Milton realized that he was subject to an inspiration over which he seemed to have no control. Every night, in sleep, his verse was dictated to him by a female Muse, whom he called *Urania*. She came to him as music, and inspired what he called "my unpremeditated Verse." When he woke up in the morning he would simply write down the verse that had been dictated to him during the night, so that the music of the poem, in this sense, is like a waking dream.

The Romantics, of course, read the poem, but what Blake particularly noticed was that there was a contradiction in the poem between the argument that was dictated to Milton by the Holy Spirit—the same Holy Spirit that inspired Moses, and gave us the Ten Commandments—and this strange female Muse. What we have in *Paradise Lost* is a female voice speaking in the unconscious—and a masculine voice speaking in the conscious. One is song, the other is argument, and they're in conflict. The argument was hard matter; the verse was the feminine soul. And one of the things that Blake says is this: song can dissolve the old argument. Soul can dissolve matter and release the energy frozen in it, release the *soul* buried in it.

To give a recent example of what Blake is talking about, do you remember what happened to us in the sixties? America burst out singing. And do you know what it was singing about? It was singing about bringing down the old Logos—the patriarchal order.

NR: The patriarchal order in Milton's case being his rigid Puritan notions about good and evil, the radical distinction between Satan and God, man and woman, Adam and Eve, and the nature of the Fall?

RW: Exactly. This was the argument of the poem, and Blake saw that Milton was locked up in it. He also saw that *Paradise Lost* wasn't about "the justification of the ways of God to men" at all. "I don't think that Milton knows what his own poem is about," Blake may be conceived as saying to himself. "His conscious mind has imprisoned his unconscious. His energies are trapped in a series of conventional attitudes and he doesn't know how to get out of them. He needs a good therapist."

You see, a poem is largely written by the unconscious. The poet doesn't quite know what it is he's saying. He thinks he understands it from a perfectly rational point of view, but from an unconscious point of view there can be something quite different going on. And that's what Blake hoped to demonstrate to Milton.

Now, a distinctive image of Romanticism is that of the *androgyne*, a figure who embraced both masculine and feminine energies in the human being. In fact, Romanticism can be seen as the enormous, painful struggle of the masculine to incorporate the inner feminine. And Blake—who is the father of Romanticism—reading *Paradise Lost*, sees the enormous conflict that Milton is having in accepting his feminine side, and that this conflict has even made Milton ill. Blake, in vision, then imagines Milton walking up and down inside his poem *Paradise Lost*, unhappy though in Heaven, trying to figure out how in blazes he is going to get out of this prison which he himself had constructed.

Then one day, as Milton (in Blake's imagination) was walking up and down inside his poem, he spied, in the little village of Felpham in the south of England, an obscure English poet who was also walking up and down in his little garden. And this poet, for different reasons, was in exactly the same kind of trap. This poet was William Blake. He'd gone to this little town partly to write an epic poem, and partly because his wife was suffering from various allergies in London and she wanted to get out and be close to the sea. So he took her there, and he found a patron who gave him, free of charge, a little cottage. It seemed splendid, the solution to everything. Only there was no intellectual stimulation, and he was bored out of his mind.

So that is Blake's situation. Due to the demands of his patron that he complete all sorts of painting commissions, he is not getting on with his epic. In fact, he is getting quite ill, and Catherine is not getting much better either. So nobody seems to be profiting from this move to the south coast.

Then Milton, who, in Blake's imagination, sees all this from his vantage point in Heaven, says as it were: "There's my man. Blake wants to write an epic. He's going to write the poem that's going to get me out of *Paradise Lost*."

This imaginal conversation with Milton, who died in 1674—eighty-three years before Blake was born in 1757—was enacted during Blake's reading and re-reading of Milton's epic. "I think I know how to get Milton out of his stuckness, out of *Paradise Lost*," says Blake. "If I can put him consciously in touch with his female Muse—his goddess energy—while he is awake, I think I can get him out of his poem."

As soon as he hears that, Milton takes a nose dive out of *Paradise Lost*, lands at the feet of William Blake at Felpham, and enters Blake's body at the metatarsus of the left foot and starts up Blake's body moving through all the chakras, the seven energy centers of the body that Blake calls "the Seven Eyes of God" that, when sealed, become the "Seven Deadly Sins of the Soul."

NR: Wait a minute now! Is this the conception Blake has of what is happening in Milton's psyche as he (Blake) reads *Paradise Lost?*

RW: Actually, it is what happens in *Blake's* psyche as he reads *Paradise Lost* aloud to his wife Catherine as, according to one legend, they sit together naked in the garden at Felpham. What I'm now describing is an actual situation about a poem that Blake wrote called *Milton*, conceived in the year 1800. *Milton* is Blake's enactment of his reading of *Paradise Lost*, in which he decides he will help this Puritan poet to unite in a "holy (healing) marriage" with his feminine Muse.

NR: Blake will fuse matter and soul?

RW: Yes. Blake says that the poem is being written in his body. Milton enters Blake's body at the metatarsus of the left foot and starts up the left leg. At the same time, Milton's virgin Muse, whom Blake has renamed Ololon, starts down the nerves of Blake's right arm into his writing hand. Blake, unlike Milton in *Paradise Lost*, is wide awake, directing his Muse, becoming sexually aroused as the bodily expression of a spiritual awakening. "Come into my hand," he commands the Muse who then descends "down the nerves of [his] right arm/ From out the Portals of [his] brain."

Milton, in the body of Blake, then travels through the seven chakras, opening each of them. In the process all sorts of strange things are going on in Blake's body, particularly in his belly where he suffers acute indigestion.

> The bellowing Furnaces blare by the long sounding clarion.
> The double drum drowns howls and groans, the shrill fife shrieks and cries:

It's a speaking body! When medication was recommended, Blake rejected it because that would be a blasphemhy against the voice of the Holy Spirit! (Compare this to today's chemical body—medicated in order to silence it). It's very, very funny, and very wonderful.

NR: Then what happens?

RW: Milton gets as far as Blake's loins. Blake gets sexually excited. And Blake says to Milton: "No, Milton, not yet. You have to make love to your Muse before you consummate your union." But Milton is a Puritan—he's used to doing this sort of thing in the dark and doing it quickly—and it's for the fallen purpose of procreation. But this is new; he's completely in Blake's body now, and Blake is in charge.

So Milton moves on through other chakras and he comes to the heart. And he has the warmest feelings which he expresses in beautiful lyric poems. And he says: "This is it!" And Blake says: "No, Milton—this is just too sentimental, too seductive. This is Garden of Eden stuff, and it got you into trouble once before. This is romantic love, and Milton, I want to tell you something. Romantic love is a sickness. It's not good enough, even as sexual love. There's more." And Milton says: "What more can there be?" "Keep going," says Blake. So Milton goes on.

Finally overcoming the temptations of the loins and the heart, Milton arrives at Blake's brain, where his union with Ololon takes place. This opening of the eighth Eye, which is the fully resurrected body, is consummated by Milton's orgasmic union with Ololon, as well as Blake's consummation with his estranged wife, Catherine, "trembling by [his] side." It is the divine marriage of the Biblical Apocalypse, the descent of the New Jerusalem "prepared as a bride adorned for her husband," and making "all things new." The reading has culminated in a commingling of their bodies from top to bottom, described by Blake as the "lineaments of gratified desire." Embraces in Eden, he writes in *Jerusalem*, are "Comminglings from the Head even to the Feet;/ And not a pompous High Priest entering by a Secret Place." The action of *Milton* is just such an embrace.

Blake now experiences himself as a fully resurrected body. He is one with the risen Jesus who now descends into his garden at Felpham, wrapped in the apparel of Ololon. He descends, that is, as the feminine Christ, the truly androgynous God who is the risen Blake constructed by the imagination.

NR: So Blake's poem is a graphic illustration of what you call the building of a "resurrected body," made possible by the poet's eventual union with his feminine soul—the soul in this case being Milton's Muse Urania, or Ololon.

RW: Yes. Milton's journey through Blake's body is the building of a bodysoul, a metaphorical body which is the epic poem *Milton*. And it is a journey every bit as astonishing as Dante's journey in *The Divine Comedy*, or Satan's journey in *Paradise Lost*, or Odysseus's homeward journey in Homer's *Odyssey*. Or, indeed, Leopold Bloom's journey through the city of Dublin in James Joyce's *Ulysses*. The danger of this journey is the danger inherent in the Romantic quest: stopping short of the goal of spiritual fulfillment so that each place of rest becomes a temptation to remain.

NR: By calling Christ "the androgynous God," are you saying that he symbolizes the union of body and soul that has now taken place within Blake?

RW: Yes, the coming together of the masculine and the feminine in a divine Inner Marriage is symbolized by Christ.

NR: What is the nature of this feminine Christ that Blake envisions and now embodies?

RW: The feminine Christ is not the Christ of the theologians. The feminine Christ has nothing to do with "a pompous High Priest entering by a Secret Place." She's not bound to a patriarchal Father. If we say "God is dead" she pays no attention whatsoever. She just goes on living. The feminine Christ is that side of God that transcends the sacrifice, doesn't become the victim of original sin, doesn't take on the sins of the world and atone for them.

In life, the feminine Christ was the Christ who surrendered rather than fought. Christ could have presumably saved his life when he went before Pilate. He could have denied what he was accused of or, if you like, he could have defended what he was accused of. But he did something that was neither overt denial nor affirmation. He refused to play the political game and he was wise enough to know that in Jerusalem (as in Washington or indeed Felpham) there was no other game in town. The androgynous God is the God who doesn't get trapped in our games, political or otherwise. He knows how to maintain his silence, particularly when the questions coming at him are loaded.

He refuses to be put on trial because if he does, not only is he betrayed but so are we.

NR: In his book on archetypes Jungian analyst Anthony Stevens emphasizes the point about Christ not being bound to a patriarchal Father:

> Jesus of Nazareth's life and teachings were uniquely concerned with the "Eros" of love and relationship. . . . Though he respected the patriarchal order in society and wished to do nothing to change it ("Render unto Caesar the things which are Caesar's, and unto God the things that are God's"), maintaining, like Jung, that the essential changes were those occurring in men's hearts, he was opposed, nevertheless, to the masculine struggle for dominance and "status."[3]

Is this the Christ that Blake believed in, and would have us believe in?

RW: Yes, that's the Christ that Blake believed in and that he tried to show Milton. What Milton was perhaps unconsciously struggling toward, Blake made conscious. In this struggle, Blake suggests that Milton was coming to a new consciousness of himself in his relationship to God. He was moving toward a new God-image. That is the meaning of Milton entering Blake's body to meet and unite with his Muse, or feminine soul, in Blake's brain.

NR: Ross, we've been on a fascinating excursion since my original question about matter resisting its soul form. Even though Blake has shown us the feminine soul alive in *Paradise Lost*, we still haven't integrated her into *our* consciousness. Haven't we instead inherited Milton's Puritanism which is still bound, as you say, to the patriarchal Father?

RW: Yes, we have. The soul, for Blake, is the awakened body, conscious matter. It is precisely what Milton, as a Puritan, could not actualize in *Paradise Lost*, a failure which he bequeathed to Puritan New England to become the great North American sexual hang-up. In our day, we have simply perpetuated the trauma of sexuality that the Puritans identified with original sin. Sexual repression carries its shadow—sexual freedom. Ironically, our sexually obsessed society perpetuates the dark, untransformed side of Puritanism. So that, as

Arthur Miller, for example, recognized in writing *The Crucible*, we remain imprisoned in an unredeemed Puritan morality. America of the nineties is still the Salem of the witch trials.

NR: You mean that we're still burning the feminine in North America?

RW: Can anyone really doubt that we are still burning the feminine? I think we're going to see a lot more witch trials before it's over.

So, you see, *Paradise Lost* still enacts us. More than that, it will continue to enact us until we have absorbed Blake's epic vision, which, if we survive, is likely to take at least another hundred years.

NR: What was Milton's *conscious* view of the feminine—the view that we have inherited and that the feminists have been struggling to eradicate?

RW: Well, Milton had some pretty crazy ideas when he started out, but his feminine Muse corrected most of them before she was finished. I can tell you a few of his crazier ones though.

He was very patriarchal. He thought, for example, that woman came from the womb of man; he thought that Eve came from the rib of Adam. He believed "he for God only; she for God in him." He believed that Eve aligned herself with the devil, with the serpent, that she became the serpent-woman. He believed she tempted her husband Adam to eat of the forbidden Tree of Knowledge and brought about the fall of man. All of this he believed was woman's work.

That is one version of Christianity—a Puritan Christianity. And Milton presented this doctrine.

But here he is arguing all of this nonsense and at the same time being inspired by a female Muse, whom he tries to resist, because maybe she's a temptress who's going to do to him as a Christian poet what Eve did to Adam. At any rate, she's a very dangerous person.

NR: Is Milton's feminine Muse going to release him from this patriarchal attitude? Is this why she's a "very dangerous person?"

RW: Yes, she's a very dangerous person because she's going to upset the apple cart. She's going to start a revolution. In the writing of *Paradise Lost*, Milton's female Muse becomes stronger and stronger. She tells him to have nothing more to do with so-called heroic verse or those old Homeric heroes. Forget all these macho men. Don't go around slaying dragons—love them. And Milton realizes he's going to have to give up war and all those heroic subjects. He's going to write instead about a different kind of battle—the battle within.

So what kind of paradigm is emerging here? What is the archetypal shift? Milton's Urania "brings nightly to [his] ear" something he has never heard before, that has never been written about before. In other words, what we have are the beginnings of a new cultural paradigm, a new understanding of the masculine in relation to the inner feminine.

In our day, Viet Nam put an end to all the old heroics for Americans. Viet Nam was a big, big step forward. The man who goes off and kills is no longer a hero. People are ashamed of him. Real heroes came back from Viet Nam but we didn't know what to do with them. And what a tragedy that was. In fact, they were something far more beautiful than heroes, but we didn't know what to call them because we had no archetype for the new masculine that had emerged in that war. So what did we do? We forgot them. We pretended they didn't exist. Archetypally, who were these people? Blake says they belong to a new culture, a new archetypal paradigm.

NR: If I understand you correctly about Viet Nam heroes, the warmongers couldn't see the inner battles those men went through trying to balance the demands of a brutal and unreasonable war with the feminine values of caring and compassion. For them these kinds of struggles didn't exist. Is this the tragedy that you see here? Is this the change of consciousness regarding what it means to be a hero that Milton is talking about?

RW: Yes. America has lived with Viet Nam as the American tragedy. The tragic heroes of this undeclared war (for who knew what to call it, how to declare it?) are its psychological casualties. Did nearly as many Viet Nam veterans commit suicide as soldiers were killed in battle?

The real battle in *Paradise Lost* goes on inside Adam and Eve. Milton referred to it as "deeds/Above Heroic, though in secret done." We are still learning about this secret battle in the souls of the Viet Nam vets. That, for me, is the battle Milton fought in *Paradise Lost*—America's lost innocence, if you like.

That is why I turn to mythopoetic literature to learn not only about the human drama (the real human actions) but also about the archetypal dimension of the human drama, a dimension that shows us, in what *is* going on, what is *always already* going on. I learn how the imagination transforms rather than circumvents human problems—transformation (as in alchemy) being inherent in the operations of the imaginative faculty.

NR: From that perspective, how does *Paradise Lost* end?

RW: It ends with the androgyne, the divine marriage, the coming together of the opposites, emerging—though still beyond the reach of Milton's conscious intent, of his "great argument."

NR: How do we know this?

RW: Because at the end of the poem Michael the Archangel comes to Adam and says something like this:

"Adam, you're going to have to leave the Garden of Eden because you have eaten of the forbidden Tree of Knowledge and broken God's command. And I'm going to give you some instruction about how you must now conduct yourself in the world, how best to conduct your fallen life. I'm going to instruct you in how you must now digest what in Eden you were forbidden to eat."

"But," he said, "this is between men only. Eve should have no part in this; she's a woman. So Eve, you go off and have a nap."

After Eve has gone Michael invites Adam to ascend the Hill of Vision, leaving Eve to sleep below while he gives Adam a long lecture on the story of humankind, right down to the Second Coming. And at the end of his instruction he tells Adam how he can build "a Paradise within thee, happier farr" than the Eden he has lost.

And so for two books of *Paradise Lost* Adam is instructed. At the end of these two books Michael commands Adam to wake Eve from her dream. Adam descends the Hill of Vision and goes off to tell Eve what he thinks is fit for a woman to know. But, to his amazement, he finds that she's already awake, and he starts to tell her certain things. And Eve replies:

"Yes, Adam, I know."

"Well, how do you know these things?"

"Because, you see, Adam, 'God is also in sleep, and [in] Dreams advise[s].'" Adam discovers that much of what Michael had told him God had also communicated in dream to Eve. All that Adam has learned on a conscious level Eve has been receiving at the unconscious level. And Adam is amazed by the things she knows. She knows that she, a woman, as Mary, will give birth to the Redeemer; that she, as the mother of mankind, will be the carrier of this redeeming consciousness, and that it will come through her body. She knows that sleep and dream are the carriers of new life that as grace transcends the purely rational limits of Adam's soul.

And he has a terrific moment of insight into what woman is, what the unconscious is, what dream is. And that there's more to all of this, to life, than just the rational mind.

Then something quite beautiful happens. Michael comes to them both, and he finds them hand-in-hand. But instead of taking Adam, he puts his arms around them both as if recognizing them as a couple, and he leads them to the gates so that they can leave Paradise together. As they walk toward the gate of birth from the Garden—womb to the world—they briefly look back at what is now a ruin, guarded against re-entry. Eden has become a scorched Earth.

In other words, once you have left that earlier kind of consciousness you can never go back into that kind of innocence again. Never. When you're no longer innocent you join the human race. Blake says, "You have entered Experience. Welcome to the world."

And so *Paradise Lost* ends very beautifully with Adam and Eve walking hand-in-hand out of the Garden together, conscious and unconscious in some kind of marriage. That is how we have to learn to live in the world.

The uniting of the two into one is also Adam and Eve recognizing each other in terms of what they have contributed to each other.

> The world was all before them, where to choose
> Their place of rest, and Providence their guide:
> They hand in hand with wandering steps and slow,
> Through Eden took their solitarie way.

For the masculine and feminine to walk out of the Garden of Eden hand in hand is to offer this world of the Fall a powerful archetypal image of its recovery. Hand in hand means that Paradise is within them—they take Eden with them.

Milton's epic had announced a new paradigm that Romanticism would further explore. Blake revealed all that was in the poem *Paradise Lost* that Milton never fully understood. Its conscious perspective is now seen from the unconscious side, an unconscious side destined to become what Marion calls "the conscious feminine."

NR: And this unconscious was the feminine voice—a voice that had been equated with evil—and whose voice had not been heard for a very long time?

RW: Had never had a voice. Never had a voice. And Romanticism rectifies this. It is the birth of the unconscious as the creative matrix to which the poet must listen, and submit. And that voice is the voice of the feminine, the feminine Muse, who is the true author of a Romantic poem.

That voice, in the combination of femininity and the unconscious, is the constellating of the healing power for all of us.

Chapter Two

The Tiger and the Lamb

NANCY RYLEY: Did the Romantic poets find anything else in Milton's poem that they felt needed to be addressed if we were ever to fully reclaim our souls?

ROSS WOODMAN: Yes, they did. Blake and Shelley felt that Milton's creative energy had gone into the figure of Satan—that Milton was "in fetters" whenever he wrote about God and angels, but "at liberty" when he wrote of Satan. Shelley therefore concluded that Satan was the real hero of *Paradise Lost*, not God but Satan. Blake argued that Milton "was a true Poet and of the Devil's party without knowing it."

The tragedy of Milton was that he had poured his enormous creative energy into a figure whom he rejected as evil. Herein, for Blake, lies the Puritan dilemma. It's as if Milton were rejecting his own power; he was using God, as it were, to crush his power.

Shelley agreed. The Puritan God whom Milton worshipped was a tyrant, the enemy of his imagination. His God had turned to stone—stone tablets, implacable laws. With such a God in charge, evil becomes frozen matter, hard matter that opposes the *energy* which is its life. Matter doesn't want to dissolve into vibrations, and cease to be matter. It's attached to its hardness, its monumentality, its implacableness.

NR: Who is this God?

RW: He is Jehovah, the Old Testament Jehovah, the author of the Ten Commandments, a "Thou shalt not" negative morality.

NR: If I understand you correctly, Blake and Shelley were concerned with releasing Milton (and us) from the shackles of this tyrant God-father that has so dominated our time as well in the form of the patriarchy. They were trying to infuse the negative morality of the Puritan faith with feminine consciousness, which is the healing energy we all need in soul-making if we are to dissolve old attitudes, old rigidities, old gods. How did they propose to do this?

RW: Through the integration of the *deus absconditus*, the hidden side of God, the neglected shadow side of human nature sometimes still associated with the feminine in its alignment with the serpent figure of Satan. "Evil be thou my good," declares Milton's Satan. Blake explores how evil can be transformed into good by channeling energies into soul-making activity.

NR: So what we have in English Romantic poetry is the recognition of the creative potential of the dark side of man that Milton (or America, for that matter) could not integrate. Is that what the defense of Satan—and of the feminine, which as you say, has often been aligned with evil—means in Blake's world?

RW: Yes. It's what Jung calls *shadow* energy. Integrating the shadow is what's going to bring you through to a new consciousness.

Paradise Lost begins with the account of the fall of Satan. God has thrown him out of heaven and Blake in effect says: "Come on, Satan, I'll take you on; I'm not afraid of that energy. It's great energy. I won't hurl you out. I'll bring you back in, because you're a part of the psyche that should not be rejected.

"And Milton, the real God is not a tyrant. I'm going to put you in touch with the God you don't yet know—the God that is not yet conscious in you. And I can tell you, he's a wonderful, loving God. You get that energy up, Milton, and you're going to see that the shadow is your friend, and that Satan is your Beloved. But we won't call him Satan—we'll give him his original name. We'll call him Lucifer, the 'light-bringer.'"

So the defense of Satan in Blake's world means the defense of energy, the defense of instinct, the defense of intuition—of all that is rejected in one's life. That is where your real genius lies. Everything that is outcast is where your energies are unconsciously placed.

NR: What does Blake think results from the repression, rather than the expression, of these outcast energies?

RW: For Blake, sickness is the result of repression of these energies. Unless we can get at this repressed energy and release it, we will all encounter the kind of sickness that both he and Milton were suffering from. The healing process is the release of what conventional society represses in all of us. "Sooner murder an infant in its cradle than nurse unacted desires," writes Blake. What Blake calls "Hell" is the energy that a conformist society makes us repress in order to live like machines.

In his poem *The Marriage of Heaven and Hell*, the greatness of Christ, says Blake, is that Christ broke all Ten Commandments. He didn't honor his father and mother. He ran away from his family at the age of twelve, and his mother went searching for him. He'd been in the synagogue preaching heretical doctrine. And his mother found him and said, "Where have you been?" And he, in effect, replied, "I've been about my father's business. But Mother, there's one thing more I want to add: Joseph is not my father." Now Christ didn't reject Joseph. He was looking for a higher Reality. He also broke the law of the Sabbath. He said, "The Sabbath was made for man, not man for the Sabbath." These are the things Christ was preaching. You name the convention—he broke it.

So another way of describing Romanticism is the defying of what's conventional by making the energy it represses available to all of us.

NR: How does Blake image this repressed energy in his work?

RW: In 1789, Blake started to write a series of poems eventually called *The Songs of Innocence and of Experience;* for every song of innocence there was a contrary song of experience. In 1794, he published his poem *The Tyger* as one of the *Songs of Experience. The Tyger* is Blake's image of the psychic energy imprisoned in the machine, as in a sepulcher, as in a prison. The speaker, locked in his "chartered" body, is terrified by his tiger energy which could demolish him in his present form or condition. He therefore experiences this energy as evil, though the real evil is his mode of perception, which images the tiger as a nightmare.

> Tyger! Tyger! burning bright
> In the forests of the night,

What immortal hand or eye
Could frame thy fearful symmetry?

The tiger takes him to brothels as the only outlet for his unruly sexual passions. Neither the church nor the state can bring them under control. The more they are denounced, the stronger they get. How can he frame or control the monster energy? What can he do with it? It's like Frankenstein's monster shaped by his own repression.

And when thy heart began to beat,
What dread hand? and what dread feet?

As the energy becomes more and more powerful, he's less and less able to control it. He is a man who is absolutely terrorized by the energies that he has struggled all his life to deny. Now they are taking their revenge on him. The poem reveals his sheer panic at being overcome by irrational drives, which he experiences as absolutely evil. It's a Jekyll and Hyde situation.

NR: But surely Blake's not telling the people to go to brothels and feel great about it?

RW: Absolutely not: that's the absolute denial of the energy. That's treating the energy as evil. Brothels, says Blake, are built with the bricks of religion understood as the repression of sexual energy.
    In lust the body is really absent. You think it's present, but it's a machine that's present, not a body. And women know it—when they're sleeping with a machine, and when they're sleeping with a man.

NR: So that part of our loss of soul, as the Romantic poets see it, is the result of this estrangement from ourselves that we experience living in a conventional society that represses so much of our instinctive vitality?

RW: Exactly. The energy is there, but it's destructive because it has no creative social channel to flow into. For example, it's raw, unredeemed energy that makes the cities and towns of America increasingly unsafe to inhabit. The United States has the highest prison population of any country in the world, outside of a dictatorship. There are 1.5 million in prison at this moment. Still bound to its Puritan origins, America remains locked in repression: you get what you reject out of sight, you put it away where you can't see it, you lock it up. But the moment you imprison that energy it becomes more, rather than less, violent. Prisons could yet overwhelm America and bring it down from within itself rather than from without.

NR: And the imprisoning of that energy goes with the conventional life-style that James Hillman calls our "white bread, have-a-nice-day" culture as depicted in TV sitcoms, the mainstream media, and the "safe," exclusive white neighborhoods of suburban America?

RW: Absolutely. That's why criminalized energy, which is a reaction to this, dominates TV and the movies.

NR: So what do Blake and the other poets tell us is the right way to release this shadow energy?

RW: Write poems. Make paintings.

NR: Making art is the expression of tiger energy?

RW: That is the expression of tiger energy. Blake's answer is that any person has the right and the responsibility to frame that symmetry, to release and shape his or her creativity, and restore the world to its original human form.

Now the tiger would say: "That's God; that's your creative power; everything that is good in you is in that energy. You must learn to channel it and to use it." The tiger is the *deus absconditus*, the God who is hidden, in need of the release we alone can bring him.

NR: Marion talks about working with this same energy in her bodysoul workshops to reconnect us to our abandoned souls. Will this creative release take care of sexual energy as well?

RW: Yes, it will take care of sexual energy. From Blake's point of view, once the energies get flowing toward their transcendent object—*opus contra naturam*, a second nature—then sexual energy will also align itself toward this goal, rather than, as in Blake's day, toward warding off despair and depression. Sexual energy is a portion of a larger energy. Isolate this energy as sexual and you have a nightmare on your hands. Brothels are only the tip of it. Go into some of them in Thailand or Sri Lanka and you'll see what *isolated* energy—isolated as sheer sexuality—is really like.

Blake would argue that sexual energy is a short-circuiting of creative power. That is to say, it's a dumping ground. Physically, sexual needs can be met in about two minutes. Then it's over. Then you can roll over and go to sleep. Forget the whole thing. Blake was absolutely appalled that all this creative energy was just something to be dumped and forgotten.

Sexuality, Blake believed, must be a part of a larger body: the imaginal body, the metaphorical body. It belongs to that sacramental order of the imagination. Once it's located there, and operative there, it's a hugely fulfilling part of one's life. But in terms of Adam and Eve putting on fig leaves and going into the bushes full of shame, that's what Blake was against.

NR: There is also the problem of our unlived or shadow energy being projected onto other people. Instead of being dealt with positively and creatively in our own lives, the shadow is often projected negatively onto Jews or blacks or women, and a huge racial or sexist problem results.

RW: That's true. We see this in the nightmare history of slavery and its aftermath, which is the American holocaust. The blacks are still not entirely free of the camps. They've still got numbers tattooed in their flesh. The blacks carried the American shadow, and those who could see that saw that the blacks were the conscience of America.

Jung argued that the shadow, if integrated, was the *transcendent* function—transcendent meaning a previously uninhabited mental and spiritual space. I think you can see that in American jazz, one of the most authentic art forms that America has produced. And what a form it is! Everything that got frozen into classicism was released there into new life.

NR: What about the sexual shadow that whites had projected onto blacks before black emancipation?

RW: It's interesting to see the image that the white culture had of the black male in the South. One of the fantasies identified with the black male was that he had a large penis and was very, very potent. And hugely promiscuous. This is the fantasy of the black seen as phallic power.

This is basically the white man's terror of sexuality. There it is. Lynch it, castrate it, do anything to get rid of it. Can't touch it, don't like the smell of it, mustn't sit in the same chair with it, mustn't use the same washrooms, the same restaurants, the same churches, the same anything. You see?

NR: Does this attitude toward sexuality all originate with the teachings of Judeo-Christianity?

RW: Oh, Judeo-Christianity played its part, but it is far more pervasive than that. If you look at the way sexuality is projected, put onto the black, and then how the black is treated, you see what the white attitude toward sexuality really is.

Jung blamed some of it on Freud who, in Jung's view, made a dogma of sexuality. He argued that Freud had substituted sexuality for Jehovah, the God whom Freud had rejected. He made a secular religion of it, an obsession of it. For Jung, sexuality was one expression of the libido, not the entire libido. Art and religion are not repressed sexuality or sublimated sexuality, as Freud believed. We're not doomed to inhabit forever a sexual nightmare, which is close to what we now have entered.

NR: Blake also wrote about the "lamb," which is traditionally associated in the Christian church with the other side of Christ, namely his compassion and gentleness. What is the association in Blake's poem of the tiger with the lamb?

RW: Blake's tiger is as gentle as a lamb; in other words, there's nothing to be afraid of. When you turn and face the shadow you will find your Beloved. "Did he who made the Lamb make thee?" Yes, because the tiger is the lamb, and the lamb is the tiger. That's why the tiger and the lamb lie down together in the New Jerusalem. It's an active state of the imagination. Blake shows us in his poem how to let it out, the goal being a conscious body—a bodysoul—an Inner Marriage of masculine [tiger] and feminine [lamb] energies.

NR: Ross, in talking about the building of a bodysoul, or conscious body, you've used examples from the work of a group of *male* poets. Does what you've been saying apply to women poets as well?

RW: Absolutely—Keats can only do so much! Emily Dickinson can do a lot more to bring Psyche back from what appears to be a world of eternal exile. So can Sylvia Plath, and Adrienne Rich, and Virginia Woolf, that wonderful woman who said, "Shakespeare's sister could have done it better!"

But the feminine and the masculine in that sense are not related to gender. They've nothing to do with male and female. It's psychic energies we're talking about. And feminine energy is that creative matrix, whether it's in the man or the woman.

NR: How does the poet distinguish between the two energies, feminine and masculine? How do you know when you're being penetrated by masculine energy, or receiving feminine energy?

RW: Masculine energy, to me, is the ability to celebrate the feminine in one-self. Masculine energy is the channeling of that creative feminine matrix, which is what all these poets are doing. The celebration of the feminine must be disciplined, otherwise that energy without the channeling is of no use to anybody. But whether it's a woman that's channeling it or a man that's channeling, it's the same process.

I'll put it another way: it's the bringing of that unconscious matrix in nature into consciousness without disturbing the unconscious, without disrupting it, without cutting it off, without becoming self-conscious about it, without becoming crippled or paralyzed. That's what's important—for that feminine unconscious to be able to flow into consciousness, into an artifact, into a film, into a poem. That is to say the celebration must go into the making of *something*.

In the sixties, Marion and I lived in London, and we went often to see Fonteyn and Nureyev dance. Nureyev was a fantastic technician, but in addition he had the most extraordinary tiger energy. When he came to London, Margot Fonteyn was about to retire. Her dancing days were nearly over. She watched Nureyev dance and something happened. She went on to become his greatest partner. She danced as she had never danced before. They enacted the new androgyne: the coming together of the masculine and the feminine. She became the lamb to his tiger.

The audience, night after night, sat there in tears, wondering what hit them, never having seen anything like this before. And when it was over Nureyev and Fonteyn picked up the flowers that had been thrown onto the stage by the audience, and they gave them to each other. It was an absolute feast. There were Eros and Psyche, tiger and lamb, united as in the New Jerusalem.

NR: But don't those masculine and feminine energies have to be consciously differentiated out from one another, and integrated into oneself, before they can be truly united in the Inner Marriage?

RW: Yes, they do. Let me give you another example from my life and Marion's that illustrates this notion of the Inner Marriage. Marion and I gave a course together in England. It was very funny because everybody, down to the last person in that room, was there to listen to Marion Woodman. Two hundred people signed up to listen to Marion Woodman—they knew her books. But if they were going to get Marion Woodman, on this occasion they were also going to have to take her husband. That was the attitude, there was no question about it. They'd never heard of me. And they thought, well, we can put up with him in order to hear her!

But also they were very curious. What kind of man did she marry? And where was he all those years when she was in Zurich training at the Jung Institute? Who was this perfectly conventional, middle-class English professor whom she could so conveniently leave in order to go about her individuation? You could just taste it—you could just see it in their faces as they looked at me.

We walked into the room filled with people and we sat down. Then, as Marion talked, they watched me to see how I reacted. Is he resentful? Is he competitive? Is he willing to take a back seat to this woman? Who is he?

Marion took about fifteen minutes to introduce me, integrate me into the workshop. I was supposed to talk about William Blake. You can imagine how interested they were in William Blake! "Are we going to have to go through all this to hear Marion? Do we have to have an hour of Ross Woodman talking about William Blake before we can get to the real nitty-gritty?"

So I said, "Blake is not what you're here for. You want to know about me, and you want to know about our relationship. You want to know how I, as a man and a husband, could endure this woman. And what this did to my ego. And how I survived her being gone on and off for five years." Of course, there was great laughter.

"Well," I said, "much of my academic training, as you have been told, was in Romanticism. I was raised in the tradition of Romantic love. Every poem I ever read said that Romantic love was a disease. It was a sickness unto death. And I said to Marion that this is what we were in. It was just a sickness unto death."

And I continued in this vein: "In so-called Romantic love, the lover seeks to recover his lost divinity, his lost omnipotence, through union with his other half, his own lost inner feminine projected onto the other person. The result in many Romantic works is death—a love-death in which death is glorified as an eternal union not realizable on Earth.

"In short, Romanticism taught me a lot about the delusions too often concealed in love. But it took my marriage to Marion to show me how delusions actually operated. We, in the name of love, were trapped in a sickness unto death. Mind you, we were in good company: Tristan and Isolde, Romeo and Juliet, Antony and Cleopatra, Heathcliff and Cathy.

"Our knowledge of ourselves and the Romantic company we were in conducted her to Zurich. In a very real sense, Marion went to Zurich to get away from me, which is to say, from her fantasy of me which was 'one flesh' with my fantasy of her. But if we were ever really to be together, we had first to withdraw our projections on one another and then relocate them where they actually belonged."

So I talked to the audience about the process of separation that began when she went to Zurich. By this I meant the process of our differentiating out from each other, and how excruciatingly painful that was. And how comfortable, by contrast, the other relationship had been. I told them that the real beginning of my marriage to Marion was not *uniting* with her—it was *separating* from her. What both of us took back by way of projection onto the other belonged, we realized, to God. That was not an easy realization, but it gave us a highly creative space in which we could function together independently of each other.

Now, as I gradually and painfully withdrew the anima projection, Marion faded from my constant thoughts, and I began to make contact with my own unconscious in a much more powerful, fearful, and creative way. I began to write again, to explore an interior life in ways that were new and strange and answerable only to themselves.

And a miracle took place: the more the projection went off, the more she was present to me as 'other,' as someone I would never fully understand, no matter how much I tried. And I learned one of the most important lessons of my life—the difference between a problem and a mystery. Our relationship had been problem-solving: 'Darling, we have a problem here . . . our problem is understanding . . .' and so forth. But there was now no problem. We discovered that we lived together in a kind of orbit of mystery. Marion became a mystery to me; I didn't know her. I knew a lot about her, but I didn't know her. What her relationship was to God I didn't know, and she didn't know mine. I only knew that the relationship was inviolate, sacred, not open to my interference. We had, through differentiating out from each other, come together in a far more profound way. Our bond was in essence the mystery of God that transcended the limits of our human attraction.

Well, at this point I looked up and all two hundred people sitting there—men and women—had tears pouring down their cheeks. And I thought, What on Earth's going on here? I was certain I hadn't moved them that much. I turned to look at Marion, to say, "Marion, what is going on here?" and found her looking at me as if what she was hearing, she was hearing for the first time. She was listening very intently: apparently that was what got to them. Later they told me that what had moved them to tears was not what I was saying so much as the fact that two people had lived together for so long, and one could still listen to the other as if hearing the other for the first time. It was the sense of freshness, of something still alive and immediate. And that, to them, was the relationship.

When we went back to the hotel that night I said to Marion, "What do you think happened today?"

And she said, "Well, it was certainly vibrant, whatever it was."

And I said, "I think I know what it was. I think we were married today."

When I had married Marion thirty-five years before—what a production that was! Two hundred students had been there all day decorating the church within an inch of its life. The place was overflowing with students, all of whom adored Marion. It was a huge spectacle. Gregorian chant, you name it. Everything was going on.

I said, "You know, Marion, it was theater. Now it wasn't pure theater, but I was aware that I was performing. I was out of myself; I was in this incredible performance."

Of course Marion was very disturbed by what I said, because I was suggesting that I had not experienced the marriage ceremony as a sacrament.

"But," I said, "what happened today was the real thing. It was the most unexpected experience. I never thought I would marry you. What happened today was an act of grace."

The next day when we went back to continue the workshop there was a lot of excitement around that room about what had happened. People said it was as if they had been to our wedding, that it was like a marriage. "Well," I said, "that's exactly the image that we came to." It had that wonderful sense of celebration, but it was not something anybody planned. It was something that just happened.

I certainly had not fully absorbed the experience, nor, of course, had they. It was as if I had suddenly experienced the sacred in a relationship that I had always inhabited as secular or profane.

Now that is what I mean by a consciousness emerging from a lifetime of work, never expecting it to happen. It's not subconsciously goal-oriented. You just give yourself to the work. And maybe it will and maybe it won't happen.

NR: You mean the work on consciousness that you've both done brought about the Inner Marriage?

RW: The work that we'd done separately, yes. The courtship, the real marriage, was through the separation: the withdrawing of the projections and the miracle of something still being there after we had withdrawn them.

The poet William Wordsworth insisted that we are, in the sight of God, "wedded to this goodly universe in love and holy passion." God is the proper object of projection, the proper action of the soul. I am suggesting when projection finds its proper object in God, our relationship to everything else changes. My marriage to Marion is sacramental in this sense. Our marriage engages us not simply in each other, but in the Creation itself, in the fate of the planet, wildlife, ecology.

I think this is what the union of the inner masculine and the inner feminine—the tiger and the lamb—is all about. That's Jung's notion of the community of the Inner Marriage.

It's also Blake's notion of building the New Jerusalem. For Blake, like Milton before him—or like any strong artist with his or her Muse—being alone with God is essential to the act of creation. The real creative work begins when you finally separate yourself out from the pressures of your environment to be alone with God. In Romantic love the other person becomes the planet. Conscious love has to be directed towards all Creation, not only towards each other.

And that's the work we all have to do if we're going to live in harmony on the planet as our home.

Chapter Three

Building Jerusalem

NANCY RYLEY: What would a poet like Shelley or Blake say about us today, given that as a society we are still mesmerized by the extroversion of science and technology, and pay little attention to the internal world of the psyche?

ROSS WOODMAN: In response to those who denied the importance of the psyche, Blake said—and this is at the core of Romanticism—you will never understand a political, economic, or religious movement until you grasp its psychological dynamic, until you grasp that vast outward world, which we call the macrocosm, in terms of what goes on in the individual psyche, which we call the microcosm.

Blake argued that, if you focus on *political* revolution, if you focus on *social* revolution, if you focus on democracy and the rights of the individual in an egalitarian society, and the overthrowing of the shackles of an *ancien régime*, if you get completely caught up in all this stuff, the energy will be deflected from its object. Desire has a bigger goal, a greater goal. For Blake that goal was the life of the imagination.

NR: How does Blake think we can break out of that limiting pattern into greater life?

RW: The building of the metaphorical body is the breaking out of that pattern. Blake called it the building of Jerusalem. *Jerusalem* was his great epic. It's a hundred plates; it's a huge, huge poem.

NR: Is this his great vision for humankind?

RW: Yes. In his poem *Milton*, Blake begins with that wonderful lyric about the building of Jerusalem.

> And did those feet in ancient time,
> Walk upon Englands mountains green:
> And was the holy Lamb of God,
> On Englands pleasant pastures seen!
>
> And did the Countenance Divine,
> Shine forth upon our clouded hills?
> And was Jerusalem builded here,
> Among these dark Satanic Mills?
>
> Bring me my Bow of burning gold:
> Bring me my Arrows of desire:
> Bring me my Spear: O clouds unfold!
> Bring me my Chariot of fire!
>
> I will not cease from Mental Fight,
> Nor shall my Sword sleep in my hand:
> Till we have built Jerusalem,
> In Englands green & pleasant Land.

Blake assembles the healing power of our energies. "Bow of burning gold" and "Arrows of desire" are weapons of "Mental Fight"; they are spiritual energies. But we still haven't absorbed Blake's poetry. His *Jerusalem* contains a culture we only partially inhabit. In its reality, his epic is the bound or outer circumference of our energy. Canadian literary critic Northrop Frye described it as the greatest unread epic in our language.

NR: Why do you say *Jerusalem* contains "a culture we only partially inhabit?" What is Blake saying that we need to know today?

RW: What's in Blake's *Jerusalem* that we need to know today is what Jung calls psychic Reality. Psychic Reality is a far larger reality than any of us can consciously inhabit. In the New Testament it's called the Kingdom of God. The Beatitudes, the Sermon on the Mount, are all about inhabiting it as a

Kingdom that dwells within us. Blake explored this inner Kingdom as his own Sermon on the Mount personally delivered to him by Christ. Every morning "at sunrise," he says in the opening of his epic, he saw Christ standing over him, "Spreading his beams of love, and dictating the words of this mild song," though it's anything but "mild."

So far as Blake is concerned this opening of his eyes first thing in the morning is a metaphor for the opening of his inner eyes. What Christ says to him as his inner sun, his inner source of light and life, is: "I am in you and you in me, mutual in love divine." Christ dictating and Blake writing is the expression of this mutual love. What he writes unveils the Kingdom within, a metaphor of which is the Kingdom without.

NR: So when Blake talks about the building of the metaphorical body, he's talking about love.

RW: Absolutely! He's talking about love. Blake's *Jerusalem* is a conscious human body that Blake calls Christ, the body of Christ. We've got to become that body. The building of it, its psychic dynamics, is the epic he constructs.

Our job, says Blake, is to recognize not simply the mineral form of the Power that created the world as atomic cohesion, or the vegetable form of this Power as cellular life, or the animal form of this Power as biological reproduction. It's to recognize its uniquely human form, which is all these other forms brought to consciousness, brought into a conscious body, which ideally is what the human body is.

The Christians have always tried to do this—ritually—by eating it, as in the sacrament of the Last Supper. *Jerusalem* is about eating Christ, about digesting his teachings. So that when I say that *Jerusalem* is "a culture we only partially inhabit," I mean we've got to learn a lot more about the digestive system. We've got to learn a lot more about what goes on in our metaphorical bodies. We have to engage in the process of digestion and see what our own unique consciousness is making of it because our metaphorical body is one that is ceaselessly transforming, ceaselessly undergoing a metamorphosis.

Above all, Blake says, we must enjoy the journey. May it bind you more and more to what John of Patmos in the Book of Revelation called "a new heaven and a new Earth."

NR: Our present raping of the planet is a huge example of *not* digesting what

Blake is saying, it seems to me. How do we enter into Blake's vision of that state of love before it's too late for us and the planet?

RW: By embracing Reality out of a love of Reality, out of a love of God, if you like. The state of the world mirrors our own inner state. We need to enter into a mutual love affair with it. As within, so without. We need to be on intimate terms with the Creation. We have to get back into contact with something as primary as the sun that rises every morning, and build from there—just as Blake builds his epic, *Jerusalem*, from there.

Blake says that if we perceived the body with the imagination, we'd ecologically transform the Earth, we would stop raping nature. We would raise nature to its human form, as distinct from the form that the machine has given it. We would learn to live in harmony with nature.

NR: Is Blake saying that all technology is destructive to us and to the natural world?

RW: Intimately tied up with technology is this business of the conquest of nature. When that notion of conquest is identified with technology and the machine, then Blake sees all machinery as destructive. A good example would be the printing press. Blake didn't want to send his poems out to a commercial press because he felt it not only brutalized the poems, it killed them. It was a form of murder. That is to say, to see his poem as he wrote it with his own hand, handed over to a satanic machine that turned it, squashed and dead and black, onto a piece of paper—like a bug you've stamped out—was a source of physical pain to him.

The question was how to get his poems into print without killing them. This was a psychic process for him, so he had to learn how to print them himself. And then he had to learn how to deal with the wounding by the printing process. He did this by painting them, which was like a healing process, and by restoring them—not only restoring them to life, but bringing them to a new kind of life whereby the printing process became an enhancement of the poem. In this way Blake was learning how to *interact* with technology, learning how to humanize it, how to engage it as craft. So that the poem was being made greater by "technology," but it was a technology that had a huge amount of soul work involved in it.

NR: By and large we've lost the sense of the soul in our technology today, haven't we?

RW: Yes, in anything mass-produced, the soul has gone out of it. But you see, the soul *knows* it's been left out and demands to be let back in. A strike, bargaining, is not just about wages. It's also about soul.

NR: Why is there a connection between our soulless technology and our destruction of the natural world?

RW: Because we want nature to exist only to serve us. It's there to be exploited, and our technology enables us to do this. It's there for the gold that's in the mines, or for the trees in the forest that we clear-cut, or the fish that we driftnet so rapaciously, and so on. So nature becomes the victim of our own rapaciousness—it gets caught up in all that self-interest, in all that greed, in the robber baron mentality.

But nature serves soul. Your garden, for example, serves soul. It's therapeutic and it's healing if we respect it and honor it as a part of divine creation. But we could certainly begin to rape your garden pretty quickly if we wanted to make it serve something else. Could we extract the opium from the poppy seeds? Could we go on the streets and sell it? I think we could. But if we do not treat nature with respect, what we extract from it finally poisons us. We reap what we have sown.

NR: So honoring the soul in nature means not exploiting it for our own ends?

RW: Yes, but more than that. It has to do with bringing the poppy to the consciousness of being a poppy, or the peony to the consciousness of being a peony. It's like Adam in the garden naming all the flowers, naming all the animals—where animals are talking, plants are feeling, Nature is speaking. They are all communing with us if we are open to them. Which is to say, nature is there to be *recognized*, and until it's recognized and named by us, there's a sense in which it doesn't quite exist yet. Human beings are a part of the Creation. Human consciousness is, in a sense, the crowning of Creation. And it's the bringing of our consciousness to all of nature around us, which is repeating the eternal act of Creation, and completing it.

NR: And included in that consciousness is the recognition of the soul in the garden.

RW: Absolutely. That's a genuine act of recognition. But, you know, I can't just walk into a garden and automatically bring consciousness to it. I can, however, settle down; and if I can quiet my own thinking and my own kinds of intrusive urgencies, I can gradually bring my thoughts into some kind of relationship with it. I'll gradually begin to speak out of it, and it will begin to hear me. And I'll be enhanced, and it will be enhanced.

NR: It will change you?

RW: Yes; and I'll change it. The flowers will have the look of flowers that are looked at. There's a difference.

NR: A difference between appreciation and love, and none whatsoever? A difference between a garden that is forsaken, and one that is not?

RW: That's right. "The Forsaken Garden" reflects the triumph of technology in the Industrial Revolution which is the triumph of the bodysoul split. Our Western attitudes toward nature are grounded in that split. You have the world of matter out there, but the mind is not a part of matter. It's imposed upon matter, as the master imposes himself upon the slave. Therefore nature is seen as an "it," a "thing" to be manipulated, forced to do our will.

What that can lead to is the ruthless exploitation of nature, the rape of nature as an insensate, unconscious "thing." This view holds that nature as mindless matter can't feel pain; it has no emotions. To perceive nature as though it did is called "the pathetic fallacy." Projecting our feelings onto nature results in a primitive, superstitious state of *participation mystique*. Primitive people might do that, but people enlightened by science don't do that. We know nature is just a mindless "thing." Flowers don't feel; flowers don't think. You cut a flower, it's not going to hurt the flower. Chop down a tree? Go ahead— the tree's not going to feel any pain. What's wrong with chopping trees down? They're just "things" out there.

The Romantics explored the dark side of this scientific "enlighten-ment," of the separation of mind from matter. And what it celebrated instead is what the poet Samuel Taylor Coleridge called ". . . the one life within us, and abroad, /Which meets all motions and becomes its soul."

NR: This is a huge jump in attitude for most people—to view the world in a more holistic and less rapacious way.

RW: Well, Blake is calling for a complete change of consciousness, what might be called a mutation of consciousness. His poetry enacts the process of being born again into a consciousness of who, in the sight of God, we are. We have to know who, as human beings, we are in order to know what nature is. Our rape of nature is our loathing of ourselves. This loathing arises from our ignorance, or rejection, of our divine origin. Blake's poetry enacts our creation, our union with our divine origin. His metaphor for this creative process is the building of Jerusalem.

He is also saying that with this kind of perception there's no substitute for the work that is required, and that it's very, very difficult. Blake calls this work ceaseless "Mental Fight."

What we are doing to the planet is catastrophic. *But there is no easy solution.* People are not going to stop cutting down the forests. They're not going to stop polluting the waters. These things are going to go on. Blake would say you cannot tell people to stop doing something. "Thou shalt not" will not work.

NR: What then is the hard solution?

RW: The solution is to re-imagine nature: turn nature from an "it" into a "thou," as Martin Buber described it. We need to recognize that we are a part of nature, that nature is a part of us, and in destroying it we are destroying ourselves. It's a matter of re-visioning nature, and ourselves as a part of it.

NR: Do you have any ideas about how to get people to do this?

RW: No, I don't. But one thing we can do is to make sure that we are each individually psychologically grounded. As must be evident by now, I look mainly to literature to ground myself psychologically. I see in literature the operation of the psyche, what Keats called "soul making." I trust Milton's feminine Muse—she's a great therapist.

For centuries we affirmed what were called the "liberal arts," the liberating arts, which released us into what we are. The horror, the fear, for the Romantics was that we were no longer on intimate terms with the arts. We no longer turned to them to liberate, to heal.

We've got to return to Milton, says Blake, and bring him back to life. Milton's struggle to move toward a new God-image is our struggle too. We not only have to bring him back to life—we have to give him a new life as a kind of progressive revelation, a progressive unfolding of a great psychic drama which embraces us all.

Because, you see, it's one song we sing—the culture of Psyche—and its orchestration is very, very rich. If the song ever stops, we're finished. So we've got to keep singing. Blake was singing when he died.

NR: Few people see what you call the "unfolding of a great psychic drama which embraces us all" as a song of adventure—what Laurens van der Post calls "the only thing worth fighting for." And what Joseph Campbell perhaps meant when he asked, "Are you up to your destiny?" As I see it, most people cringe before the demands of psychological work, and of "soul making." Why is that?

RW: Because we're used to the quick sell—advertising—where the most extraordinary promises are made. We are a culture of easy fixes, which means that nothing gets fixed. What I'm talking about is the sweat shop, where the real work is done. It's hard work. Love your enemy, yes. Integrate your shadow, yes. But don't think it's easy. There's no easy fix. God will not cheat us out of ourselves, deny us the dignity of our own pain.

Love your shadow? Forgive your enemies? These are very difficult things to do until you consciously understand who and what your shadow is. The process of coming to understand, says Blake, is the process of forgiveness. In your desire and need to understand your enemy you are forgiving; when you understand your enemy in terms of what that enemy has constellated psychologically in you (and that is the work of therapy)—that is forgiveness.

What does it mean to forgive the father? It means that I have absorbed that internalization of him in myself, and that I no longer need to act that out. I no longer need to project my father onto the world and do battle with him out there. Nor do I need to collude with the inner power principle he represents, and allow him to bully and victimize me in my own life.

Paradise Lost is a monumental epic, and extremely complex. It's a struggle within Milton's soul—a tremendous battle. Blake read that poem with all the concentration of his being. He said: "I've *got* to *understand* this." That is forgiving Milton. That's love. Love is not a sentimental thing. Love thy neighbor? Come off it—that's habit, an outward thing, a motto on the fridge.

NR: What's the connection between the hard work of "soul making" and saving the planet?

RW: I confess I'm becoming increasingly uneasy about the use of that word "save." God does the saving, not us. It's His and Her planet, not ours.

NR: Is it really up to God to save the planet? Surely *we* have a huge responsibility. "God helps those who help themselves."

RW: Yes, but the idea that *we* can save the planet is very destructive because that's hubris. From my point of view, we are not in charge. We are not in control. If it were in our hands, the game is over. But I don't think it's in our hands. I think there is a providential operational scheme, a master plan infinitely more benevolent than anything we can imagine or execute. We didn't create this planet. We are not the authors of it. We are the stewards of it, the custodians of it. But we're bad stewards. We ignore this reality at our peril when we attempt to take over, steal, what does not belong to us. Private property rights cannot extend to the planet itself. We cannot own it. International cartels cannot own it.

If anyone wants to take on the planet, if they really want to take on the planet, like Atlas with the world on his shoulders, do they know what they're saying? Have they really harnessed within themselves the energies that are required to carry the planet around on their backs?

The work of saving the planet, which is clearly the work that most engages us, must, I think, be grounded in our relationship to God. Certainly I would want to know something about that relationship before I could have any opinion about what one hopes to achieve in terms of saving the planet, and how one hopes to achieve it.

NR: Do you think, given the relatively unconscious state of our society, that the task is hopeless?

RW: No. No, I don't say the task is hopeless. I would say that there is a visionary center where the task is always already done. The oak tree is always already in the acorn.

NR: You mean the visionary center that Laurens van der Post calls the "master pattern" within each person? Or what Jung calls the "Self"? Or that James Hillman calls the "daimon"?

RW: Yes. And if you're in that, it's a very different story. It's a totally different story. But if you're not in it, then for God's sake, for the sake of your own welfare, leave it alone.

NR: But surely each of us has to do what he or she can to help heal the planet, no matter how advanced (or retarded!) we are spiritually. How does a person actually make contact with "this visionary center where the task is always already done"?

RW: Jung said, and I would agree with him, that the visionary center is ultimately a religious center. Until his analysands (those, say, over forty) moved into that center—where like Blake and Milton they were grappling with God—they had not yet found the way to the *core* of their problems, their neuroses.

I believe, as Jung believed, that we have a huge investment in our neuroses. We stake our whole lives on them, build an entire life-style around them. To overcome or resolve a neurosis is like stepping out of who we are, or think we are. Christ called this stepping out of our habitual self a Second Birth. If we want out of our neuroses, he said, then we must be born again.

What I'm saying is this: poets of the highest order—Milton, Shakespeare, Dante, Wordsworth, Blake, Rilke, Emily Dickinson—take us into their sacred groves where God is present and let us see what goes on there. That is, we are taken in literature into the author's sacred place. Even though we cannot claim it as our own, what it shows us is that we too have a sacred grove, "a visionary center," where we are alone with God. Most of us are not given the genius to enact the sacred core of life in a literary way. But—and here's my point—everyone enacts it in *some way*. That's the mystery of the actual. I know God is there in the mystery of the actual; by *actual* I mean every living form of life.

So we can help save the planet by getting to the core where God is, where it always already is saved. "Let go and let God" is the way some describe it.

NR: So the fate of the planet—like our soul's life expressed in great poetry—is ultimately in sacred hands, and we have to honor that mystery in every aspect of our lives. That takes enormous faith and dedication, Ross.

RW: I know from my own experience that without God it cannot be done. There's a delusion about doing in which the doing is an undoing, a perpetual canceling out. Someone described it as endlessly carrying water in leaky vessels.

NR: You need a little help?

RW: It isn't that we need some help. It's that we are instruments. Now, the more impure we are as instruments, the more we sweat, the more trouble we have, because we're just not channeled for it. Blake, for some reason, was an extraordinary channel.

Blake's body, the body Milton entered and traveled through, was, when Milton entered it, a very sick body. The journey of Milton to Blake's brain was a hugely transformative trip. This planet as a giant human body is very sick, sick unto death. What has now to take place in it, as a healing process, is every bit as radical as what takes place in Blake's body as Milton journeys to his brain to meet and unite with his Muse. We, like Milton's Muse in Blake's brain, can bring a healing consciousness to this sick planet. That, I think, is our task.

NR: You say that we must "let go and let God." Does that mean that we shouldn't be making attempts to stop what we can, do what we can?

RW: No, it's a sense of first giving ourselves over to what is being attempted in us: we are a huge experiment. We are all enormously creative, hugely creative.

NR: Few of us are creative visionaries like Blake, though. As I see it, most people these days are either drugging their creativity into silence, or are only able to find the time to be creative in very small ways. Most people would say they don't have great opportunities in their lives for building an imaginal body. What is the answer for people who say this? If saving the planet means first connecting with those deep images within ourselves that give us life and energy, how does the normally harassed person do this?

RW: A blade of grass is a greater painting than a Titian, if you get to the core of it, and getting to the core is what we all have to get to eventually.

But you're right; only Blake could write *Jerusalem*. But that doesn't mean that the sun only shines on William Blake, that the Sermon on the Mount was addressed to William Blake and to no one else. Christ doesn't come looking for Blake, saying to hell with the rest of us. Blake despised any idea of an Elect.

We've each got our own version of Jerusalem to build, even if it's just a shack without running water, or making a loaf of bread by grinding our own wheat, or buying some second-hand clothes at the Good Will shop and making them over to fit us. The point is, we've got to make some sort of human habitation for ourselves. If the Biblical version of Jerusalem, which was Blake's model, is too vast, well then, consider "the lilies of the field" (Matthew 6:28).

Whatever we do to make ourselves into inhabitants, into citizens, of the planet, we have to put our very best effort into it. If I have a thimbleful of talent and Blake has a barrelful, then it takes just as much effort for me to fill my thimble as it takes Blake to fill his barrel. None of us can get off the hook by comparing ourselves to Blake in order to claim that we can't do anything that really matters.

Blake knows that what he is doing is not easy. He knows that it would be easier to pull the covers over his head because the sun is hurting his eyes. "The mutual love" arises only when the Power that created nature is recognized as the same Power that created us.

NR: Is Blake's Jerusalem ever built?

RW: No, Jerusalem is never built; it's always being built. Like Romanticism, the great emphasis is upon process rather than product. Product is always finally the enemy of process. The form will always freeze the content. In other words, Jerusalem is something that we're all doing all the time.

But it gets deflected into sexual intercourse. It gets deflected into political revolution. It gets deflected into social activism. These things in themselves are all right, but they tend to become the object; they tend to become the goal. Once that happens, the energy gets congealed. And once energy is congealed in a political stance, a political platform, your tiger will roar. Energy can *not* be contained in political forms, gender forms, social forms, religious forms. *It will not stay there.* You can imprison energy, but the moment you imprison it the tiger will roar. *And he will be heard.*

NR: What does he say?

RW: "Let me out." We have to live with the tiger, otherwise we get sick. That's it. There is no alternative. You may call it a curse, but *we are all artists* in this sense. And there's no point in trying to deny it, because it will get you in one way or another.

     We all have it. We are all infected with a divine discontent. But to know how to use it? That's the key.

NR: So that the struggle to build Jerusalem, both within ourselves and on the planet, is always going on?

RW: Yes, the struggle to keep trying to build Jerusalem will continue, always. And as our planetary crisis gets more alarming, that will make us take more action. But from the psychological point of view this is the arena in which the psyche is already at work; the struggle is going on now as it always has been, and that doesn't really change much over time.

     Blake would say that without contraries there is no progression; what we want is the ceaseless "Mental Fight," and as long as we're in this world we're going to be in that struggle. The great virtue of the crisis we're in is that it makes the struggle all the more demanding; it makes us more alert. Yet we go on with it—that's our triumph. And when we can't fight any more we die, and it's a good time for us to die, when we have ceased to fight. But there are always young people coming along, so that the fight will go on—not *against* nature but rather engaging *with* nature.

     No, Jerusalem is never built. From the psychic point of view the struggle is always going on.

Chapter Four

New Life in the Dreaming Earth

NANCY RYLEY: Ross, our conversation up until now has been focused on Blake and Milton as harbingers of a changed consciousness for our time. If we humans aren't going to end up destroying the Earth, it's obvious that there is an urgent need for what Blake saw as a mutation in our consciousness. How close are we to achieving this?

ROSS WOODMAN: A culture reaches its fruition when the body/soul split is healed on a new level of integration. There comes a time in every world culture when the two really do come together, when the inner and outer worlds mirror each other.

A genuine global culture toward which, in the name of survival, we are now moving requires a level of conscious understanding previously dreamt of only by visionaries but never actually achieved. People like you, Nancy, confronted in your particular case with environmental illness are, of necessity, working toward it. That necessity is your own survival. I think of you as a canary in the global mine warning the rest of us of what lies ahead.

NR: As a consequence of the way we've mistreated the Earth, environmental illness, cancer, and other environmentally related diseases are now afflicting millions of people on the planet. How do you view this dark side of globalization?

RW: I think that this dark side is, alas, necessary to any real growth of consciousness. It's the nightmare that forces us to wake up and face our condition. When we are forced to see what we are doing to nature, we are at the same time forced to see ourselves as citizens responsible for the welfare of the planet. The sickness of nature, especially when it becomes immediately and particularly our own, awakens us to the planet and our responsibility for it.

I believe that such is the chaotic state of the world right now that more and more people are realizing that a new order, a new Creation, has to be brought out of this chaos. We're back at the beginning with the primeval void, back in that state mythically described in the opening verses of Genesis. Some people know that's where we are, and they're ready in their own way to do what Blake did. It's a huge task and we would be madly inflated if we believed we could undertake it on our own.

NR: When do you think people will really start to recognize the planet as their home and realize that in order to inhabit it we must make some radical changes?

RW: I will tell you: When we can no longer breathe. When we can no longer eat. When our environment is so poisoned that cancer has become a plague, only one of many that threatens us all.

I think when people face their own extinction, face their own deaths— and I'm talking in the literal sense, I'm talking about a polluted atmosphere, I'm talking about ozone pollution, I'm talking about when it's no longer possible to perform your natural functions—when your body is poisoned and you become largely dysfunctional (which is what most of the human race is becoming, whether they know it or not)—when this happens, then something quite spontaneous will begin to operate. We will begin to draw on something that we haven't been in touch with for a long time, and that something is called survival instincts. Then we'll experience what a mutation in consciousness is like, when what is happening globally threatens our very existence. If necessity is the mother of invention, survival is the mother of change. But until our survival is directly and immediately threatened, not much is going to change.

NR: Well, survival is certainly an issue when you have environmental illness.

RW: Yes, what you have is the global culture's illness in microcosm. Its problem is explicit in you, except that it doesn't know it yet.

NR: You mean that the global culture really doesn't know what's happening to it?

RW: That's right. You're ahead of the society. You're a cultural canary in the late twentieth century's global mine. What you're saying to people through your illness is: "We have to look at the culture because it's being destroyed."

NR: Or it's self-destructing. Right now there are increasing numbers of "canaries" who can't go out of their houses, or who have to wear breathing masks when they do. People are having their lives slowly ruined by the illnesses they are getting from toxic chemicals sprayed onto our foods, into public places, used in building materials—the list goes on and on. The result is suppressed immune systems which lead to many of the degenerative diseases people are suffering from these days. We're no longer the vigorous people we once were. Working on this book, there were some days when I didn't function at all—the symptoms from some inadvertent chemical exposure were too bad. Unfortunately, poisonous chemicals don't always arrive flagged.

For example, I recently had my blood tested for chlorinated pesticides, and found that my levels for Endrin—which is a pesticide sprayed on crops—is three times the population average. I was shocked because I don't eat anything but organically grown food! The obvious conclusion is that although a certain farmer may be growing pesticide-free crops, the poisonous chemicals being sprayed onto adjacent fields are spreading onto his crops, and we're eating them.

RW: Can you do anything to get rid of these chemicals?

NR: Well, for starters you can get into a sauna and sweat them out for four hours a day, for six weeks—or longer. It sounds simple, but four hours a day in a sauna can cause complications with blood pressure and possible kidney failure. To say nothing of the cost: under medical supervision, about $8000 would probably cover the total cost of a six-week program in the United States.

RW: And when you step out of the sauna you go back into the polluted world. That means you've got to keep doing this therapy all the time, which puts you in the impossible situation of your body being in opposition to the environment. And when the body is against the environment, so is the psyche.

NR: That's exactly what happened to me before I was able to escape into unpolluted surroundings. I started to perceive my surroundings as my enemy, and I still do when I go to the city.

I hate to sound like a doomsday Cassandra, but I really think that if this society is going to survive, it's going to have to voluntarily give up all the things that the environmentally ill are *forced* to give up. All the things that have turned North America into a consumer paradise are what it needs to reject as its *raison d'etre*. Because, although health problems may not yet be evident in many adults, they are increasing to an alarming degree in children who have been handed a legacy of the poisons that their parents have been ingesting for decades because of our polluted environment. So it's a tragedy of the first order, isn't it?

RW: Yes, it is. The culture's loss of a spiritual connection to the planet has allowed us to launch an assault on the Earth that is reflected in our damaged bodies because psyche and soma are one. The split between soul and body is played out in the society through all these diseases. The healing, if not yet the cure, lies in embracing the Earth as our own body and working with the two as one.

Wordsworth, for example, begins his fourteen-book epic poem, *The Prelude*, by describing a "gentle breeze" fanning his cheek as if it were "half-conscious of the joy it brings/From the green fields." The breeze joyously awakens him to nature's benign presence after he had been imprisoned for a long time in London where he remained "a discontented sojourner." Like you, Nancy, Wordsworth experienced what he called "the vast city" as the site of his own kind of environmental illness, and his epic begins with a celebration of his relief—like you going to your island home, or to your home in the Canadian Rockies. "I breathe again," he cries, as I am sure you have cried many times.

For Wordsworth, "I breathe again" is a joyous moment of rebirth. As the external breeze becomes his own inner breath, he senses his renewed relationship to nature and realizes that the breeze (not your gas fumes!) is the "sweet breath of heaven" which has its "correspondent breeze" within himself. In this visionary realization, the fourteen-book *Prelude* is conceived and born. I recommend it to you, Nancy, for your healing.

NR: Is the emphasis on the breath as the focus of healing part of the mutation of consciousness that you're talking about?

RW: Yes, the focus upon breath as the breath of life, the breath that the God of

Genesis breathed into the nostrils of Adam so that he became a living soul rather than a clod of clay, requires a mutation in consciousness from the physical to the psychic, from physical breath to soul breath. It involves a shift from the physical, or literal, to the metaphorical dimension. Most people who practice any form of meditation—Yogis, for example—understand this.

Shelley's *Ode to the West Wind* is another example of the healing operation of breath when breath is attended to as sacred. In it he invokes the west wind as a "thou," calling it the "breath of autumn's being." In the surge of this wind in an autumn storm, he sees the coming death of his own declining Western civilization in terms of autumn leaves, sent by the violent west wind to their "dark wintry bed," like "pestilence-stricken multitudes." But the west wind that acts as a "Destroyer" is also a "Preserver." The "dark wintry bed" of fallen leaves, "yellow, and black, and pale, and hectic red," protects and nourishes new life in what he calls "the dreaming Earth."

Shelley here is inviting us to absorb nature's life and death process into our souls so that it becomes our own internal process. To enter the realm of the soul—your own soul process, Nancy—is to view the Earth in winter ("the winter of our discontent," the pestilence that is environmental illness) as nourishing new life in the process of destroying an old one. Shelley's "dreaming Earth" carries as dream the potential spring within winter. This ceaseless mythopoeic vision of life as the potential hidden within it, waiting to emerge, is what Shelley means by soul life.

NR: So that poetic vision, far from being fantasy or superstition as the rationalists insist, is essential to our survival because it sees life in terms of what lies waiting within it to be born?

RW: Yes. Because for you, Nancy, not to know yourself as pregnant with new life—not to see your environmental illness as a very difficult pregnancy and labor—is to commit yourself to death, a winter without spring. Not to imaginatively inhabit Shelley's offered vision is to resign yourself to pestilence, and to number yourself among his "pestilence-stricken multitudes." What Shelley wants you to see is the new life, Spring, behind Winter— ("O Wind,/If Winter comes, can Spring be far behind?")—pushing slowly forward to your own rebirth. This is surely what this book is about.

NR: That still leaves me with the physical reality of a poisoned environment which I, and all the other people with environmentally related illness, are trying to grapple with. You can't breathe spiritually if you're dead, Ross! What you're saying could be interpreted as letting people off the hook as far as dealing with the contamination of the planet is concerned.

RW: The healing of the planet, which is what is involved in the healing of your own body, is, I think, far more difficult at the literal level than it is at the metaphorical level that the Romantics describe. Indeed, I really don't believe there can be any real healing at the literal level unless it first enacts itself metaphorically in the human imagining of it. To execute a gold medal high jump at the Olympics, the athlete must first imagine the jump in his mind. The winner is the one who is capable of literally enacting the highest and best metaphor of it.

What I'm suggesting is that we have to believe in the reality of the imagination in order for it to perform a healing function. We cannot, Christ says, enter his Kingdom unless we become like little children.

NR: Do you mean we have to *imagine* a cure for ourselves, and the planet, before it can actually happen?

RW: Yes. The knowledge of the physical world, which includes our own bodies as the highest, most complex form of it, is not enough. If, for example, you could get rid of all the chemicals that are poisoning your body and be restored to physical health, would you have achieved your own ultimate goal?

Physical survival is a basic "Darwinian" instinct. We must be "fit" enough to survive while, at the same time, seeing to it that the environment is "fit" enough for us to survive in. This struggle—Darwin's "survival of the fittest"—now requires a huge mental effort, a mutation of consciousness, if we are not soon to be extinguished by the poisoned gases we are releasing into the environment as our most dangerous form of germ warfare. Blake enacts this mutation, as do the other Romantic poets.

Of course, it's not easy. It's no longer a simple matter of unconsciously breathing in and out, in and out; it now requires a *consciousness* of what it is we are doing when we breathe. We must at a certain critical point attend to the fact that breath is the gift of life, the miracle of Creation itself, and therefore in some very real sense sacred. We need an awareness of what is being received and of what is being given back if life is to be perpetually renewed as, for example, Blake, Wordsworth, and Shelley renewed it.

NR: Are you saying that even if we were to clean up the environment tomorrow, we're unlikely—in our present state of consciousness—to find cures for environmental illness, or cancer, or any of these twentieth-century plagues?

RW: I don't believe that we are because I don't think we have yet fully imagined them.

NR: In other words, by focusing on *cures* we might be overlooking new perceptions of Reality that are being born in us through our illnesses?

RW: Yes. We must, the Romantics assert, awaken to the Reality that resides in the "dreaming Earth." Our survival now depends upon embracing this vision of death in the service of new life if we are creatively to grasp the providence that resides in the calamity that has overtaken our planet, and all that it nourishes and contains.

NR: The "providence" that resides in the "calamity?"

RW: Yes. The Persian prophet, Baha'u'llah, put it this way:

> My calamity is My providence.
> Outwardly it is fire and vengeance,
> Inwardly it is light and mercy.

NR: Light shall come out of this present darkness?

RW: Yes. This "providence," I suggest, can be found in a powerful image in the final book of the Bible, the Book of Revelation, which gathers into itself the entire burden of the Bible's meaning:

> And there appeared a great wonder in heaven; a woman clothed with the sun, and the moon under her feet, and upon her head a crown of twelve stars; and she being with child cried, travailing in birth, and pained to be delivered. (Rev. 12:1-2)

Nature as the Great Mother containing the sun, moon, and stars, "travailing in birth, and pained to be delivered" does indeed offer us a powerful image of our own endangered planet at this moment in time. To describe it (or her) as "a great wonder in heaven" is to perceive her as the Reality she is in the archetypal imagination of the poet. To tap into that inner imagery, which is the language of the soul, is to tap into the healing ground of the psyche where the full burden of an environmental illness is offered up as a new birth in consciousness.

The woman in labor in the Book of Revelation is, archetypally speaking, at once yourself and the Great Mother, Nancy—yourself mothering yourself. In what you have revealed about your struggle with environmental illness, I have gained some very real awareness of your urgent need of the support of the Great Mother, and of the very real danger of experiencing her as entirely negative or life-destroying. In India, for example, it is quite possible to view the Great Mother, Kali, as entirely destructive, a Mother who wantonly destroys her entire creation. In reality, however, she is, like Shelley's West Wind, both Destroyer and Preserver and, of course, the ultimate Renewer like Wordsworth's "sweet breath of heaven." I think that you, and other ill people like you, need to meditate on the Great Mother and to work on your creative relationship to her. May the feminine force be with you!

NR: Thank you, Ross. When I think of "calamity," I also think of the biblical story of Job. Many sick people that I know feel Job's trials as their own. Are you not also telling us that, like Job, it is through suffering and pain that we will be reborn into a new relationship to the Divine?

RW: The knowledge that suffering can be redemptive constitutes a major shift in consciousness—a new birth. It's an excruciatingly painful process, but there's a huge grace operating in it. However, ultimately, I think that Thanatos (death) is in the service of Eros (love); that God is ultimately Love. Right now it is not easy to affirm this, even as it was not easy for Job to affirm it. But he did.

I think that our affirmation, unlike Job's, however, must now come from an affirmation of what Marion calls the *feminine.* Job belonged to a patriarchal world; he was himself a great patriarch addressed by a severe patriarchal God constellated by trauma. He spoke out of Job's trauma as a voice out of a horrendously destructive whirlwind. There was more sheer power than love in that voice. You, Nancy, cannot identify with that voice, nor should you.

What is now happening—and Marion is very much a part of it—is that this patriarchal voice of God is being brought into a new relationship with the feminine. Mechanistic science, like the patriarchal voice of God, has tended to treat nature with power rather than with love. In treating your disease as the enemy that must be conquered, you have tried to make nature (your body) your slave. In other words, in bending it to your will you have entered into a master/slave relationship with it. It is essential to avoid settling into this destructive scenario lest you become the very thing you are fighting. This can lead to despair, and despair can usher in defeat. You end up defeated not *in* your struggle but *by* your struggle. I have seen it happen. Therefore I'm suggesting a new model of behavior in which you recognize the "providence" in the "calamity."

When Marion was diagnosed with metastasized cancer, she had to face up to what appeared to be the imminence of her death. It was suggested that she should do whatever she most desired to do. What she most desired was to go on doing what she had been doing most of her life. The realization that she had not left undone those things she most loved and wanted to do was a source of great inner peace. She knew that, even if her cancer could not be "cured," she herself had been "healed" by this affirmation of her life.

Someone in a workshop confronted her very directly, saying in effect: "Mrs. Woodman, how can you stand here and talk about healing imagery when you have cancer? How can you do it? Imagery is not healing you. You look sick. The longer you talk to us the paler you get. You've got rings under your eyes and you look exhausted. And yet you stand here talking about healing images."

NR: How did Marion deal with that?

RW: She distinguished between *healing* and *curing*. She said, in effect, "I am talking about healing, not curing. I could die of cancer tomorrow and be healed. Healing has to do with soul, and the soul becoming whole. And I can tell you that cancer is a leap towards wholeness in me, meaning that I am more embodied in my soul because of this. And I'm ready to go."

NR: I know from talking to her that having cancer brought her to a consciousness which she didn't have before.

RW: She had it before, but it certainly got more focused. Marion's soul life was what had always been important to her, and she knew that cancer could not take it away from her. In the very midst of death, she experienced her own inner abundance of life. Her very confrontation with death enhanced that experience. Marion knew she was a whole (not a perfect) person in touch with her own growing sense of being. She called this growing sense of being "the pregnant virgin," which is the title of perhaps her most influential book.

In her confrontation with cancer Marion became even more deeply involved in her own on-going soul life. She saw in the possibility of her imminent separation from her beloved physical body an experience that found its most natural analogy in the separation of the embryo from the mother's womb. She was prepared to thank her body for the life for which it had prepared her, in something like the same way that the mother's womb prepares the embryo for a life beyond it. I watched Marion during this period more fully imagine the heaven she was always already in. The wonder that she experienced in childhood became the power of her true womanhood.

Let me say that as a result of having, on a very different level, gone through this experience with Marion, I now see her as someone who inhabits a life-after-death world. And that life-after-death world that she is now learning to inhabit is intimately connected to what I think of as our new planetary life arising out of the "death" of our old tribal and nation-state existence. Coming through their "death" to a global reality is, I think, analogous to what Marion has been through. It's the "providence" in the "calamity" of cancer.

Now, if you can get into that mentality, if you can get into that consciousness, there's the sense of *wholeness,* of our relatedness to the planet, to all of life, including immortal life.

NR: Are you saying that ultimately, like Marion, we have to experience a rebirth in consciousness; and that if we do, we will then enter into a renewed relationship with the Earth which will be beneficial to her, as well as to ourselves?

RW: Yes. I'm suggesting that within this process of ensouling the body lies a new *planetary* consciousness (the Earth itself as *conscious body*) which resides in our growing awareness not only of the reality of the human soul but of the divine presence (the Kingdom of God) manifesting itself in that planetary reality. I am quite persuaded from my own experience that the planet, like our bodies, urgently needs the new consciousness that is now opening to us in multiple ways. I suspect that the planet, and our bodies, have been waiting a very long time for the kind of recognition this new consciousness can offer.

NR: If we alone can bring a conscious understanding to planet Earth, what is our task with regard to her future, and ours?

RW: Our task now is to recognize that the planet Earth is one country and that we are its citizens. A great metaphor of that is the photograph of Earth taken from the moon.

NR: I know the photograph you mean, and I'll never forget it. It shows this glorious orb set like an azure jewel in the immensity of space. What it doesn't show are the clear-cut forests and the depleted oceans. Nor does it show the national boundaries and war zones, and all the other things that divide and fractionalize us on the globe. Do you think that humans will see that wonderful imagery as a metaphor of the unity in diversity that we consciously must adopt in order to survive?

RW: Jung believed we were moving into a new stage of psychic Reality marked by the coming together of all the peoples of the Earth. He saw physical reality as the outer embodiment of psychic Reality. He did not, therefore, entirely rule out the possibility of something out there that, as a mandala, answered to a collective unconscious projected yearning for world unity, a collective image of unconscious human desire. The new mandala assumed its most concrete form, perceived by our senses, as the circular Earth seen from the moon, floating in space. This new lunar consciousness was a giant step for humanity, for it symbolically signified—as a phallic thrust into outer space—a marriage with the feminine, a true coming together of the masculine and feminine in a *hieros gamos*, an Inner Marriage such as he had been studying in alchemical texts for many years.

Jung was in this respect participating in the making of what most would call a new science fiction, which he considered to be the myth of a new age, the archetypal depiction of a new age like the myths of the gods in earlier civilizations.

NR: What is Blake's vision with regard to our future on the planet?

RW: Blake's vision is the building of Jerusalem. Jerusalem is the city of God. It is one city, one country, one humanity, one religion, one God. "The Earth is one country, and humankind its citizens." We are all citizens of the planet Earth. The source from which Milton and Blake drew their inspiration will become the unifying source binding us as one family inhabiting one globe together. Blake called this vision of the Earth as one country "the great harvest of the nations." He took his vision from the Book of Revelation. His poem, *Milton*, ends with a vision of this "great harvest and vintage of the nations:"

> The ovens are prepared, the wagons ready.
> Lions and tigers sport and play.
> All animals are prepared in all their strength
> To go forth in the great harvest and vintage of the nations.

This is the new consciousness. We went to the moon to find out where we are, to photograph the Earth. We now know we're members of the planet, that the planet is our home, and that there are no borders, no boundaries on this planet that we cannot cross.

"The Earth is one country, humankind its citizens." We either live together or die together. For a house, a planet, divided against itself will not stand.

THE GLOBAL BODYSOUL

MY TALKS with Ross Woodman at first felt lofty and cerebral, but in the end it was his humanity that reached me and was responsible for a large shift in my consciousness; his role in my soul's journey was to be as a catalyst for change. Gradually I realized that I was being shaken by some of his insights: Christ as a feminine deity; we don't save the planet—God does; and so forth. The spiritual teacher Gurdjieff once said that "shocks are good for you." So I plunged on with our talks, hoping that Gurdjieff was right and that I would be able to keep up with the imaginative vision of this remarkably erudite man. In the end I grew with our talks—they stretched me and pulled me out of old thought patterns. But it wasn't easy!

One thing that Ross said which keeps resonating in my mind, was: "What I'm talking about is the sweat shop, where the real work is done." That comment reinforced what I already had gleaned for myself: that soul work takes all the dedication and love we have to give it. Nor can we short-cut the labor that goes with it by looking for quick fixes for our spiritual condition. Near the end of our talks Ross revealed much to me about his own struggle for psychic wholeness, and from this I realized to what an extent he had trod this path before me. By agreeing to participate in this book he was in fact reaching a hand out to help me, a fellow traveler.

The problem of dealing with environmental illness at a physical level is beyond the scope of this book. Suffice it to say that for years after I first became ill, the practical side of coping with this disease completely absorbed my attention as I desperately tried to detect what food or chemical was causing my symptoms *that* day, *that* hour, *that* minute. Ross Woodman made me realize that spending all my time adjusting to a poisoned environment was too Self-limiting. The "deep meaning of environmental illness" is that, at both an individual and a collective level, this disease is a spiritual malaise as much as a physical condition. This does not mean that the reason people get sick is because of some spiritual or psychological failure. After all, saints get ill and sinners stay healthy! It does mean, however, that our state of consciousness can determine whether our illness will take us down or become a powerful stimulus to our transformation.

As my understanding of Blake's concept of the bodysoul grows, it never ceases to amaze me how my own body gives me exactly the symptoms required in order to put me in touch with my soul's needs. For example, in many of the treatment modalities concerned with my illness, the emphasis has been on my poor digestion. Now here was Ross Woodman telling me about Blake's poor digestion, and his own, as indicators of a huge spiritual need.

I had not been brought up, as Marion had been, in a deeply religious household, so I had no traditional container for my spiritual yearnings. On the other hand, I was a true child of my time in that most of the people I knew were having trouble "swallowing," let alone "digesting," any of the myriad religious practices available to choose from. It reminded me of the story about Bertrand Russell who, upon being admitted to a British jail for some act of civil disobedience, was asked by the jailer on duty what religion he followed. When Russell replied, "Atheist," the jailer scratched his head, and said, "Well now, that's a new one on me. But I guess we all worship God in our own way, eh!"

Worshipping God/Goddess in my own way was precisely the problem. What way would that be? Finding the answer to that question led me right into the real "sweat shop" that Ross had talked about. If the end result of the "sweat shop" was what Marion called "a vibrant life," then perhaps dragging myself from doctor to doctor in the long search for help for my body would also heal my soul. Ross, and my own negative dreams about relying exclusively on medical modalities to heal me, would change that. Gradually I dropped a lot of those outside sources and turned inward to work with my own inner healer imaged as Chiron.

Ross had shown me that in my emphasis on the connection between my sick body and the sick planet, I had failed to meditate on the Great Mother, who was the Preserver of life, as well as its Destroyer. The "providence" that he had found in the "calamity" of Marion's illness had revealed another side of the Goddess: her ability to transform us through suffering. Through Ross's insights into the death/rebirth cycle in nature, I became aware of the possibility of deep renewal in myself. Within the "dreaming Earth" of my own body lay the beginnings of "new life" which were emerging out of the painful experience of environmental illness.

My encounter with Ross Woodman alerted me to the crucial need for an increased planetary consciousness as an enlargement of our own life dramas. The mounting damage to the global environment is forcing us to shift our attention from the exclusive care of the individual human soul to a concern for the collective soul, the *anima mundi* or world soul. Indeed, we are now beginning to realize that the popular appetite for self-help therapies may increase rather than diminish our alienation from the environment. By withdrawing exclusively into ourselves in search of some inner healing we run the risk of participating—through neglect—in the destruction of the environment upon which our physical, emotional, and mental lives depend. We exaggerate the very mind-body split that is the cause of our accelerating malaise.

In our conversations Ross Woodman had taken me on a guided tour of the concept of building a bodysoul through the Romantic poet's imagination. In Blake's poem *Milton*, what happens in Blake's body as the English poet John Milton travels through it is an enlargement of the body until it becomes the bound or outward circumference of Blake's (and Milton's) energy. Passing well beyond the conventional limits of the five senses, the action of Blake's body—its lungs, its heart, its stomach for digestion—becomes the action of the *anima mundi*, the animating soul of the world bringing the New Jerusalem to Earth. Blake's body becomes the "global village" of communications guru Marshall McLuhan, the village we all now inhabit, whether we know it or not. The present information revolution that is unveiling the vast, interconnected, interdependent life of this planet is a revolution that prophetically took place in Blake's bodysoul two hundred years ago. The same revolution is happening now in our own bodysouls.

In Ross Woodman's reading of the Romantics, the enlargement of the body as the form or container of the soul is the return of the feminine. The body as a dangerous machine forced to obey the commands of a brutal and tyrannical master—like that of the monster in Mary Shelley's *Frankenstein*—was a body that the Romantics associated with the Industrial Revolution. The transformation of this body into a city and a bride—as a place where the masculine and the feminine come together in a marriage of opposites—is, Ross Woodman has argued, a transformation that has taken place in many Romantic texts, including Blake's body viewed as a text, as the site of his poem.

The subjugation of nature as the subjugation of the feminine to the masculine that culminated in the Industrial Revolution, was opposed by the Romantics, who initiated the feminist revolution that is only now coming within sight of its goals.

The Semitic religious tradition (Judaism, Christianity, and Islam) is fundamentally patriarchal and carries within it a long history of masculine rule or dominion. Indeed, it requires no great stretch of the imagination to see in the treatment of nature—in and as the Industrial Revolution—a dark mirroring of the treatment of women in this tradition. The worship of the feminine, of the Goddess as distinct from God, has at times in the Semitic tradition been viewed as a form of idolatry. Nowhere did this idolatry seem more evident than in the tradition of courtly love, a tradition in which the masculine virtues of the epic gave way to the feminine virtues of romance. Intimately related to this tradition, in which the enshrined and forbidden lady became the object of the knight's worship, was the rise during the twelfth and thirteenth centuries of the worship of the Virgin Mary as the Mother of God. The Great Mother who gave birth to God was a divine Mother who, as Mother Church, was destined to become the Bride of Christ.

As the Reformation would demonstrate, the Mother of God as the Bride of her Son contained within it sufficient forbidden psychic phenomena to make it an object of anxiety as much as of veneration. Protestantism was in some measure the restoration of an epic masculinity to a "romanticized" or "femininized" parody of itself. It was a restoration, as Ross Woodman suggests in tracing the journey of the poet Milton through the body of Blake, that Milton attempted in composing his epic, *Paradise Lost*. Milton's "verse," however, was dictated to him by a female Muse while he slept. It is in large measure the content of that feminine "verse" with which Milton, in Blake's body, has to come to grips. Romanticism in this sense completes the heretical revolution that began with courtly love. The Christ who returns to Earth in Blake's *Milton* is a Christ appareled in the garment of his Bride. He returns as the "feminine Christ."

What Ross Woodman has offered us in his innovative reading of the English Romantics is an extraordinary psychic paradigm of the world we now inhabit, a world in which the masculine and feminine are struggling to achieve a new and balanced partnership in which neither one tyrannizes the other. He has offered us a vision of the inner dynamism of the *anima mundi*, the global soul that is now—in the bodily form of an endangered global environment—struggling to maintain its own inherent wholeness, its own balance of yin and yang, feminine and masculine. The masculine-feminine dynamism of the world soul, expressing itself in and as the world's body, is the dynamism that governs us all in ways we are only beginning to understand.

Moving from his reading of various Romantic texts to an equally revealing reading of the text of his own life—particularly in relationship to his marriage to Marion Woodman—Ross Woodman has attempted to close the gap between literature and life. In writing *The Recluse*—an epic that he never finished—William Wordsworth described himself as composing "in lonely peace" what he called "the spousal verse/of this great consummation." The "great consummation," as Wordsworth describes it, is the marriage of the mind to nature, of mind to body as the healing of the great divide between them.

Wordsworth wrote "in lonely peace" because the hour of this marriage had not arrived. He knew that the coming together of mind and body—masculine and feminine—would take time. Ross Woodman suggests that the time has now come. The isolation that Wordsworth experienced is no more. The release of the feminine into consciousness has already happened; it is all around us; we are living it; we are feeding off it; but we are still not conscious of it. As the feminine archetypal image is evolving in our time, it is accompanied by a similar transformation in our image of the masculine archetype. No longer suitable for the global culture that is emerging out of the patriarchal structures that have dominated the Earth for centuries, the old authoritarian sky god is not a deity comprehensive enough to embrace the consciousness of Gaia which is manifesting in our time. The old God is dead, but he is being replaced by a new image of order, law, and authority which is coming to us through modern science and its penetration into the dynamics of the universe.

Today, the Romantic vision has become the actual. It resides where Wordsworth said we must find it, not in a "History only of departed things,/ Or a mere fiction of what never was," but in the "simple produce of the common day." Blake declared that the New Jerusalem celebrated in the Book of Revelation was to be found in "a Wild Flower" and "a Grain of Sand." Coleridge said that rightly to perceive a wild flower was to repeat in our finite minds the eternal act of its creation in the mind of God and the womb of nature. The Kingdom of God on Earth lay in the cleansing of "the doors of perception," so that with our five senses, we could see beyond them into what they embodied as a portion of the soul. Ross Woodman offers us a practical guide to the soul's perception of itself as a body. In that perception, he suggests, resides what now exists around us as the Kingdom of God, the globe itself still threatened by an obsolete, one-sided, patriarchal perception of it.

Ross Woodman, Ph.D., Professor Emeritus at the University of Western Ontario, is the author of many articles on Canadian art, including an extensive, published interview with London artist Jack Chambers. He has also written numerous articles in various journals on religion and world civilization, and has been the recipient of Canada Council Senior Grants as well as a Nuffield Fellowship. His books include *James Reaney* and *The Apocalyptic Vision in the Poetry of Shelley*. In 1993 he received the Distinguished Scholar Award from the Keats-Shelley Association of America.

NOTES

[1] Theodore Roszak, *The Voice of the Earth*, New York: Simon & Schuster, 1992, p. 220.

[2] Ibid., p. 242.

[3] Anthony Stevens, *Archetypes*, New York: Quill Publishers, 1982, p. 207.

PART FOUR

ABANDONED PLANET,
ABANDONED SOULS

*"Our soul's life is dependent on the divine splendor in the
natural world and our access to that world."*

THOMAS BERRY

A Culture of Lost Souls

WRITING THIS book has made me realize that I have sought a sanctuary in nature all my life. Some of my earliest memories are of the plainchant of the Trappist monks in the pre-dawn hours as they paddled their canoes down the magnificent Ottawa River near my parents' home in Quebec. Later, living in a busy urban environment, I longed to find another retreat like the one I had known as a child. Beyond escaping to a cottage for a few weeks every summer, I never managed it. Imagine my distress when I finally moved away from the crowded bustle of city life, only to discover that my newfound paradise was under siege.

In the mountainous region just outside Banff National Park where my husband and I spend our winters, a river winds beneath 10,000-foot peaks that rise sharply on either side of a heavily treed valley. Biologists call the rich bottom land which surrounds this river, and which is the natural habitat of coyotes, wolves, and elk indigenous to this area, the *montane*. The feminine principle would share this precious ribbon of arable land with all the wild creatures which come here to feed and rear their young. The masculine principle would defend and protect the creatures' right to be here. The tragedy is to see both principles being violated by corporate developers and merchants who are filling the valley with resorts, shopping malls, and condos that will soon obstruct the animals' entry into these grazing lands.

There is tremendous unconsciousness in people who will allow their addiction to profit to take precedence over the survival of other species. Particularly threatened in the Rocky Mountain parks are the remaining populations of grizzly bears, moose, and wolves whose access to a "wilderness highway," which they urgently need for their survival, will be blocked if expansion continues. A wildlife corridor of connecting international park preserves, currently planned to extend the full length of the eastern Rocky Mountain ecosystem from Yellowstone Park in Wyoming to the Yukon Territories, could be blocked right here in the Bow Valley because of excessive human population and greed. Except for a few groups of naturalists and other ecologically sensitive individuals, no myths of Goddess or Hero are evoked by the people here to challenge the "myth of progress" that Thomas Berry tells us in his interview so dominates the soul's landscape in our culture.

Few people seem to realize that, contrary to our hopes for global harmony, we are at war on the planet, with those committed to saving the environment pitted against governments aligned with corporations and entrepreneurs in a battle for the remaining wild spaces and resources of the Earth. As the millennium approaches, we are becoming more and more polarized into those who see the planet (no matter what the cost) through the viewfinder of the old rapacious paradigm, and those who see the Earth as a living entity with needs of her own that must be respected if she is to continue sustaining us.

Cultural historian and theologian Thomas Berry is very aware of the seriousness of our situation, and because of this I was determined to seek him out. The dream imagery which had originally propelled me to England came back to me as I recalled the figure of the priest "dressed in ordinary clothes" who had also been present in my dream about Laurens van der Post.

Thomas Berry's courageous and impassioned defense of the Earth in the face of our mindless despoliation of her had affected me deeply. Inspired by his book *The Dream of the Earth*, I impulsively decided to phone him to ask if he'd be interested in taking part in this book. Unhesitatingly, he said yes. Here was a man who spoke regularly at prestigious universities such as Harvard, addressed conferences of eminent theologians in Europe, even conferred with environmentally concerned officials in the White House, extending his hand in support and friendship to a complete stranger. As David Abrams, author of *The Spell of the Sensuous*, said in the preface to his book: "the great-hearted Thomas Berry gave essential encouragement"! Over the many months that we've conversed, "essential encouragement" is exactly what Thomas Berry has given me as well. My soul, which had gone "into hiding" when I first became ill, has dared to come out and voice its protest against our treatment of the Earth as I have resonated to the integrity and uplifting ideas of this wise and compassionate man.

I did not actually meet Thomas Berry until a year after our initial conversation, when he came to Vancouver, British Columbia, to lecture. By that time we had discussed the state of the Earth many times on the phone, so when we finally met, we embraced each other like old friends who had already been through a few planetary wars together—which we had! The talk he gave on our need to "befriend the Earth" was as inspiring as the man himself. The audience—many of whom were young environmentalists committed to fighting the clear-cutting logging practices of the British Columbia forest industry—gave him a standing ovation.

I originally came to the West in order to get away from the poisoning I was experiencing after years of living in an urban environment. Unfortunately, the places where we chose to settle are now threatened by contamination as well. For people like myself, the danger of ingesting chemicals, like those released from the pulp mills near my summer home, is that it could add a critical load to an already compromised immune system. The problem of pollution from the excessive numbers of cars which will accompany the increased population in our Rocky Mountain valley poses a threat to our survival here as well. Like the animals, and the indigenous people before us who were hounded out of these areas by the mining companies and the railway builders, the environmentally ill will soon have few places left to go; which means that none of us will have clean places left to go because in the not-too-distant future we'll all be ill from environmental poisoning.

Writing this book hasn't been some sort of intellectual head trip for me; to find answers is, I believe, a matter of life or death for all of us. Without finding ways to cleanse ourselves and the Earth of toxic contaminants, I, for one, am not going to survive. Neither is anyone else.

Thomas Berry's mystical view of the Earth as a sacred trust extends to include the soul's response to the universe itself. It was the kind of vision I knew I needed to explore if I was ever going to link my inner quest to an external Reality I could also believe in.

We are linked in our consciousness to the Earth, and to the universe, partly through myth and its power to change our vision of the world. Myths have their roots in the archetypal world of the collective unconscious, where the patterns for the great dramas that we enact during the various stages of our lives—love and heroism, conflict, and the search for God—have their original impetus.

Myths are stories told collectively, from the soul's point of view, of the way a society relates to the larger world beyond it. Every society has its guiding myths, whether it lives them out consciously or not. Myths which are not consciously constellated, however, have the power to destroy entire nations (to say nothing of individuals). This is illustrated by what happened, for instance, when the Nazis in Germany became possessed by the Grail myth and turned Hitler into a god.

It is obvious that our society is in the grip of a myth which it neither recognizes nor understands. It is what Jung called the Faustian myth, and which Thomas Berry refers to in the interview that follows as "the myth of Wonderworld"—in which we've sold our souls to science, technology, and corporate control in a senseless drive for more and more things. This has become such a world-wide phenomenon that even tradition-bound countries such as China and India are abandoning their ancestral ways of life, lured by the seduction of our advertisements for the good life. James Hillman describes this destructive aspect of our living out of the myth as: "Faust going to the Orient, whereby we've *sold* to the world and *de-souled* it at the same time."

An equally disturbing aspect of our living-out of this myth of ever-accelerating growth is what happens to our sense of place in the world. With increased access to twenty-four hour services—satellite, cable TV, and the Internet—at our fingertips, we no longer have a sense of space and time which has boundaries. With these destroyed, we do not have a relationship to a particular place, or to a special contour of land to give us roots. We live without pattern in patternless consumerism, where every place we go is the same as every other place, and where we no longer feel at home no matter where we are. Close ties to community, and to the land, are one answer to this. Humanity's need for a cosmic story, a new myth which will give our souls a universal sense of belonging, is another.

In their book *The Universe Story*, Thomas Berry and Brian Swimme write that contemporary science has revealed that we are not alone, as nineteenth-century scientists believed, in an indifferent universe filled with dead matter that is running downhill into entropic disorder. Instead, what we see all around us is a world of structured intricacy, an elegant integration of mind and matter that is still evolving and of which we are a fundamental and crucially important part. This is the heart of my interview with Thomas Berry, in which he talks about his belief that only through connecting to the central myth of our time, which is the story that our empirical scientific studies are giving us of the universe's unfolding over 20 billion years of development, can we find our souls' proper place in the cosmos, and end our destructive behavior towards ourselves and the planet.

For Thomas Berry, a society that can believe in the myth of progress at the expense of the natural world is a culture of lost souls. What we are doing to the macrocosm (the planet) can be seen in the microcosm of my own mountain valley. The people who are carving up this peaceful wilderness for their own advantage are not evil, but most of them have lost any soul connection to nature. As one of the most significant thinkers about planetary issues of our time, Thomas Berry has been called "the conscience of the Green Movement," and a "giant" with respect to the effect that his thoughts are having on changing environmental ethics in this century. Recognizing that all creatures have conscious awareness to a greater or lesser degree, he has also become a crusader for the "rights" of the non-human world.

In the mountain park near my home, a grizzly bear recently tore into some tents at a popular campsite and injured several of the campers who were staying there. The story that unfolded is a sad illustration of "rights" being denied to any creatures but ourselves. The day after the bear attack, a park warden who investigated the scene was reported as saying that there was "no reason" why the bear should have done this because the campers were "following the rules" by not having food in their tents, not baiting the bear in any way, and so forth. Several days later another report was issued from the park authorities that the bear they "thought" had attacked the campers had been caught, and that they had killed it because it had "not been provoked by the campers to attack." The report went on to say that the park authorities had also killed her eighteen-month-old cub because of the fact that "it had learned its aggressive behavior from its mother," and might in future be harmful to humans. With approximately one hundred grizzly bears left in this area, and more than five million visitors to our Canadian mountain parks every year, it seems that the odds against the bears surviving here are rather doubtful. As for their rights, I do not mean to imply that bears have the right to tear up campsites and injure campers. But one has to ask what right we have to be in their territory in such large numbers in the first place? Do the animals not have the right to defend their homeland on which we, as humans, are increasingly encroaching? After all, the national parks are there to protect them, not us. (As it turned out, the wardens discovered later that they had killed the wrong bear and her cub, for which they were remarkably unapologetic.)

Fifty years ago, trying to protect our forests, U. S. Supreme Court Justice William O. Douglas spoke up for the rights of trees to go to court "to sue for their own preservation." His argument was ignored in favor of giving large forestry companies the right to clear-cut in perpetuity instead. Trees breathe out oxygen and sequester carbon, which means that where there are trees there is less carbon dioxide in the atmosphere. Carbon dioxide is a greenhouse gas which both poisons us and adds to global warming. This is a critical issue for everyone, but perhaps especially for the environmentally ill, where surviving becomes a daily challenge in the face of the continued degradation of the planet.

For Thomas Berry, loss of soul and loss of the flora and fauna of the Earth are the same thing, for we are so inextricably connected at a psychic level that any diminishment of them diminishes us. In the history of environmental protection, Henry David Thoreau and John Muir stand out as giants in their defense of the American wilderness, while in Canada, Grey Owl and Ernest Thompson Seton saw that the destruction of wilderness meant the disappearance of a critically needed psychic experience for human beings. Like our indigenous peoples, they believed in a mystical communion with nature, seeing groves and altars as places for worship in her great forests and mountain expanses, rather than as resources for unlimited exploitation. Thomas Berry echoes this sacred feeling about the natural world when he says that contemporary loss of soul is fundamentally a loss of "reciprocity" between the human and non-human worlds in which both morality and reverence play a fundamental part.

Since our health is intimately connected to the well-being of the planet, in making individual moral choices about the environment, it is especially important to understand what's at stake each time we fail to put the planet's needs first. Envisioning the Earth as an extension of our own bodies—its forests our lungs, its oceans and rivers our bodily fluids—should make us think harder about poisoning her further. Recognizing that our individual souls are also in jeopardy each time we allow another planetary rape to go unprotested might be another incentive we need to change our ways. Thomas Berry shows us a new way to relate to the natural world around us, and offers us a vision of how to live on the planet with compassion and integrity.

CHAPTER ONE

THE MYTH OF WONDERWORLD

NANCY RYLEY: Thomas, before I ask you about the myth of "Wonderworld," I'd like to talk to you about the Christian doctrine of the millennial age of abundance and human perfection, and how this has affected our relationship with the planet. Could you describe that particular doctrine and its impact on our present-day exploitation of the Earth's resources?

THOMAS BERRY: Well, the millennium ideal belongs to the apocalyptic tradition of the Bible, which describes the expectation of a cosmic cataclysm in which the ruling powers of evil are destroyed and the righteous are raised to life in a messianic kingdom. It begins largely with the Book of Daniel, but its final explanation is in the Book of Revelation of St. John in the New Testament; particularly in the last chapters, as regards the dragon and the woman, and the conflict with the dragon.

NR: Who is the woman in this conflict?

TB: Well, she's the woman clothed with the sun, with the moon under her feet, crowned with twelve stars, and so forth. The woman bears a child, and the child is assaulted by the dragon, and the whole conflict of good and evil is described in terms of the woman and her child and the dragon. It's an apocalyptic image of the redemption process and the community of the redeemed, which has been adapted in Christianity to the Madonna figure.

The important thing is the fact that there would come a period of a thousand years during which the saints would reign and the dragon would be chained. During this thousand years there would be peace, and justice, and humans would experience a relief from what we call the human condition—which is to say the ordinary pains of life, the difficulties, the challenges, and all its threatening aspects.

This myth has lived in Western consciousness for centuries. It's the drive, largely, of western history, and it's one of the explanations of why the Western world has such historical dynamism.

Now early Christians thought that the second coming of Christ—to occur at the end of this thousand years of peace and plenty—was going to happen in their lifetime. But of course this never happened, and it took a while before Christians could accept the fact that history was going to continue: to their minds the Messiah had come, and it should have been the end of the world. That's one of the reasons why St. John wrote the Book of Revelation, which was to tell Christians that there was a history ahead of them, and that there would still be a great deal of struggle to come. But that there would also be this thousand years of peace which would occur just before the termination of the created world—when the earthly Jerusalem would be transformed into its heavenly setting.

NR: When this millennial vision didn't occur by divine grace, what happened?

TB: Well, humans decided they'd raise it up themselves. The millennial myth was absorbed into, and found expression in, the modern doctrine of progress —which has seen humans trying to bring about this promised state through their own efforts by exploiting the resources of the earth.

That's the whole dynamism of the modern world. The millennial myth was the drive behind the founding of America. It was the drive behind Marx and communism. It's very fascinating that the historical drive back of both communism and capitalism is the same thing: the millennarianist drive that is going to create Wonderworld.

NR: Is *Wonderworld* your word for the plethora of shopping malls, factories, superhighways, and sprawling suburbs that most people are living in now?

TB: Yes. The myth of Wonderworld that is behind the creation of this world is the myth of interminable growth brought about by our technological wizardry. It's this myth, or vision, that is fueling the drive towards the endlessly high consumption of goods that characterizes our society.

NR: What has been the result of this myth on the way we've treated the Earth?

TB: Obviously the result has been total exploitation. The millennial vision of a beatific future that we would accomplish ourselves through prodigious effort implied that all things on Earth, as we found them in their natural state, were in an unacceptable or unholy condition. Everything needed to be changed. As a result, every effort of science, technology, economics, and politics was to be bent towards effecting these transformations of the natural world. The drive behind this whole mechanism was to take all our natural resources and transform them by industrial methods into products for a society that has an insatiable hunger for more and more things.

NR: This drive obviously has a deep spiritual yearning behind it, or it wouldn't be so strong, would it?

TB: That's right, it's religion turned to the service of secular purposes. We have to have these physical things because we're spiritually so unfulfilled. We're so diminished in our soul values that these other things hold a huge attraction for us.

Our idea of the market economy is sacred to us; we now have sacred values that are associated with our modern, commercial, mechanistic way of life that go right back to the original myth.

NR: How does technology serve this?

TB: By making life easy for us. Technology is the instrument by which we build Wonderworld. A comfortable, painless life becomes the transcendent purpose of our technology. But obviously we're ending in Wasteworld, not Wonderworld. That's the tragedy of it.

NR: You say "transcendent." Does that mean that it's a technology that has had no limits put on it?

TB: That's part of it. But mainly when you talk about the "transcendent" purpose of technology you're talking about its aim, which is to "transcend" the human condition. Because at the bottom of this there lies a profound hidden rage against the human condition. This idea of reaching for a world beyond the human condition is the pathology of the Western soul; it manifests as continual dissatisfaction, which is now deep in the Western psyche. There are awesome forces at work in our society, and they all go with this unrest, with being unable to accept life as it is given to us.

Therefore, we're going to make this a better world, a better world than the natural world, a world transcendent to the natural world. As soon as we can get the instruments, we're going to take the planet to pieces and put it together in a better way. And that better way will be Wonderworld.

NR: The power of the millennial myth seems to have surfaced most powerfully in our worship of the modern corporation. Why does the corporation exert such control over our deepest psychic structures, so that no matter what the cost to the Earth we go along with it?

TB: The corporation is supposedly the main instrument for taking us into Wonderworld. It takes us closer to fulfilling the American dream of building a paradise on Earth. It's the corporation that builds the shopping malls, the factories, the developments, and all the elements of the humanly created industrial paradise that we can no longer live without.

Also, the corporation has a grip on us psychically because it has taken possession of the planet. It gives us our jobs; it runs the world that we live in; it pays our salaries. It has established itself as the context for our survival. And so everything else must give way to the corporation. Governments must see that the corporation remains the supreme reality to be protected. Everything else must suffer in order for the corporation to prosper.

NR: Therefore consumption too has come to have something "sacred" about it.

TB: That's right. We're caught in a round of production and consumption which feed into each other in a never-ending cycle. And the whole process is kept going by advertising, which activates our desires and encourages people to spend to get more things. You see it in people with children; the parents just deluge their children with toys. Whereas before, a child might have one or two or three toys to play with, now you see children's rooms so stuffed with toys that they couldn't play with every one in a period of ten years. We're just overwhelming life with things.

NR: Do you think that people make any connection at all between all the things that we have and the damage that we're doing to ourselves and to the

Earth?

TB: Very seldom, it seems. But there are moments of depression and moments of radical dissatisfaction when people almost go into a frenzy because they suddenly feel an emptiness of soul. At such moments they experience a lack of fulfillment, and a longing for something better, and then they become frustrated. They literally pound the walls, and pound each other, because a certain desperation comes into their lives. They just don't know where to go, what to do, or how to manage.

In this dissatisfied way their worlds fall apart. Marriages fall apart, families fall apart, personalities fall apart. The fact is that "the ten million things" cannot fulfill the needs of the soul.

NR: I notice more and more that advertising agencies use certain associative terminology and concepts from the world of the sacred, and from the world of nature, to sell us all these "things."

TB: Yes. They use Christmas. They use Easter. They use Mother's Day. They use every possible sacred celebration, and every sacred moment, and turn it into a commercial indulgence period. They use all the sacredness of childhood to advertise their products. They use the sacredness of the feminine body and its attractions to stimulate desire.

NR: Many ads make it very clear that if you don't purchase their products you'll never experience "peace" or "joy" or any other state of spiritual fulfillment that one expects from living in paradise. The message is that the only way to enter paradise is to *buy* your way in.

TB: Well, sure. It's all based on a sense that all this is going to make a person happy. I think that the supreme expression of this is the advertising for the automobile Infiniti, which uses the phrase: "Just slip into the driver's seat and be happy ever after." But it's pure fantasy to think of being happy forever after in an automobile!

NR: Using the sacred to promote secular ends—how does this harm us ultimately?

TB: Well, it evokes our deepest expectations and leads us into ultimate frustration. Its promises are so great and the expectations are so sublime, and then everything crashes into nothingness when the bubble explodes and people realize they have nothing. And they realize that for this they've given up their most precious things: their most precious moments at home, and their enjoyment of the natural world.

We've given up all the basic realities in order to get these trinkets, and the trinkets dissolve, and we're left empty. It's that emptiness of inner being that is the pathology.

NR: What about the fact that our souls are tied to corporations that are plundering the planet? What is it doing to our souls when we collude in our workplaces, and in our lifestyles, with the destruction of the whole nonuman world around us?

TB: Obviously, it's leading us into increasingly disastrous personal, social, and spiritual situations. Our sacred soul-life is tied up not only with corporate, but also with national goals, which in the name of the millennial myth of progress are also violating the planet. It becomes a sort of religious fervor to defend one's country, and one's job, even when both are plundering the planet's resources.

NR: A lot of people would say that with our high standard of living, the scientists, engineers, and technocrats who have been altering the Earth have left us with a heaven-on-Earth as the myth promised.

TB: On the contrary, they've left us with drowned rivers and poisoned soils, plastic waste and toxic trash littered everywhere. It's a terrible irony that the doctrine of millennial fulfillment should end in the trashing of the Earth. Religion has a dangerous side as well as an exalted side, you know.

With all their knowledge, and the kind of power that only God and nature held in former times, these people have failed to bring about a state of affairs on Earth that is life-enhancing for both the human and the nonhuman world. The result is that we've corrupted the entire planet. And what's amazing is that we still haven't learned. What's amazing is that the universities are still educating people for this type of world, this type of life. Educators still haven't the slightest idea of how to educate. Universities are not preparing young people in the professions for what they should really be doing.

NR: And what should they really be doing?

TB: Well, take for instance the law profession. It should be clear that the American Constitution, which is the ultimate referent for social order in our society, is based on a totally inadequate jurisprudence. What we're guaranteed in the English traditions of common law are participatory government, individual freedom, and property rights. But these are guaranteed to humans at the expense of the natural world.

The greatest single error across the board in every aspect of our lives is the establishment of a discontinuity between the nonhuman and the human, giving all the rights to the human to advance itself at the expense of the nonhuman. We need a *continental* constitution, such that every mode of being on the continent enjoys the benefits of the constitution. As things stand now, however, nonhuman beings have no rights in our perception, leaving them totally vulnerable to human aggression.

In reality, however, we two are so bound together that if anything happens to the nonhuman it also happens to the human. Our exploitation of the natural world leads to counterproductivity, to self-destruction. We have to realize that this is one world, this is one community, and get rid of the idea that we are the only beings that matter. Other creatures, other modes of existence have rights and needs, too. We aren't the only ones.

That's what universities should be teaching their students, rather than teaching them how to go out and make money by perpetuating the present system.

NR: Why, in your view, are universities failing to teach these things?

TB: Because they're funded by the same commercial interests that are tearing up the planet. Business now funds our educational institutions. Not only are universities supported *by* the corporations, but students are being prepared by the universities for service *in* the corporations. Their future rests with their capacity to support the corporate enterprise.

NR: Are you saying that therefore the corporations have a real stranglehold on university curricula?

TB: Certainly they do in the economic field through the various business schools. The whole teaching of economics in our universities is disastrous. They don't even know the first law of economics, which is to preserve the integral economy of the planet. You cannot devastate your basic planetary economy and expect your derivative human economy to prosper, because the human economy is a subsystem of the Earth economy. It's absurd, but they don't teach that because corporations generally can't see beyond the financial bottom line to the ecological bottom line.

NR: What do the corporations and the educational institutions say that our future on Earth will be? How do they keep the myth of progress going?

TB: They try to persuade us that unlimited progress alone leads to a more creative and fulfilling future for humans; and that in their commitment to profits in the name of serving human needs and purposes, they are willing to alter the planet completely in order to make it a better planet. But we can't go on altering the planet radically, as we have been doing, because we don't have either the knowledge or the wisdom. We've run the world into this absurdity because we haven't the slightest idea of the real consequences of what we're doing.

NR: I have heard people say, "Don't worry about this oil spill, or that radioactive leak, or more depletion of the ozone layer; science will take care of everything."

TB: Well, tell them that science has been taking care of things for some time now, but things keep getting worse and worse. The arrogance of scientists is that they have the power to significantly affect the entire functioning of the Earth, and because of this they think that they're totally able to control, or rectify, any disasters that come about because of their interference. What about the birds that died as the result of being covered with oil from our leaking oil tankers? What about the 20 percent of all living species that we will have driven to extinction by the year 2000?

That we should be destroying nature at the rate that we are is beyond all comprehension: rain forests felled at the rate of an acre a second—forests which contain half the living species on Earth; the extinction of ten thousand species a year around the world. This is *power*—the power we have to alter the whole chemical and biological makeup of the globe. It is a destructive patriarchal system that exists solely for the purposes of fulfilling the original millennial vision.

NR: How does one strike a balance between trying to control nature and letting nature overwhelm us totally? Before the advent of science and medicine we had minimal control, and the human condition was one of extreme vulnerability. You say that our difficulties arise from our failure "to accept life under the conditions it is granted to us," with its pain, sorrow, and insecurity. But surely there must be some happy medium between that acceptance and the desire for total control, total security, complete comfort, and the willingness to do anything to nature in order to have these things.

TB: Well, humans have a right to defend themselves against the destructive aspects of the natural world. But the whole of the natural world has a tension relationship with everything else; every being is under stress from other beings. The solution is for us to learn how to enter into this tension relationship with other modes of life creatively, and not to devastate the planet in the process of finding our place within the complex of planetary forces.

It's becoming more and more obvious that the whole industrial plundering of the planet is disastrous because it's built on the extractive economy. The extractive economy is a terminal economy; it's one that's not renewable. It's based on resources that are limited—once used they are no longer available. The only viable economy is the ever-renewing organic economy.

For example, the petroleum that we extract is the basis of just about our whole life process, and it's going to be gone in fifty years. Petroleum makes our whole way of life possible: our food production is petroleum-based, so is our clothing, our energy, our transportation (all those beautiful automobiles!), and so we've become totally petroleum-dependent.

Now people will say, "We'll find substitutes." Well, there are limits to the substitutes, and the stakes are being raised higher and higher and the devastation is becoming more and more comprehensive. We're making a dismal, terrible future for our children.

NR: I know. We don't seem to care. That's what puzzles me.

TB: It's because we're lacking leaders; we're lacking educators; we're lacking religious people; we're lacking lawyers. That would seem to be the difficulty.

NR: How do you think we can turn this thing around and bring ourselves back into connection with the Earth?

TB: There's no formula that I know of, but the first thing we need to do is to awaken to the fact that something is missing.

I talk about North Carolina, where I live now, and I say, "We need to come home to ourselves." They've got a beautiful situation there, but they're tearing the whole countryside to pieces. It's one of the most magnificent parts of the continent and it's being devastated. And people think that this is progress. They're building roads madly. They're tearing up immense areas of land for shopping centers and these big stores—Wal-Mart and K-Mart. It's just unbelievable what they're doing. All this is happening because we have this disastrous notion that "more is better."

NR: We're going through the same thing here. It's what Marion Woodman calls "the addiction to more and more matter." Laurens van der Post says that our collective pursuit of endless growth is like a cancer gone wild. He says it's no wonder that cancer has become rampant in our time; it's the outward expression of what our souls have become.

TB: Absolutely—he's absolutely right.

NR: How has our bedazzlement by Wonderworld affected our attitudes to nature?

TB: The fact that we've separated ourselves from an intimate association with the natural world shows up in the way we trivialize it. Nature is a place to get away to on a vacation from the real business of life, which is our work in the city. Or nature is of passing interest when the leaves are turning red in the fall. Both of these attitudes are all right, but they're shallow. The world of nature shouldn't just be useful to us as an escape from reality, because if that's all it means to us, then the deep psychic connections which would lead us to honor the natural world and defend any violation of that world will never occur.

NR: Do you think that one of the reasons for the wanton and incomprehensible destruction of our natural places is that for a lot of people real nature doesn't measure up to the Wonderworld imitation of it fabricated in places like Disneyland and the West Edmonton Mall?

TB: Places like the West Edmonton Mall and Disneyland are dream-worlds, worlds of play and fantasy, where there's no pain, no sorrow, no demand for sacrifice—where nothing is left of the original spontaneities of nature. In that sense it's a totally non-threatening world.

NR: They're worlds without any soul in them, aren't they?

TB: That's right.

NR: Does this Wonderland vision of nature serve some purpose for the industrial-commercial world? Does it help them perpetuate the myth of progress?

TB: Of course it does, because in such an illusory world, people are able to forget that the real world of nature is being irrevocably damaged all around them. The fantasylands that we've been talking about perfectly serve the purposes of the commercial world because they keep the illusion going that we are entering Wonderland, rather than Wasteland.

NR: What do you deduce from the fact that most people accept Wonderworld's false portrayal and harsh treatment of the natural world?

TB: The fact that we don't put forth the Earth's integrity as the most important priority in our lives is a sign of severe personal and cultural pathology. The radical discontinuity that we have established between ourselves and the natural world is the problem; that's the pathology. After all, at a very basic physical level, what can be more important than the uncontaminated quality of the air we breathe, the food we eat, and the water we drink?

NR: As you know, Thomas, I have environmental illness, which means that almost everything that defines Wonderworld—from superhighways reeking of car exhaust, to food additives, to chlorinated water—makes me ill. In your view, is environmental illness caused by what you call "our severe personal and cultural pathology"?

TB: In my view, there is a practical, organized effort in our society which is directed towards the conditions that cause environmental illness. In other words, the corporations are supporting the conditions that cause this illness. However, very few people are relating these things in a direct way. The people that are suggesting, in their critiques of the present situation, the necessity for spiritual adjustment are saying something that is quite valid. But if we don't get to the existentialist source in the functioning of the establishments that are creating this situation, then nothing will be done. The four establishments—economic, political, intellectual, and religious—are all either supporting the forces that are causing environmental illness, or accepting them.

NR: Are you saying that all the guardians of the culture have let us down?

TB: Completely, because none of them have been concerned with the planet. As a result, our institutions have all become so dysfunctional that we can no longer trust them to guard us adequately against the twisted values of the commercial-industrial powers that run our world. We can't trust the business community. We can't trust any of the professions. We can't even trust the religious community to adequately critique this deleterious situation. Most of all, we can't trust our legal system to stop the present poisoning of our soils, air, and water systems.

NR: Why do you say that?

TB: Because the legislative and judicial systems in this country now exist to support the entrepreneurial enterprise. Multinationals have no restraint put on them because they have no allegiance to any government nor to any nation. As a result, global corporations have become the controlling enterprises of the entire human venture, of the Earth project itself. In this endeavor they're aided and abetted by the courts, who weaken any legislation that threatens corporate profit. In other words, the legal system in this country is supporting corporations who are taking the planet apart. Tragically, there is nothing in the Constitution to stop them.

NR: Is this why those who are fighting so hard to save the environment and who are also trying to protect the interests of the community—by saving the trees, conserving the fish, and so forth—aren't more successful?

TB: Yes, because any protest against the entrepreneurial enterprise is seen as an act of rebellion. It's considered unacceptable both politically and legally. If environmentalists protest the devastation of the forest, for example, they can't get anywhere because the law supports the plundering.

NR: You've used the word "trust" several times with regard to other groups in our society, besides the legal profession, which you feel have also let us down. Do you feel that these groups also could have done more to protest the violation of the planet?

TB: Certainly they could have, but they're in denial. Take the medical profession: when the breast milk of women becomes a source of possible contamination for their babies, one would have thought that the doctors as a profession might have raised their voices in protest, but they haven't done this in any adequate manner.

NR: I can certainly relate to what you say about most doctors. A few doctors whom I know are trying to help the environmentally ill, but hardly any of them ever speak out publicly about the harm that toxic chemicals are doing to people's health. Most doctors deny that the problem of environmental illness even exists, despite a recent study which found that, for example, "twenty percent of the Canadian population suffers from chemical sensitivities."[1] As things stand, many environmentally ill only survive by making huge efforts, at enormous personal expense, to do so. But none of us are being cured.

Actually, the people who help us the most are the various conservation groups like the Sierra Club and Greenpeace, because they're the ones who are trying to clean up the planet.

TB: The reality is that there's a great deal of active opposition to changing the status quo. In fact it's not only active, but in some cases quite intense.

NR: From which quarters?

TB: From the universities, from government, from labor—from all those who stand to gain the most from our continuation of the present system. The leaders of the establishment give very few indications that they're aware of the disastrous situation in which we find ourselves. This refusal to alter their mode of thinking about our treatment of the planet is one of the chief obstacles to making the changes necessary to turn things around.

The fact is that industrial progress, regardless of the price we pay for it in our diminished health and spiritual well-being, is an accepted thing. Most people have bought into it, and they've bought into it for the full term; in other words, until our natural resources run out. The pollution, the sprayed foods, the toxic waste, the acid rain—these are all considered to be of marginal concern, accepted blindly as the condition of survival in Wonderworld. Jobs are the only reality. The rest is romantic idealism about nature that they say no one can afford.

Such is the strength of the myth that has us in its grip. The supreme driving force behind Wonderworld is neither economic nor political, but visionary.

NR: Tell me more about the "visionary" aspect of the Wonderworld myth. As you say, the fact that there is so little opposition to what we're doing to the planet indicates that we're in the grip of a very powerful, unconscious drive. Are we into addiction?

TB: Yes, we're addicted; we've been what I call "psychically entranced" with the idea of unlimited material progress.

There are four terms that I sometimes use to describe the present situation and that indicate the effect of the hold that the millennial myth of progress has over us.

First, it's *counterproductive:* our institutions and professions are producing the opposite of what they should be producing.

Secondly, it's *addictive:* once we're into this Wonderland way of life it seems impossible to disengage.

Third, it leads to *paralysis:* it destroys so much of our own psychic energy that it becomes extremely difficult to overcome. In fact, it takes heroic psychic energy to establish an alternative.

The fourth term I use is *pathology;* our present situation is the manifestation of this deep pathology that I've been talking about. That's the way you know pathology: life becomes counter-productive, addictive, and paralyzing. That's why people in a pathological state can't act, which is the present state of our Western society.

NR: Instead of soul values—some inner directive defining us—we seem to get our sense of values now exclusively from our roles as producers and consumers. Is it the *unconscious* power of the myth that's driving us to be this way?

TB: Yes, it's the unconscious power of the myth. But then, that's what pathology is. It's a distorted energy that takes control of us. People in the grip of an unconscious drive have no independent inner energy to act on their own. They are submissive to whatever forces are acting upon them, as we're submissive to all the advertising that controls us. We don't have the power to overcome the activation of our energies that is produced by advertising, so we spend, spend, spend—and collect an infinite number of things that ultimately are burdensome, rather than fulfilling.

NR: You're describing a state similar to drug addiction.

TB: That's exactly what our addiction to commercial-industrial progress is. Mythic addictions function like drug addictions. Even when they're destroying us, the psychic fixation is such that we cannot get away from it. So we deny that any of this is happening; at present we are in a real state of denial about the severity of planetary destruction for which we are responsible.

NR: Is there no way to counteract the power of the Wonderworld myth? Could we defeat it with a more consciously arrived at ethic?

TB: We've all heard how agonizing it is to give up an addiction. But the cure lies in consciously going through the pain, and making the sacrifice required, to bring us through to the state of health that lies on the other side of the addiction. This is a huge achievement for an individual to manage, to say nothing of accomplishing it on a global scale.

And so we must re-invent ourselves and ask what it is to become a human being. Any culture that devastates its air and water and soil, and refuses to even admit that it's behaving in an unreasonable way, is pathological and needs to be re-invented.

We have to re-evaluate the most basic orientations in our lives because we lose our souls when we lose the forests and the animals, when we contaminate the natural world with poisons and pollution. It's not just an aesthetic loss, or an economic loss that we have to be concerned about. It's the survival of the soul that's at stake. That's what our destruction of the Earth is all about: loss of soul.

CHAPTER TWO

THE SOUL IN NATURE

NANCY RYLEY: Thomas, you made a very strong statement recently in which you said: "We're the most destructive presence on Earth. We are the affliction of the world—its demonic presence. We are the violation of the Earth's most sacred aspects." How has this come about?

THOMAS BERRY: Well, I don't know of any single species that has such awesome powers of destruction as the human. The basic biological law is that every species should have opposed species or conditions that limit it, so that no one species, or group of species, could overwhelm the others. But humans, by their technological cunning, are able to subvert that basic biological law. That is what has enabled us to bring about such vast destruction in the life systems of the planet.

NR: You also said: "The result of our interference in the planet's functioning is the possible termination of the last 65 million years in the geo-biological development of the planet Earth."

TB: The visible life periods on the planet are generally divided into the Paleozoic Period, which would be roughly 600 million to 220 million years ago; the Mesozoic Period, which would be 220 million years ago to 65 million years ago; then the Cenozoic Period, which extends up to the present.

Two hundred and twenty million years ago there was a collapse in which 90 percent of all species were extinguished. Sixty-five million years ago something quite similar occurred. It was not as severe as the earlier one, but this terminated the dinosaur period, the reptilian period. After that we entered into the mammalian period and the period of the birds, trees, flowers, and so forth as we know them now. This has been the geo-biological period that has provided the background for humans, who came in the later phase of that development.

We humans have existed for only a very brief time, but during this time we have interfered so much with the functioning of the planet that we have caused serious dislocation to its biosystems, chemistry, and climate. E. O. Wilson at Harvard, Peter Raven of the Missouri Botanical Gardens, and Norman Myers of Cambridge, I consider to be among the foremost biologists who know, in a comprehensive way, all the life systems of the planet. These three indicate that nothing this significant in the extinction of life forms has occurred for the last 65 million years.

NR: Can we go back into history to look at some of the reasons why this devastation of the planet has come about? In your book *The Dream of the Earth*, you said that "the ultimate basis of our ecological difficulties lies in the roots of our Christian spirituality." What are the main Christian teachings that led you to this conclusion?

TB: In original Christian teaching there were rightly considered to be two scriptures: the scripture of the natural world, and the scripture of the Bible. Nature was seen originally as both created by the divine and as a primary self-presentation of the divine. The Bible itself indicates in the Book of Genesis that the human is created within the natural world and has a certain bonding with the whole of the natural world. So there is a rich connective basis in the Christian tradition between the divine and the Earth.

But since the sixteenth century, Christianity has focused on the Biblical revelation of the nature of God, not on the scripture of the natural world. The result is that we have distanced ourselves from the intimacy that should be ours with the phenomenal world. When the Christian world puts a verbal revelation in a dominant position over the revelation of the natural world, it distorts the whole process. Our experience of the Divine should take place in and through the natural world because the natural world is the primary revelatory experience.

NR: You also wrote that since the sixteenth century it has been Christian belief that humans have a special covenant with a transcendent Father deity. Has this covenant adversely affected our relationship with the planet?

TB: Yes, it has. Through the covenant we were given a sense of our divine mission that we were to carry out into the world; we saw ourselves as having a spiritual destiny beyond that of other members of the created world. All of this increased our feeling of superiority and undermined any sense of being part of a total Earth community. In North America, for example, we ignored communion with, and protection of, the natural world—including its indigenous peoples—when it conflicted with our proselytizing zeal.

The American continent was ready to communicate a profound spirituality to the Europeans who first came here. It still had something of its primordial vigor, something of the innocence that older civilizations had lost long ago. In the grandeur of its forests and rivers, in the magnificent variety of its wild creatures, in the splendor of its mountains and valleys, North America was a more immediate manifestation of the divine than the European culture of the explorers and settlers had experienced for centuries.

However, as divinely appointed messengers of the Christian faith, these incoming peoples saw themselves as bearers of "civilization" to this untamed world. Bibles in hand, they thought they already knew everything that they needed to know. Otherwise, they might have learned something of the spirituality appropriate to this land from the native peoples. Their failure to enter into a rapport with the primordial world they found here meant that the possibility of a communion relationship with it was lost, and a "use" relationship with the continent was established instead. This has been the deep source of our present problems of both sustainability and spirituality on this continent.

NR: Did their attitude lead directly to our present assault on the planet?

TB: Well, one couldn't say that our present assault on the planet was exactly caused by the Biblical-Christian revelatory experience, but it did establish a context in which the natural world could be seen as merely an external object and therefore open to exploitation.

After all, this devastation through industrial plundering did not happen out of a Buddhist world, nor a Hindu world, nor a Chinese world. It came out of a Biblical-Christian, classical, humanist matrix. So obviously the cultural tradition that we're heirs to is vulnerable to this type of excessive emphasis on human rights over the natural world.

NR: *The Dream of the Earth* also contains a strong indictment of the church and its patriarchal leanings. What exactly are you indicting it for?

TB: Patriarchy on the whole has had little regard for either the well-being or personal fulfillment of women, or for the destiny of the Earth itself. In fact, there is what I consider to be a patriarchal dominance in the whole tradition of the church.

In the Paleolithic Period and in the Neolithic Period which extended up until 5,000 years ago, you had the maternal goddess tradition; the universe was considered to have evolved primarily out of a maternal nurturance process. But the biblical tradition begins the Creation narrative with the Earth Mother of the eastern Mediterranean being abandoned in favor of a transcendent Heavenly Father.

NR: What happened to the feminine world of the goddess religions?

TB: It went underground where until now it has remained with the folk traditions—hidden traditions which the church has considered destructive and therefore unacceptable. We lost a fair amount of intimacy with the natural world when that happened, although this did not take on severe dimensions until later times.

NR: At what point did real aversion towards the natural world appear in Christian thought?

TB: As I see it, the real difficulty with the Christian view of the goodness and accessibility of the natural world occurred at the time of the Black Death when, between 1347 and 1349, one-third of the European population died in less than two years. At the time, people had no explanation for this. They didn't know anything about germs. They could only figure that the world had gone wicked and that God was punishing the world for its transgressions. It was a traumatic moment in divine-human-Earth relations, a moment when suspicion occurred about the benign aspect of nature, and alienation from the natural world began.

After the Black Death, religious redemption became the most important fact of the Christian experience. Uppermost in most people's consciousness was a need to get out of the world that had turned on them. But the emphasis placed on redemption was at the expense of a divine presence in, and through, the natural world. The Christian story was no longer the story of participation in an Earthly community. Instead, the emphasis had stretched to life after death in the heavenly community. Preoccupation with salvation out of the world through a personal savior transcended all interest in Earthly matters.

An exaggerated emphasis on the spiritual then began to take place. The fifteenth century was a period of intense piety in Europe. In Protestant Puritanism, and then in the Catholic form of Puritanism called Jansenism, a deep aversion occurred towards the natural world because the natural world contained a great deal of pleasure, and beauty, and celebration of which people were very suspicious. This aversion has continued into modern Christianity.

NR: At the same time, didn't the Black Death give birth to a secular scientific community that had its own solutions to the problem of what it saw as aberrant nature—as untamed nature out of control?

TB: Yes, the other response to the Black Death was the creation of a scientific priesthood that would understand and control the physical world. When Francis Bacon came along at the end of the sixteenth century, he said that you don't deal with the natural world by a spiritual escape from it. Instead, you defend yourself from the threats that come from nature by learning to control it. You "torture nature" in order to make it give up its secrets so that you can exploit it and make the world a more suitable and less painful place for humans to live. And scientists had a free field; they could do anything they wanted to because, by now, Christians had become indifferent to what was happening to the natural world.

The idea of nature as the carrier of numinous modes through which our souls could commune with the Divine was progressively lost in the religious life of the West after this time.

NR: Did scientific thinking by this time replace the idea of a divine presence in nature with the notion of a clockwork universe?

TB: Yes, in the seventeenth century the philosopher René Descartes said that there are only two aspects of reality: mind and extension, and what's not mind is extension and matter. The universe is a mechanical process that functions because of some creative principle, or creative reality. But there's no soul in nature.

This idea became central to the whole development of modern thought, particularly in England and France, which adopted Newtonian physics, first presented in 1687. The whole secularist, anti-religious trend followed, supported by a humanism that kept a moral tone but which had very little religious insight.

NR: And the classical Western idea that every living thing contains a vital inner principle, or anima, or soul, completely disappeared?

TB: It was totally denied by Descartes and his followers, and he was followed extensively. The soul that had been such a rich part of the pre-scientific, mystical world-view was now taken out of the universe and out of all living and non-living beings.

Two centuries after Descartes, Darwin demonstrated through his principle of natural selection that life was simply a struggle for survival without any conscious or psychic meaning inherent in that struggle. The universe itself was only a random sequence of events to which one could ascribe no divine purpose.

NR: Has eliminating our perception of the soul in nature had a direct relationship to the amount of damage we've done to the Earth?

TB: Yes, of course it has. The result of viewing of the world as both mechanistic and soulless is that the whole of the natural world has become vulnerable. What has followed in the centuries since Descartes has been an assault of Western scientific engineering on the whole world around it.

NR: Is this all because the spirituality of the natural world has been obliterated in terms of religious consciousness?

TB: That's right. Our response to a persistent inner drive for some rational understanding of the universe has been a world we are no longer able to commune with. Instead, we have a world that is dissected, measured, observed, and exploited in the name of progress. We have a universe which is emptied of its grandeur and significance because it is reduced to a mathematical expression, pure and simple.

It was not until the eighteenth century that the spirituality associated with the natural world began to show up again with the Romantic movement. Although the Romantic movement was not exactly religious, it did have a religious aspect expressed in the works of people like William Blake, William Wordsworth, and Samuel Coleridge.

NR: Blake in particular was very concerned with the fact that mechanistic science had eliminated the soul in nature, because it meant that we no longer had any self-imposed restraint about violating something sacred when we plundered the Earth.

TB: Yes, by Blake's time our manipulation of the environment had become a preoccupation, starting with the factory system. By using energy from coal, we had developed the iron industry that he talks about in such strong terms as "dark Satanic mills." Then came railroad building, steamship building, and all these mechanisms. This developed right up through the nineteenth century.

But you get the real meeting of science and scientific technology around the 1870s when Thomas Edison established the first research laboratories. After that there were two main developments: the electronics industry and the chemical industry, when DuPont set up his chemical factories. Then, in 1904, Ford came along with his factory productive processes. All of this was to have enormous deleterious influences on the planet. People had no idea what they were doing when they invented the automobile—no idea it would turn into such a disaster.

NR: Was there a point where you think we should have stopped?

TB: Definitely. We should have considered what we were doing and what it was leading to as soon as we developed petroleum. The first oil well in the U.S. was sunk in 1859. We began to use oil for gas lamps in the second half of the nineteenth century. Then we began to develop the gasoline motor and the internal combustion engine. But we had no idea of what was happening. We live to our detriment with air pollution now. But the scientists then should have been able to tell us more about what was going to happen if we took the petroleum out of the Earth, burned it, and released its residue into the air.

NR: Do you think the responsibility for the contamination of the planet lies at the feet of the scientists?

TB: Not all of it, perhaps; they're driven by social ideals. But the scientists definitely have to bear a lot of the responsibility.

Let's take the example of chemical fertilizers. The scientists gloried in the fact that they could throw chemicals on the soil and temporarily produce an abundance of crops. But they should have known that the organisms in the soil were needed; they should have known that chemicals would kill the soil. But they just brought us into these activities without warning us of any deleterious consequences.

Nor did they tell us what was going to happen if we changed the larger functioning of the planet by taking the petroleum out of the Earth. If there is any single issue that the next generation is going to have to deal with, it's the macrophase problem of what happens when we upset the basic chemistry of the planet by taking the petroleum and other fossil fuels out of the earth, use them, and then throw the residue out into the air and water and soil. We seldom think about the residue. We just assume that somehow or other it will be incorporated into the chemistry of the planet. So yes, it is my belief that the chemists have been negligent in their basic role in maintaining the integral functioning of the planet. The same applies to the biologists. Apparently it's not their concern either.

NR: Everything you're saying has real meaning for the environmentally ill. Contamination from fossil-fuel residues probably accounts for more chemical sensitivities in people like me than from any other source. As for chemical fertilizers, the more chemicals in our bodies, the worse our problems become. Instead of "better living through chemistry" (as the old DuPont ad claimed!), what should the scientific community have advocated?

TB: A life more in harmony with the integral cycles of the natural processes, where we learn to interact creatively within the organic processes and rhythms of the natural world, rather than trying to interfere with these processes through the use of poisonous substances.

NR: Thomas, you have lived in China and made a deep study of Chinese culture. Do the Chinese have a richer legacy regarding the proper function of humans vis-à-vis the natural world than we in the West have inherited?

TB: Well, Confucius had a marvelous insight one day concerning the necessity for an intimate relationship between humans and nature. One of his students said to him, "You tell us all these things; you overwhelm us. Couldn't you make it simpler?" Confucius said, "I'll give it all to you in one word—reciprocity." Reciprocity—what a beautiful word! If you take, you must give. That's the trouble in our relations with nature; we only know how to take from it. But if we take from the soil we must give back to the soil. Confucius taught his students that in the sixth century B.C. and we still haven't learned it!

NR: In the drive today to make nature more controllable and predictable, have scientists and technologists—acting in the service of commercial-industrial interests—destroyed the reciprocity between ourselves and the planet as it once existed?

TB: Well, to return to the soil—soil is a magical substance where alchemical processes occur which enable living things to grow and prosper. We thought we could nourish ourselves from the Earth without reciprocally nourishing it in return in accordance with organic principles. We haven't done this, and the result has been impoverished and eroded soils with depleted nourishment for everyone.

That's why I say that the first principle of our relationship to the Earth is reciprocity, and we come to that by having esteem for every mode of being. Every mode of being has its own rights. Trees have tree rights; birds have bird rights; insects have insect rights. An "object" has no rights. A "subject"—that is to say, something that has a center of spontaneity, what I would call a center of attribution, of action, that has an identity, a soul—has rights. It has dignity.

But we no longer see the Earth as having any dignity, let alone a soul. Soil is something almost for contempt. It's there to subserve humans, purely and simply, rather than primarily being a substance of a mystical nature.

The same with the rivers. To dam the rivers is to destroy the dignity of the rivers. If we destroy the dignity of the rivers we destroy the dignity of the humans. There's no ultimate benefit for the human if we ruin the rivers, and ruin the salmon, and over-fish the seas. It's just self-destruction.

Without reciprocity we cannot survive, and the Earth cannot survive. Our lack of understanding of this fundamental fact has led to our devastation of the planet. This has been our legacy from the scientific-technological community and our loss from an earlier age that saw humans as simply an integral part of the whole Earth community. Intimacy with the entire non-human world around us—on its terms, not ours—is what we have to revive as the prerequisite essential for our survival.

NR: To re-establish intimacy with the planet, you say that we need to return to a fifteenth century, pre-scientific, mystical experience of the universe and immerse ourselves in its mystery. But it seems that the part of us that would respond to the mystery is dead, or at least numb. Would you say that as the result of the way we've treated the Earth and its creatures that we ourselves have become lost souls, estranged from the natural world?

TB: Totally. Our spontaneous, instinctive responses to the natural world have been smothered by our contemporary mode of living. We no longer hear the cries of the animals and birds as we hunt them to extinction, or the voices of the trees as we clear-cut whole forests for profit. We've died to some inner principle that ties us to other forms of life. We couldn't cut down the forests, or extinguish the animals and birds with such callous insensitivity, if we hadn't.

   We've lost our fascination with existence, and because we can't enjoy the world of plants and animals around us, we're wiping these things out at a horrendous rate. We don't have the butterflies, or the songs of birds, or the fragrance of the honeysuckle, or the stars at night any more. Our lives are shriveled. And in this shriveling of life everything loses its meaning. Everything is trivialized.

NR: Do you see any hope for another life period in the future when this might change—when we would find our proper place in nature and start to act differently towards the planet?

TB: I have proposed a new Period that I call the Ecozoic Era. It's a term I thought up some time ago to succeed the Cenozoic Era. What the Ecozoic Era seeks is to bring the human activities of the Earth into alignment with the other forces functioning throughout the planet in order to achieve a creative balance. Because if we don't enter this projected age, we'll just go more deeply into the devastation of the present. And if we go more deeply into the devastation of the planet it will mean an extensive collapse of the major life systems of the Earth as we know them.

The Ecozoic Era is the moment when the small self meets the Great Self. It's when the needs of the planet and the needs of the person meet. We cannot separate or isolate human destiny from the destiny of the planet because we come out of the identical dynamism. We prosper or fail together, we live and die together, because the planet is ourselves. We are the Earth.

NR: Is the Ecozoic Era connected to the millennial myth?

TB: Well, the Ecozoic Era is the same myth, but in a valid form. The millennial myth is in our consciousness, and, to my mind, is never going to be obliterated. It's the dream, and the dream drives the action towards our building a viable society. But we have to transfer that millennial ideal into an acceptable mode of expression. The Ecozoic presentation of the millennial myth is the only thing that can save us, because we need something as dynamic as that to give us the energy required to confront the mythic power of the industrial vision. It will not be the perfection of existence that the original myth suggested, but it will be as close as we can come to it. The Ecozoic Era will bring us back to the primary purpose of the Creation itself, which is to create a world of delight in existence. Once we accept the Earth this will happen. The song of the birds is a delight in existence. The flow of the rivers is a delight in existence. Humans are supposed to identify this delight in a conscious form, and to celebrate it as the cosmic liturgy. That's how I see the Ecozoic Era.

NR: At the present time, aren't we instead entering the period of "conflict" prophesied in the millennial myth? In other words, do you see a final battle coming between those who would exploit the Earth for her resources, and those who would conserve those resources—a conflict between good and evil in the apocalyptic sense?

TB: I don't see it coming—I say we're into it. We're into an apocalyptic era of strife between the creative and the devastating forces—between those who see the world as a collection of objects and those who see it as a communion of subjects. But I'm not concerned with our extinction as a result of this conflict. I'm concerned with the degradation of the planet. Extinction is possible, but degradation is inevitable. It's the degradation of the Earth, while the people who are bringing it about fill their lives with trivial Wonderworld conveniences; that is the tragedy.

NR: You have said that the ultimate goal of the Ecozoic Era is "not simply to end the degradation of the planet, but to alter the mode of consciousness responsible for the devastation"—that what is needed isn't "simply adaptation, but transformation at its deepest level." Is this happening yet?

TB: Definitely, there is a change of consciousness going on. But it doesn't yet have the power that it needs, and it's not going to have that power until a whole change of mind and heart has taken place in the larger community. What's needed isn't simply a more clever adaptation to an ever-weakening biosystem. What's needed is a transformation that will end the patriarchal pattern of humans' drive to disturb the entire functioning of the globe.

We have so much control in proportion to the amount of our consciousness. We have to learn how to live in the universe on its terms, instead of ours. But we have a long way to go before we learn how to restructure every human task and every human institution until they function in a harmonious relationship with the requirements of the planet.

It's by far the most difficult issue humanity has ever had to face.

NR: As things are now it's almost as though we were entering another period like the Dark Ages. Is there something we can learn from that interval of history?

TB: In the eleventh through thirteenth centuries people were engaged in what they called a Great Work, which was the establishment of a finer civilization after the chaos of the Dark Ages. One of the great values of the ecology movement today is to have a Great Work available that people can be involved with in all kinds of ways; because everybody has an ability, everybody can join in.

NR: Is a Great Work something that engages people's souls?

TB: Their souls, their hearts, their bodies—every aspect of themselves. There is a medieval story about three people carrying stones who end up building a cathedral. The story is about the motivation of the three people. The first person is asked what he's doing and he says, "carrying stones": his is a life of physical labor. The second person says that he's supporting his family: he's the average person concerned with looking after his loved ones. The third person says that he's building a cathedral.

All three people are doing important things; you don't negate one in terms of the other. But in their consciousness of what they're doing, they're all quite different. In times like these we need people who have the energy and the type of dedication it takes to build a cathedral; in other words, we need people who realize that we are shaping a new order of things. It's a question of whether people are only going to work carrying stones, or raising families—or whether they're going to be aware of, and inspired by, a Great Work as well.

NR: In your own work, do you believe you're inspiring people to get involved in the Great Work of saving the planet?

TB: The whole purpose of my work is to provide an ennobling or inspiring direction for people. Because if we're going to have to give up some of the harmful things that we're doing—as well as some of the comforts—and take on some of the more severe disciplines, we are going to need a deeper sense of why we're doing this. It isn't enough just to be tough or disciplined. People will need to go further than this and feel the type of dedication that comes from doing something wonderful and inspiring.

NR: Doesn't increased ecological awareness bring with it an obligation to address, as well, the utilitarian aspects of sorting out the damage that our bedazzlement with the myth of progress has created?

TB: We've got to address these things, of course: we've got to recycle; we've got to cut down energy use; we've got to cut down on the use of chemical fertilizers; we've got to do what I call "the ten thousand things." But microphase changes—for example making cars that use less fuel—are totally insufficient by themselves. The needs of the human community are going to be so great with increased populations that we will need some really fundamental change in ourselves if we're going to effect change in our environment. We have to remember that while we do "the ten thousand things," it's not enough. *We* have to change: it's a soul change that's needed. If the soul change doesn't take place, then these other things cannot succeed.

NR: Is the foundation of this soul change a return to the mystique of the land?

TB: Yes, a return to the mystique of the Earth, to the dynamism and wisdom of the natural world, is a primary necessity if we are ever to establish a mutually enhancing human presence on the planet. It took more than four billion years for the Earth to establish that brilliant interaction of genetic codes that existed in the late Cenozoic period when we came into existence. To think that we, with our limited insight into this mysterious process, could take control of the life systems is a supreme arrogance. We have tried this for the past century in agriculture and ended up with the most absurd agricultural program ever invented. This is the consequence of making economic use our primary attitude toward the natural world. Such an attitude violates the deepest instincts of our being.

We came into being in the loveliest moment of all Earth history. We were made for the beauty that surrounds us. We could not experience the fulfillment of our souls except through the experience of this beauty. We may destroy this beauty, but we cannot destroy our need for this beauty. Our need, even our longing for immersion in the awesome world that surrounds us, is manifest in our immediate and most intense response to the natural world—in the admiration, wonder, awe, and reverence we experience immediately when we hear the song of the mockingbird, when we see the coloring and grace of a butterfly in flight, when we see Mount Rainier, when we walk through the forests of the Northwest, when we feel the wind on a summer evening.

In these experiences we find our deepest human fulfillment. That is why we go to the sea or to the mountains, to some place distant from city turmoil, to be healed and inwardly renewed. There we find our deeper selves. We are caught up into the world of the sacred. Only in this experience will we obtain the insight and the energy we need to alter our commitment to absolute devastation of the Earth in search of economic gain.

CHAPTER THREE

THE SACRED UNIVERSE

NANCY RYLEY: Thomas, why is it important for a society to have a universe story, or creation story, about its origins?

THOMAS BERRY: Well, a universe or creation story is a narrative that tells people how things were in the beginning, how things came to be as they are, and the human role in the story. A creation or universe story does many things for the members of a society. By giving them a sense of their proper place in the cosmos it provides their lives with meaning and purpose. It gives them goals and values, and reinforces their feeling of belonging to a larger system so that they know who they are.

NR: The creation, or universe, story then is fundamentally an attempt to relate humans to the larger cosmic picture?

TB: Yes, it's a primary effort in intelligibility, in how humans identify themselves so that the whole universe is experienced as a single, integral process. The basic challenge of humans is to discover how to identify their own role in this cosmological process.

NR: What was the nature of the creation story for early peoples? How did they see the universe?

TB: Traditional societies saw the universe moving in ever-renewing seasonal cycles—a process that always was and always would be. The basic perception seems to have been that the universe is an ever-renewing, self-sustaining process that goes through a sequence of changes, particularly seasonal changes: from a springtime expression, through a florescence, and then through a diminishing phase—a kind of cessation or dying down. And then a renewal began the whole cycle all over again. This became the great liturgy of the universe, and humans found themselves within this great ritual.

NR: Did this story of the universe give people a sense of connectedness to the sacred sources of life?

TB: Yes. It connected them to some Great Spirit, to some ultimate nourishing principle. That was the basic idea. This ultimate nourishing principle found its expression in the different powers of the universe, which were considered to have a mystical dimension—like the wind and the sea and the stars. And these powers began to be identified in personal terms which were expressed in art and in religious rituals, all of which had a cosmic connection.

It's still a very personal universe to indigenous peoples. A universe story still functions as a mythology for their societies, connecting them to the natural world through a mystical bonding to that world.

NR: Did the realization that the universe is sacred in its origins have a transformative effect on the soul of the individual in these cultures?

TB: Well, it was a guiding fulfillment for them. It brought about a transformation from a lesser to a greater sense of fulfillment in the life experience of each person.

As the child educator Maria Montessori indicates, the primary need of the child in all cultures is for a sense of the universe; this is the answer to all questions. This is the fulfillment of the human process, not simply in the phenomenal order, but also in the trans-phenomenal mystery that is expressed in the phenomenal world. As soon as the child begins to respond to this vital universe, the child's mind is elevated. The child's mind is oriented—the emotions are excited by the stars, by the wind, by the sea, by all the natural phenomena. The child then experiences this expansion of soul, this expansion of mind, this expansion of imagination, and that is the basis of all education.

Without this experience of the numinous aspects of existence, the psychic energy that the child will need for support through the difficult times in life won't be there.

NR: With the demise of the Christian myth as the basis for an understanding of our place in the universe, what has happened to the creation story in our time?

TB: At the present time we are in between stories. Since our traditional creation story no longer carries any meaning for many people, we need another story that will educate, heal, guide, and discipline us, just as the Genesis story once did.

NR: What kind of new story do you think we need?

TB: A story with a wider vision than we have had for several centuries—a story such as contemporary science has provided for us—one that will carry our imaginations both into the celestial realms of space, and into the deep psychic depths of the human, and unite the two. We need a narrative that will provide a sense of personal meaning, as well as inspire us—as some of the greatest contemporary scientists and naturalists have been inspired—with a sense of reverence and awe at the grandeur of the universe.

Neither the redemptive-religious nor the Newtonian-scientific communities were able to give us these things. As a result, our children have not been taught to be entranced by the wonders of the universe. And we have felt free to assault the Earth at will.

NR: What has happened to our society as the result of having renounced the story of our origins in a creative universe and having adopted the Cartesian view of a spiritually meaningless universe instead?

TB: We have lost the world of meaning. The inner satisfactions of life have disappeared, replaced by comfort, replaced by power in the physical order, replaced by building this magical world of matter.

There is no longer a soul in the human, any more than there is a soul in anything else. Because the human has been reduced to a production of the blind forces of matter, the values have become mechanistic values, not tied to any sense of spiritual meaning. The spiritual and moral values that once sustained us have disappeared. We've become lost, adrift in a society that has lost its guidelines, its rudder.

NR: You said that the new story we need to guide and heal us is going to come through contemporary science. How will today's scientists guide us towards the reclamation of our souls?

TB: The difficulty is that most scientists got caught up early on in the mechanistic view of Descartes whereby the whole planet was desouled. So then the question becomes: "What is a soul?" A soul is the informing principle of an organic body. Just consider this: take an acorn. Scientists can analyze the DNA; scientists can analyze the material composition in an infinite amount of detail. But they can never write a formula for the unifying principle that makes that complex organism able to function as a unit and do those thousands of operations involved in sending down roots, and raising the trunk, and extending limbs, and shaping leaves—each one different—and setting seed, and so forth, all of which is a perfectly coordinated single organic process.

Most scientists insist that there's no inner principle organizing all of this. They are totally oblivious of the fact that without an informing principle guiding, containing, and organizing this, none of it could possibly take place. There is an informing principle but it isn't a principle you can see, however; it can't be put into a formula; you can't hear it or taste it or experience it directly. Aristotle pointed out that you cannot perceive this with the senses; you can only recognize that there's a soul there, there's a principle there—through intelligence or intuition. You know that it's there because you know something has to hold these things together and enable them to function to shape a tree. Gregory Bateson recognized this informing principle and called it MIND, and he was rare among scientists precisely in doing that.

NR: What do *you* call it?

TB: Well, of a tree I call it the form, or the soul. Every animated being is by definition an ensouled being. *Anima* means soul—if it's "animated" then it's ensouled. The soul is the guiding principle, the self-organizing principle of every living being in the universe. And each soul is part of the self-organizing process of the universe.

NR: How did science finally evolve to the point where quantum scientists recognized that the nature of the universe was different than they had supposed—that the mechanistic universe, as they had conceived it to be, had some other story to tell?

TB: Continuous exploration of the function of the universe during the latter half of the nineteenth and throughout the twentieth centuries enabled scientists to penetrate deeply into its material constitution. During that time the whole functioning of the natural world was quantified and analyzed in the work of such men as Hubble, Planck, and Einstein. By virtue of the increased sensitivity of their instruments which enabled them to listen—to have an empirical contact with the phenomena of the universe—they were able to arrive at the awareness that the universe is not simply placed there and moving in ever-renewing seasonal cycles. Instead, they realized that the universe is a "coming to be"—more cosmogenesis than cosmos.

What this new narrative related was the sequence of *transformations* through which the universe had gone from the time of its origin until the present. Like any story, it told a sequence of events through which a thing passes in the self-shaping transformations that enable it to be what it is at the present time.

NR: "Self-shaping" seems to accord with the description you just gave of a soul as "the informing principle of an organic body." In that sense, is this new narrative of the universe from contemporary science telling us that the universe itself has consciousness, has a soul—*anima mundi?*

TB: Yes, it is. The universe in the phenomenal order is self-organizing; it is self-directing; it is self-fulfilling. Over time it has shaped the galaxies and the planets, formed the elements, built the continents, fashioned the plants and animals. The universe is the only self-referent mode of being in the phenomenal order; every other being is universe-referent; that is, every other being takes its identity from within that context. That's why having some sense of the universe is absolutely primary.

NR: Did the universe give itself existence?

TB: No; although the universe is self-organizing, there's no way in which a phenomenal cause could account for its own existence. Why is there a universe rather than no universe? That's the ultimate mystery, and science, of course, has no answer for that.

The realization that the universe is not meaningless, determined, nor random, but instead has had its own consciousness from the beginning, has brought about a unique transformation of the human mind in our time. Nothing like this has occurred, it seems, since the beginning of human intelligence. I say that the story of the universe, which the penetration of quantum science into the world of sub-atomic physics has revealed, is the greatest moral, religious, and spiritual event to take place for many centuries.

NR: Is that because quantum physics provides a basis for accepting the universe as a transmaterial, spiritual reality?

TB: Yes, and it's an awesome revelation. It's what I call the "primary revelation." The story of the unfolding of the universe over time and space is a story which, up until now, has not scientifically been known to us, but which, in its mythical dimensions, is of paramount importance in changing our behavior towards the Earth.

NR: In *The Universe Story*, you and Brian Swimme have written that one important aspect of what modern physics has discovered about the nature of the universe is called "quantum non-separability." What does that mean?

TB: Quantum non-separability in the universe is the awareness that the subject (knowing) is integral with the reality (known). This is not a "knowing" subject simply "knowing" an object that's out there in space. It's a question of a rapport between two subjects in intimate communion with one another.

NR: How will this provide us with the basis for a new spiritual myth that would guide our behavior in our relationship to the Earth?

TB: It's a way of getting beyond the sense of the universe as a collection of objects, and into the perception of it as a communion of subjects. In that sense, through quantum non-separability, modern physics is taking us back to earlier centuries with the awareness of a mystical bonding of the entire universe within itself.

NR: Quoting from *The Universe Story*, do quantum physicists actually talk about "harmonies in the universe existing beneath the apparent chaos of the sub-atomic world?" And about "each mode of being resonating with every other mode of being," as though they were living in the pre-scientific fifteenth century that envisioned the world in this way?

TB: Definitely. In quantum theory every atom is immediately influencing every other atom of the universe. Every particle is connected to every other particle, every galaxy to every other galaxy.

NR: Does this lead to the conclusion that everything in the universe is interconnected?

TB: Absolutely. It's all quite mysterious, but there it is.

NR: How does this inability to separate the "knowing" subject from the object "known" translate into meaning for the forms of life on Earth?

TB: It translates into organizing centers. Everything exists as an organizing center of spontaneity, of integration. Everything is organized within itself in relation to everything else, so that everything has its *particular* mode of "being," and its *universe* mode of "being." It takes a universe to make any entity in the universe. We are what we are because everything else is what it is!

NR: Besides every single thing in the universe having what you've called a "cousin" relationship to everything else, we also have this inborn dimension which connects us to the larger whole?

TB: That's right.

NR: Could you talk about a specific animal and its inter-connectedness with its home environment?

TB: Well, let's take a bear as an example. Put it outside its temperate forest home and its life becomes meaningless. Inborn in that bear are the love of the salmon that swim in the rivers there, and the love of the wild berries that grow there, and so forth. The environment makes the animal and the animal makes the environment. This is the mutuality of the universe.

NR: Looking at our own case as humans, the Buddhist Thich Nhat Hanh observes that people who spend any time in the forests know that "forests are our lungs outside our bodies." And in *The Universe Story* you wrote about how the pond of the dragonfly shapes and influences the mind of the dragonfly, and vice-versa, making the point that you can't separate the two and make any sense of either the dragonfly's life or the pond's life if you do.

TB: That's right. Some people understand this in the human order. I believe an architect, maybe it was Frank Lloyd Wright, said that we make our buildings and then our buildings make us. We make our automobiles and then our automobiles make us. That's the catastrophe that people don't recognize when they make something, they are made by that thing.

NR: Could awareness of the inter-relatedness of things make people who live in urban environments aware of our close bond to the planet?

TB: Yes. It could make us aware of the fact that if we devastate our environment, we devastate ourselves. It could bring home to us the fact that if we live in a world of pollution then we'll be polluted, and that we should therefore be very, very careful about making the world over into parking lots and vast areas of contamination.

It should also make us aware that if we lose the vision of the stars, we lose our souls, we lose our imaginations, we lose our minds, because the experience of the stars is one of the most sublime and transforming experiences that humans have.

NR: Some Eastern religions—particularly Buddhism—as well as many indigenous peoples from all around the world, have understood the universe in its creative unfolding mythically and intuitively. They didn't have to analyze it as we have done in order to understand it. Is it also important for us to understand the *mythic* basis of the contemporary scientific explanation of the nature of the universe?

TB: Heavens, yes! Myth is the only way in which we can understand anything in any depth. It's the mythic telling of the scientific story that makes it comprehensible to our emotions, and to our total understanding on every level—emotional, spiritual, intellectual—of the world around us. Only as "story" does it carry with it a sense of meaning, a sense of the sacred.

The universe story was intuited by earlier peoples as the myth of the

Great Mother. The Great Mother archetype symbolizes the maternal or nurturing principle that ties together the whole of the natural world in a mystical bond. For those early peoples, the Great Earth Mother was rich in symbolic meaning as the image of matter. Through that symbolization, humans found the emotional and spiritual identification with the Earth which we have now lost. For us, no voices emerge from the plants and animals, from the mountains and rivers, to tell us their stories. Our contact with the psychic energy that came as the result of our connection to those meaningful images is gone.

Restoration of belief in the sacredness of matter, and of our bonding to the Earth through the Great Mother myth, is essential today if we are ever to defeat the Wonderland myth which has caused so much devastation through its power-driven negation of the Earth's needs.

NR: Has quantum science come up with an equivalent of the Great Mother myth?

TB: In modern physics the concept of the great curvature of space is the principle that holds everything together in intimate relationship to everything else. The universe as we know it is an expanding universe, sufficiently closed so that it can hold together, sufficiently open so that it can keep expanding. What gives us the curvature of space is the balance between the expanding and containing forces. All this is poised in an infinitely exquisite balance—what I call "creative disequilibrium."

The curvature of space enables things to be present to each other. At its lowest level, we talk about it as gravitation. Gravitational attraction is what holds things together at the physical level. While this bonding together sustains everything in intimate relationship to everything else in a physical sense, it does so in a psychic sense as well, because all things in the universe have a psychic or a spiritual dimension. Without gravitation there would never be any human affection. Affection is ultimately sustained by what we call gravitational attraction.

Fundamentally, then, without that curvature of space there would be no universe, no bonding, and no human affection. And because the curvature of space contains and holds things together in a kind of maternal embrace, I suggest that the curvature of space is our modern metaphor of the Great Mother.

NR: Some of Marion Woodman's analysands have had dreams about Buffalo

Woman as the Great Mother, as well as dreams about other Indian archetypal figures. You have said that, "The Indian carries a primordial tradition of great significance for the entire human community." In what ways can they guide us back to an awareness of the sacred quality of the universe that we have lost?

TB: Our indigenous peoples live in a magnificent universe. They perceive everything in this dimension as communicating the deep mystery of existence, as communicating the Great Spirit. For indigenous people, unlike ourselves, it's not a question of a sacred versus a secular order of things: they live in a sacred universe. It's composed of both constructive and destructive forces, but it is ultimately a benign universe. For them, the sense of the numinous, the divine voice, speaks through every phase of cosmic existence.

NR: Even today, in our modern world, do they still have this sense of connection to a sacred universe ?

TB: To a surprising degree they do. Several years ago I met Lame Deer, one of the more renowned visionaries of the Sioux tribe, at a conference which was held in the cathedral of St. John the Divine in New York. He spoke about the difference between how white people worship Divinity, and how tribal people prefer a different setting for their worship of the Great Spirit. While he praised the cathedral, he also remarked on what an over-powering setting it was for communication with the Divine. For his part and for tribal peoples, he said, they prefer to worship under the sky within the surroundings of the natural world. The sun dance, for example, is carried on out in the open with the center pole and the dancing back and forth. This is the center where the divine and the natural and the human come together. It's a cosmic renewal ceremony. Out in the open among the sounds of the creatures, and the smells of the Earth—exposed to the wind, and the rain, and the sun—worshipping in nature is a profoundly different experience from worshipping in a church or a cathedral.

What he said made an overwhelming impression on me and made me wonder about what we have lost in the lifestyle that we have adopted.

NR: You write in *The Dream of the Earth* that the indigenous people have kept in touch with the depths of their own psyches, with the archetypal world of the collective unconscious, whereas we have, by and large, lost this connection. Why is this important?

TB: Well, it's important for a very basic reason. You see, the pre-human modes of being—plants and animals of the non-human order—are guided mainly by what we call their instinctive world, which in turn is guided by their genetic processes. Humans are genetically coded towards a further trans-genetic cultural coding whereby they become human. That is, we have to be taught; we have to be taught language; we have to be taught relationships and social conduct. We need to learn so many things in order to become articulate human personalities. That's why we have such a long childhood.

Now the bond between genetic coding and cultural coding is the archetypal world. We don't just invent our cultural world without any guidance from our genetic coding. That guidance comes from what we call the archetypal tendencies of the unconscious. It's the world of the archetypes which guides us in building a viable culture.

NR: So that if we've lost touch with the archetypal images of the unconscious we can't make appropriate decisions about the kind of world we want to live in?

TB: That's right. Jung points out that our tendency to over-rationalization has destroyed our capacity to respond to those numinous ideas and symbols that would give our culture the kind of wholeness and sound values it so badly needs. Our reason overwhelms our deeper intuitions. Through over-rationalism and ego we tend to lose the immediacy of things that we know instinctively.

NR: What effect does losing touch with the imagery from the archetypal world of the unconscious have on the way we treat the planet?

TB: Well, that's why we devastate the planet. Archetypal energies are unique energies because they activate our deepest instinctual bonds with all forms of life; instinctively we tend to be in awe of the planet, we tend to be reverent towards it. But once we begin to have a certain amount of rational control, then we begin to become arrogant. It's human arrogance that is causing the trouble.

NR: Would you say that if we fail to pay attention to the archetypal images that we will also lose touch with what's meaningful in our lives?

TB: Yes, I would. Archetypes are patterns of energy that influenced our behavior long before we developed a reflective consciousness, and they still do. The archetypal symbolizations of the Great Mother, the Tree of Life, the Mandala or Center, and so forth, are the ways we all have of orienting our lives to the greater dimensions of Reality. Without receptivity to their energies, our existences become fragmented and too narrowly circumscribed. The human psyche loses its moorings, and our individual lives lose their meaning.

Having lost touch with the archetypal images means that we have lost touch with the genetically coded source of our connectedness to the universe. In our narrow, materialistic self-preoccupation we've cut ourselves off from the forces that would guide us. Without a conscious relationship to the realm of the archetypes, the culture we've produced has become pathological rather than nourishing.

We are now caught in a unique situation: no humans ever had the power that we have; no humans ever had an understanding of the universe as emergent process. But we don't know how to use our power because we have lost our sense of the controlling elements.

NR: Can indigenous peoples show us how to reconnect to these eternal patterns in ourselves?

TB: Indigenous peoples experience life in a profoundly different way than we do because of their deep receptivity to the numinous psychic energies embedded in the natural world around them. They discover themselves and their own identity within the identity of everything else. Through intimacy with the natural world, the Indian is able to penetrate the spirit world which lies beyond the phenomenal world, and whose symbolic images then surface in visions and dreams. These images are then given external form in rituals, chants, and various other forms of religious expression. That's why their poetry is so magnificent. As Brian Swimme has written:

> To find oneself in the icy sea in a skin-covered kayak when the dark surface parts in the winter evening and a vast sleek presence appears, to be suddenly staring, eye-to-eye with this spirit from the depths of the ocean, was cause for years of celebration. The

song transmitted in that instant was the meaning and the fulfillment of a lifetime.[2]

This is the kind of communion with the Earth that sustains and gives
meaning to life: the entering into the life-enhancing forces of the universe
through a subjective communion with the entire non-human world—with
the rain, and the wind, and the birds, and the sea creatures. Existence as a
celebratory expression—that's what life is all about.

NR: It's sad, but most contemporary people can't, or don't, have experiences
like these. Living as we do, so far from that kind of contact with nature, how
can we make use of indigenous peoples' knowledge and wisdom in our lives?

TB: Unfortunately we don't live in a universe like theirs; the Earth is not
singing for us. To occupy a certain territory you have to know the song of that
territory. Compared to their life of mind and soul we are greatly diminished.

Even so, we can still adopt a sense of mutual presence towards the
natural world wherever we are living. We can do this by seeing that we do not
alienate ourselves from the dynamics of the natural systems, by diminishing
the absurdities of urban life, by diminishing automobiles and road building,
and all these other things. For the stars in the night sky over our cities to be so
blocked from view by particle and light pollution is not simply a loss of the
passing visual experience, it is a loss of soul. We can only remedy this by
recovering a sense of the birds and the flowers and the wind and the stars, so
that we recover the poetry of life. Only in this way can our existing cities be
transformed in such a way as to return to some livable form of expression.

Mainly, what we can learn from the native peoples, then, is a certain
basic humility before the deeper forces of existence. That's the main thing
they can teach us. And it behooves us to pay attention.

NR: Essentially then, on what do you believe our survival depends? What is
most important for us "to pay attention to" at this time?

TB: I believe our survival depends on our psychological and intellectual "entrancement" with both the mythic and the scientific presentations of the universe story. Scientists have begun to enter into this realm of the mythic and
the sacred with their recent awareness that the evolution of the universe is the

epic of our times. Without a narrative that evokes our excitement about the splendor of the world around us, a narrative which engages our deepest psychic energies in a discovery of our spiritual place in the universe, we cannot hope to end our present entrancement with the myth of progress which is presently destroying our world. Only fascination with the mythic dimensions of the universe story can counteract the myth of Wonderland.

So we have to go back to a primary sense of awe and wonder at the universe—a primary sense of the universe as sacred. If we don't develop that, then I don't know how we're going to manage. But recovery of the sense of the sacred is primary. And the universe itself should teach us that.

CHAPTER FOUR

CELEBRATING THE UNIVERSE

NANCY RYLEY: Thomas, does the universe story replace earlier traditional religious teachings—Buddhism, Christianity, and so forth—as the focus for our worship of the Divine?

THOMAS BERRY: Well, we have both. The universe as a sacred story is an enrichment, not a negation, of the great religious teaching traditions. St. Thomas, the greatest of the theologians of the medieval period, tells us that the integrity of the universe is "the ultimate and noblest perfection in things." He doesn't say humans, he doesn't say Christianity, he doesn't say religion, he says the universe. So what is needed now is a kind of meta-religious horizon under which all religions of the past can achieve a new mode of being and learn to function in a new context. I think this is provided by our new understanding of the universe. I think of it as a sacred story. It is revelatory. And I think that we have to work out of that.

NR: Are people ready to accept that, do you think?

TB: Our difficulty is that our religious traditions are all retreating back into neo-fundamentalism. They're not willing, or not able, to enter into this new sense of the universe in some integral way, and of establishing an intimate sense of who we are. But we're never going to understand who we are except through this new story of the universe.

NR: Is communing with the universe going to be "a solace and a comfort for the afflicted," as they say in the Christian prayer book? What most people seem to want is a personal savior.

TB: Well, this is not going to negate that dimension of things. Religions can still keep their personal saviors. But we do need both, because the contemporary scientific view doesn't deal with the suffering of the world. You must go to the various religious traditions for that.

Buddhism, for example, is immersed in the fact that the three basic characteristics of the universe are that it is transient, sorrowful, and unreal. Buddhists express compassion like no other people on Earth for plants, animals, and for all living things. The Bible also tries to deal with suffering and pain, and to assign them a moral cause.

NR: Does the fact that we need our religions imply that the universe itself shows little compassion?

TB: Not at all; nature is very compassionate.

NR: In what ways?

TB: By the way in which it provides for our needs. By the way it gives us solace in our pain. What do we do when we're sorrowful? We go to the sea or to the mountains. Or we bathe in the river. Or we go for a walk under the stars.

NR: The universe is such a lofty, impersonal concept for most people, and that makes it very hard for us to relate to it. But in *The Universe Story*, you and Brian Swimme give examples of the "service," or sacrificial dimension, that the universe demonstrated as it was evolving, which could be interpreted as a kind of model for human behavior. Can you tell me something about that and what we can learn from those events?

TB: The universe has gone through many crisis moments. I'm thinking particularly of the supernova moment of the first-generation stars. The first generation of stars was a dead end. Nothing more could happen to them because they only had the simple elements of hydrogen and helium, whereas we needed ninety-some elements to have a planet Earth, and life, and consciousness. So some of the first generation stars collapsed in enormous heat to create those ninety-some elements.

There was one particular star (astronomers have never given a name to this star) that Brian Swimme and I called *Tiamat*, that underwent this type of sacrificial collapse, and exploded into space as star dust. Then the gravitational process came into play and created our sun, which is a second generation star, and which had these little planets around it, including the Earth. So the sacrifice of Tiamat gave birth to our solar system. Its supernova explosion sent us most of the atoms we have in our bodies, and made our existence possible. Sacrifice is a quality that is built right into the nature of the universe.

The challenge of the whole emergent universe is that there's the catastrophic side and the creative side. There's constant disequilibrium; nothing creative would ever have happened in a state of equilibrium. It takes great disasters to bring forth great creativity. For instance, if the dinosaur age had never ended, humans most likely would never have appeared. Mammals would never have developed in the way they did. So it's important to know and be inspired by the story, and to trust the story.

NR: Like the universe, are we going to have to accept the idea of "creative disequilibrium," and make sacrifices and accept loss if we are to continue the privilege of living on this planet?

TB: Well, we certainly need to realize that if we're going to survive, we need to transform our present way of life, and give up a lot of things that we now think are necessary for life but which are really killing us.

NR: In what other ways do we as humans reflect the consciousness of the universe?

TB: That's the entire purpose of human intelligence—to enable the universe to reflect on itself through us. It's not so much the human knowing the universe, as the universe reflecting on itself in human intelligence. The whole purpose of the human is to enable the universe to have fascination with its own beauty and its own aesthetic qualities; to have the experience of intimacy with itself, and with that ultimate numinous source from which it emerges.

NR: You are talking as though the universe were a creative entity which expresses itself as consciousness in our imaginative lives—in our art, in our poetry, and so forth.

TB: It does! From the quantum point of view, an artist's awareness can't be separated from the universe of which the artist is aware. We delude ourselves that *we* have created a painting or a poem when, in fact, our creations are echoes of the creativity present in the entire universe. We are only able to capture a tiny fraction of this. The psychic aspect of the natural world is activated in our awareness, and in turn responds to our awareness of it.

NR: Is this a reciprocal relationship?

TB: Yes, it's a reciprocal relationship between ourselves and the universe. Only mechanistic science believes that we are disconnected from the deeper dimension of things around us—that we are here, and that reality is out there, neither affected by us, nor affecting us in the act of knowing.

NR: Is that what you mean when you say in *The Universe Story*, "The human being within the universe is a sounding board within a musical instrument"?

TB: The idea of a sounding board is simply that the whole is written in each part of the universe. The part and the whole are reciprocally related. Each part of the universe is the expression of the total universe, in a particular way.

The difficulty comes when we mistake the sounding board for the whole instrument. We forget—caught up as we are in fascination with our own accomplishments and knowledge—that it is the numinous dimension of the universe which activates us, and that we do not act independently of its influence.

NR: By "the numinous dimension of the universe" do you mean the world of myths, visions, and dreams that poets, artists, and indigenous peoples remain connected to but which we have lost?

TB: Well, yes; it's so clear in the total story of human experience that humans have been at their most creative in relation to this sense of the universe. This has happened throughout the classical civilizations of the past, as well as in the societies of the indigenous peoples of the world.

NR: *The Universe Story* contains a wonderful passage which I'd like to quote because it seems so fundamental to an understanding of how you feel our creativity—our soul's expression—only truly emerges by the grace of our connection to the surrounding cosmos.

> We now know that the interiority of any mammal is the result of a long and complex process of creativity beginning with the star-making powers of the Milky Way. Walt Whitman did not invent his sentience, nor was he wholly responsible for the form of feelings he experienced. Rather, his sentience is an intricate creation of the Milky Way, and his feelings are an evocation of being, an evocation involving thunderstorms, sunlight, grass, history, and death. Walt Whitman is a space the Milky Way fashioned to feel its own grandeur.[3]

TB: Well, that's the grandeur of things. One of the things that makes the great literature great is that it presents the human process within the cosmological process. You have this in Whitman. You have it particularly in the Homeric epics, and in Virgil, and Dante, and Shakespeare, and Dostoevsky. An example in American literature would be *Moby Dick*. When Melville takes us deep into the story of Captain Ahab's efforts to destroy the Great White Whale, he takes the story into its epic dimensions and into its cosmological dimensions.

NR: What does the whale symbolize in Melville's story?

TB: The whale symbolizes the demonic aspects of the natural world.

NR: But the whale isn't a demonic presence in nature.

TB: No, but we see the natural world as having a demonic aspect. This feeling of the demonic aspect of nature is an integral part of our American experience. That's our view of it, because we have become predators on the natural world. This assault on the natural world, rather than an integration with the natural world, is what is central to so much of American literature. But it is particularly powerful in Melville's *Moby Dick*. In his story the whale destroys us. It turns on us. But it also is "stricken" in the process. So Melville is dealing with that ultimate relationship of the human with the natural system. That's precisely what we've lost in much of our literature today. We've lost the sense of the cosmological dimension of things. We have the scientific measurements and technological skills, but we've lost the universe in any meaningful context.

NR: Does what you're saying about how we must look at human life within the context of the whole cosmological process apply to other areas of modern life as well as literature?

TB: Yes, of course. Take economics: economics is a noble function. It deals with the way in which things nourish each other in a reciprocal way; that's part of the intimacy of beings with each other. But this degradation of economics to a pure money-making function destroys the whole meaning of the process.

Similarly, in our laws and our jurisprudence we've lost the feeling that the order of the human is an extension of the order of the universe, the order of life, the order of the planet Earth.

When we lose the sense of our integral relationship with the larger context of the universe, we become trivialized. Right now my critique of our human situation is that we have simply become trivial; we've lost our depth of meaning, our soul's connection to its Source.

NR: As individuals, how can we grasp anything as awesome as the spiritual dimension of the universe?

TB: As soon as we see the stars in the heavens, as soon as we hear the singing of the birds, as soon as we experience the feel of the wind, as soon as we have any experiences of the natural world, our first reaction is all admiration, sensitivity, and delight. All these forces within us naturally respond; children have these and they scream with delight at the stars and the wind. So we obviously have an instinctive response to nature from our first moments.

Later, our education tells us that we have to approach nature as though it were a mechanism, as though it were something to be manipulated, something to be used. We are educated out of our primary experience, but our primary experience is something that goes beyond the mechanistic context in which our education encases us.

The question is, how do we preserve the immediacy of this early experience? It's something that's experienced as a sense of the beautiful, a sense of the entrancing that activates something in our souls, that activates something that cannot be expressed in any scientific formula.

NR: You have written about the effect of climbing a mountain on the soul of the climber. I hike and ski a lot in the mountains, but I've never been able to articulate what happens to me there, except that it's a pretty deep experience at a spiritual level. There's a wonderful section by Brian Swimme in *The Universe Story* about this experience:

> A human being, for instance, can climb a mountain and get hit by something so profound, at so deep a level, that the human will never be quite the same. This precise feeling will not occur on the ocean or in a cave or a valley. Other sorts of experience will take place there. This specific mountain moment will emerge only in the presence of the mountain; it is evoked out of potentiality by the mountain. The dynamic of the mountain is accomplishing something in the universe, is acting, is altering reality. . . . Poetry and the depths of soul emerge from the human world because the inner form of the mountains and the numinous quality of the sky have activated these depths in the human.[4]

TB: Yes, we don't create these profound feelings of oneness, of elation, of awe and reverence, ourselves. They come about as a result of the interaction between ourselves, the mountain, and the universe.

NR: That's what I think is so important for people to understand: the fact that we live in a spiritually alive universe, and for this reason our interaction with it affects what we become. Bringing conscious recognition of this to the wilderness changes our Reality. It alters our whole view of our need for nature because, as you say, through the natural world the soul finds its connection to its Source. Besides working to save it for its own sake, isn't this the fundamental reason for trying to save the Earth?

TB: That's right. Human beings are made whole in nature. That's where we complete ourselves; that's where we find ourselves.

One of E. O. Wilson's books, *Biophilia*, is about the inborn affinity we have for nature, and how, in its turn, nature draws us to it; how it lives in us, in our intellects, our imaginations, and our genes. The word *philia* comes from the Greek word *philos*, meaning "loving". Biophilia is our capacity for intimacy with, and relatedness to, other forms of life. That is what intelligence is. It's what emotions are. It's the capacity to be intimate with some other being as "other."

To the extent that we think of everything around us as objects, instead of as subjects to be communed with, we deny our own sensory experience, our own capacity for intimacy. We then become oblivious or indifferent to the existence of anything but ourselves.

NR: Who's in charge of what happens to the Earth, do you think? Are we?

TB: Certainly not! Obviously we have a lot of power in relationship to the natural world. Otherwise we couldn't devastate it so terribly. But it is sheer arrogance on our part to think that we have the ability to deal with the complexities of the Earth's functioning—to think that either individually or as groups we can solve anything. We really can't, any more than we can cure a person. The planet will develop and heal itself in its own way. There's a lot we can do to help it heal, but ultimately it has to heal from within, and if we don't obstruct this process it will do that. Although we must take responsibility for what's happening to the Earth, it's simply not up to us to heal it.

NR: How can we creatively enter into that healing process?

TB: The creativity that is manifested throughout the planet is not emerging simply out of individuals, nor out of groups. It's a deeper force, and that's what's important about the universe story. It tells us that there are forces at work, forces governing the structure of human consciousness. It's not simply the *voice* of the Earth, it's the *power* of the Earth that is dealing with the crisis we're in. Unfortunately, it's very hard for us to become attuned to that voice and that power because we have lost our basic intimacy with the natural world and have entered instead into a destructive relationship with it.

NR: You have said, "In moments of confusion such as the present we are not left to our own devices but supported by the ultimate powers of the universe as they make themselves present to us through the spontaneities within our own being." What does that mean in terms of where we can look for guidance for the task of healing ourselves, and helping to heal the planet?

TB: It means that even our basic reasoning processes are ultimately governed by those pre-rational, or pre-conscious, instinctive forces within us, acting in concert with the larger spontaneities of the universe. All organisms are guided by the interaction of these forces.

Take the monarch butterfly, for instance; its migration covers thousands of miles. In some instances the butterfly that returns years later to the tree where its grandparents were born is two generations away from the butterflies who originally left there. How does it know where to return to if it's never been there? How does it know how to go to this specific grove, to this specific tree? It knows because:

> The winds speak to the butterfly, the taste of the water speaks to the butterfly, the shape of the leaf speaks to the butterfly and offers a guidance that resonates with the wisdom coded into the butterfly's being.[5]

There's some kind of genetic determination operating here, but it still needs the guidance of the landscape.

NR: How does this apply to how *we* are guided by the landscape?

TB: The Earth is here to be communed with. Everything in it has its own voice—we must simply listen. How do we do this? By allowing ourselves to be guided by the inner spontaneities in us that respond to the integral functioning of the whole system. We need to develop our receptivity to the point where we open ourselves fully in response to the psychic energies deep in the structure of Reality itself. It's not control through an intellectual knowledge of the environment that we need. We need to tune ourselves, so that we can respond creatively to the unfolding of the Earth process, not trying to control it, but working cooperatively with it.

That's why I say we are taught by the Earth; if we listen to the outer world it tells us so many things. In our literature, in our economics, in everything, we learn from the Earth.

The planet Earth is primary. It's the primary healer, primary economic reality, primary religious reality. It's the primary legal and moral reality.

It's primary in everything.

NR: How does the rain speak to us, or the sun? What do they say?

TB: Well, first of all, they speak to us through their presence. They communicate a sense of beauty and order and warmth and life-giving qualities, like the blossoming of flowers or the flow of the wind. They reveal to us the basic creativity and fertility that is at the basis of existence, and that the universe is ultimately a celebratory reality. It's not ultimately a utilitarian thing; there's no special utility in flowers blooming or fish swimming or butterflies or whatever. It's just a gorgeous expression of existence.

NR: Thomas, you have obviously "tuned" yourself to hearing the messages of the Earth. You told me that several years ago you spoke to the assembly of Canadian Indian tribes at Cape Croker in Georgian Bay, Ontario, about these things, and that it was a great occasion for both them and you. What did you say to them?

TB: Well, I said that I didn't know what to say before I came, I didn't know what they expected of me. I told them that right up to the night that I spoke to them I still didn't know what to say.

So I asked the moon: "What should I say?" And the moon said: "Tell them the story." And I asked the wind: "What should I say?" And the wind said: "Tell them the story." And before I came into the tent to speak I asked the clover in the field: "What should I say?" And the clover said: "Tell them the story, my story. And the story of the wind, and the river, and the bay. And tell them their story, the universe story."

And then I got up to speak and I said: "What I say here is not important. What the stars say is important. What the wind says is important. What the river says, what the ocean says, all of this is important."

Then I said: "The difficulty of my generation of Euro-Americans is that we've become autistic; we can't hear these stories; we can't be guided by them."

Later on that day, after I had talked, one of the Mohawk chiefs spoke and he said that this was the first time that he had ever heard a non-Indian speak so much like the old chiefs, like their grandfathers and the old chiefs.

NR: What a compliment. That must have been the most wonderful thing for you to have heard.

TB: It was. It was one of the highest honors I can recall in my life. So there has been some close rapport between myself and the indigenous people. I don't know where it comes from, to tell you the truth.

NR: Indeed, where does your sensitive rapport with nature come from?

TB: Well, as a child I was very fortunate to have had woodlands that I could walk through, and enjoy, learn from, and be excited about. As a child I had a lot of experiences that children now might not have.

NR: Did you have other experiences when you were young that perhaps drove you more deeply into nature and directed your path away from the world?

TB: From the time I was quite a young child, I experienced the commercialization of everything. I was born in 1914, and as early as the 1920s, it was clear that this country was dead set on commercialization. I needed time to think because I couldn't envisage myself in the world that was coming into being. My abhorrence of the ideals that went with a consumer society was so strong that in 1934, when I was twenty, I went into a monastery. The main idea was to have time to think through what was happening, and to establish my personal response to it.

So my life has been governed by a sensitivity that was activated quite early in this century. I've lived through this century quite conscious of the things that have happened in each of its decades, and I feel I know something about it. I've gone through the whole thing, and I have witnessed it, and experienced it, and thought about it.

NR: Was dropping out of society a hard decision for you to make?

TB: No. For me it was easy, because I had been kind of counter-cultural from the time I was born—certainly by the time I was seven or eight! By the time I was nine years old I had a thickening stack of catalogs showing all the equipment needed for going to the Northwest, which was for me the only uncorrupted wilderness left in those days.

NR: You were going to run away from home?

TB: No, I was just going to go there when the right time came.

NR: And did you go?

TB: No, I never did. It turned into a mental or a soul thing, you might say. I always thought of the Northwest as a better world, where I'd find the type of insight I needed. But now I say that the Northwest came to me when Brian Swimme, who's from the state of Washington, came to New York where we studied together and designed *The Universe Story*.

NR: What happened that made you decide against going to the Northwest yourself? What choices did you have to make there?

TB: Well, I was a brooding personality—at least, I'd adopted that identity! I was very absorbed in the thought world, and I began to identify my work with writing and teaching. But first of all I had to learn something myself, so I stayed at the monastery for ten years before I went back home for a visit.

What there was in monastic life that appealed to me was a movement into the liturgy of the universe. The liturgies of the monastery were coordinated with the day-night cycle, with the dawn, the meridian, the sunset, and the midnight. We'd get up in the middle of the night, and the psalms and the wonderful, beautiful hymns that were written through the course of the centuries, were portioned out through our day. We also followed the seasons of the year: the springtime, the summer, the fall, and the winter. It was a very profound experience of the cosmological order.

One of my deepest attractions to the Catholic tradition is because of the strength of its cosmological foundation. This means that if we have any idea of divine Reality we get it from our experience of what we see or hear around us. St. Thomas says, "There's nothing in intelligence that was not first in some way in the senses." And that's where I come from.

NR: Can you tell me more about your sense of participation in, and appreciation of, the story—and the glory—of the universe?

TB: My primary experience is the universe itself—the great liturgy of existence, which is a sense of delight and a celebration of participated consciousness with everything else. It's a mystical thing. Everyone has this to a certain extent if they open themselves to it.

All the great civilizations were built on this perception of the natural world. People in the past were able to participate in cultures that were founded in this. That's the lost element, the lost soul in our culture, because we don't connect with anything except ourselves. People try to find themselves *in* themselves instead of finding themselves in their Great Self—the Great Self which is the Universe self.

The human story and the universe story are a single story; that's where we discover our larger being. In other cultures the individual is able to express this by participating in a sequence of celebratory moments, but we don't do that in our society.

NR: What would meaningful ritual and celebration provide for us?

TB: The way back to our connection with the Earth. You asked me earlier about what the indigenous peoples could teach us. Well, that's what they can teach us: a celebratory appreciation of the wonder of Creation, and of the interconnectedness of all life. Celebration expressed in our music, our dance, our poetry, and in our religious rituals is the highest form of gratitude for the life that has been given to us.

Celebration is our tie to our own sacred grounding in the Earth. Indigenous peoples express this grounding either by pounding a stick, or their feet on the ground, or by striking a drum—all of which connects them with the psychic energies of the Earth. Intimacy with the natural world expressed in these ways transforms the soul.

NR: In *The Dream of the Earth* you said:

> We look back at the stories, the revelatory dreams of earlier peoples—at their efforts to establish contact with numinous energies governing the phenomenal world through shamanic performances and rituals, with disdain. We were the sane people, the dreamless people. It is a bitter moment to awaken to the devastation this has caused, all because we thought we deserved a better world.[6]

There's something terribly poignant about that. What do you see for us in the future? Do we need to become dreaming people again in order to find our way?

TB: We have to remember that the guidance comes from the dream—that the dream guides our actions. We have always turned to the dream, or the revelatory vision, and to the shamanic personalities in our societies to bring us into contact with the numinous powers that govern the phenomenal world around us. In every civilization, poets and artists have evoked the spirit powers in their most exalted creative moments, and brought them forth in every form of symbolic imagery.

Since we can no longer trust our culture to guide us, I think that the next phase of evolution will also depend on the shamanic insights of the scientists. It will be their sensitive understanding of, and response to, the greater patterns at work in the natural world that we will need in order to heal it and ourselves. They are the ones who will fathom the deepest mysteries of the universe and bring back the vision and power needed by the human community. They are the ones who will lead us back to experience "the dream of the Earth" in the depths of our own being.

NR: You have also said that we are going through a period of "awakening" at this time. What did you mean by that?

TB: There's a way in which the universe chooses its moments, and chooses its people. It's important to realize that we didn't choose the time in which we would be born. We didn't choose to have this responsibility put upon us; we were given it. But there's something wonderful about the givenness of the situation in which we find ourselves. We don't know what the outcome will be, but we do know that it is a mission of extreme importance. We are indeed in a great moment of awakening. Although there are precedents in history for "awakening," there is a newness about our time, and we need to be sensitized to the awesome transformation that is being required of us.

We must also remember that the universe in this process has never failed to provide support for the mission that was to take place. The Earth in its celebratory dimensions has a positive creative aspect and will give us the guidance that we need.

NR: You said in one of your lectures that what we are living through right now is "an opportunity, a moment of creativity that rests on the primordial disequilibrium—the wildness—of the universe." What did you mean by that?

TB: What I meant was that wildness is a component in all creativity. As Thoreau said, "In wildness is the preservation of the world"—not wilderness, but wildness.

     We're living in a wild time, and those who are most intimate with the wild know that you don't fight the wild. The wild has its own ways. It's the wild that will punish you; the wild that will beat you; the wild that will make demands upon you. But it will also carry you. It will also thrill you. It will also guide you if you just know how to interact with it. It's that sense of "in wildness is the preservation of the world" to which I think we need to attune ourselves.

     All this is beyond the existing formalities of any of the religions of the world. But it's what all the religions of the world are built on eventually, and it's speaking new things to us now and taking us into new adventures. Children have this sensibility, and we need to keep it alive, we need to help them develop their own individual modes of interacting with the wild. In this way, I think that the issues that take place in our world can turn into exciting adventures, as we go through this difficult century and on into the new century, the new millennium, into what I have called the Ecozoic Era. Rather than acting out of a fear of the past, we need to move forward out of an entrancement with the future.

NR: So you do see a way for us to reclaim our abandoned souls through a renewed connection to the Earth?

TB: I see a way, but only if we listen to what the natural world is telling us. We must become as enchanted again with the natural world as we were when we were children. That's where we come to the fact of the universe as a great liturgy, a great celebration. Celebration: that's what everything is all about. That's where we can introduce joy into life in a new, comprehensive way. And that's where everything begins and everything ends.

Epilogue

Re-visioning Nature

THOMAS BERRY'S reverence for the natural world was infectious. After talking to him, I found myself going out more frequently at night to look up at the stars. Gazing at the radiance of the mountaintops lit up by the full moon transported me into a state of ecstatic wonder of the kind I imagine early peoples must have felt in their encounters with the cosmos. Thomas Berry revived in me something that I thought I had lost—a sense of awe at the grandeur of the universe.

Before I met him, I had attended a workshop on cosmology and spirituality given by Brian Swimme in Victoria, British Columbia, near where I live. A brilliant mathematical cosmologist concerned primarily with the large-scale structure and functioning of the universe, Brian Swimme is unlike most scientists in that he sees the whole story of evolution as the basis for a passionate belief in the sacredness of the cosmos. An environmentalist and a philosopher of science as well, he also believes that it is because we do not see the cosmos as revelatory that we are having all our planetary difficulties. In this he acknowledges his indebtedness to the teachings and writings of Thomas Berry.

Later, I was able to see Brian Swimme's twelve-part video series, *Canticle to the Cosmos*, which was a deeply moving and stimulating experience, and a milestone in my journey towards consciousness.

The scientific paradigm for the last three hundred years has been that the universe is a mechanistic, clock-like entity with no inner principle of life or consciousness. By accepting this view, we have in fact been programmed to lay waste the planet—something we are doing with alarming speed. Thomas Berry tells us that, by contrast, we must now perceive the universe as the epic of our times—a sacred story that fulfills, in the twentieth century, the purposes of the creation stories of other peoples from primordial times on through to the present.

How the original fireball took shape is the ultimate mystery. But quantum physics has shown us empirically that matter and energy—which early tribal peoples thought of as gods and goddesses with vast powers to give shape to the world—are creative, continuously spawning galaxies and bringing forth life in spontaneous outbursts of intelligence.

The amazing revelation for our time is that over vast eons the universe has been expanding and developing in a self-organizing, self-aware way. In the same way that a "master pattern" structures our archetypal psyches, there is an underlying ordering principle that activates the dynamics of the universe. Scientists now know, for instance, that if the speed of the expansion of the cosmos had been increased by a trillionth of a trillionth of a trillionth of one percent, the universe would have exploded. On the other hand, if the speed of its expansion had been decreased by the same amount, the universe would have collapsed.

The judicious care with which the whole universe, including ourselves, was fashioned must bring about in us a reverence and an awe when we consider the magnitude of the intelligence behind the creation of this magnificent work of art. Our study of quantum physics reveals, however, that this is no engineer with a set of blueprints at the source of our Being. Development in all of nature comes from within. Matter and energy, linked to the self-organizing dynamics of the universe, are what animate everything around us.

The One Reality from which all life in the universe sprang also generated the great variety of modes of consciousness throughout the planet, including ours. Our present understanding is that everything in the universe—a trillion galaxies or so—emerged from the original fireball as a single differentiated energy event. Implicated in the fireball is everything that presently exists; the original fireball is revealed in the universe of the present. But we can only understand the fireball through what emerged from it. And since the fireball has expressed itself in consciousness, then the universe must be a consciousness-producing process.

In the new story of the universe, it is only through our encounters with one another that the Reality of each is evoked. In other words, our conscious participation activates the Reality latent in any other part of nature. Without this interaction, matter remains inanimate to us. Re-visioning nature pre-supposes a mystical view of the universe, but it is now backed by the new scientific paradigm. Blake's vision has become the new physics. If, on the other hand, we see the natural world as Thomas Berry says, "like a collection of objects rather than a communion of subjects," it becomes vulnerable to our exploitation.

In nature, there is a community of differentiated modes of consciousness, rather than a simple overall consciousness participated in through quantitative differences of more, or less. Consciousness is the capacity whereby one being becomes present to another being as "other" without ceasing to be itself. Rocks, for example, have their own distinctive form of consciousness which they communicate in terms of their qualities of hardness (as in granite), beauty (as in marble), or semi-preciousness (as in amethysts). All these are different ways in which rock expresses itself. Rock communicates its essence to *us* when we see a mountain lit up by the sun. We can then commune with its luminous presence, which ignites our souls and inspires our imaginations. Through this encounter—if we are sensitive to it—we can meet and acknowledge each other's being.

Indigenous peoples, as Thomas Berry has pointed out, have consistently lived in a world that they consider sacred, and they therefore enter into relationship with it in an intimate way. Buddhists also teach that nature is alive; atoms and electrons are always moving. For them, stones and water and the rest of the inorganic world (which we consider inanimate) are consciousness itself.

That the universe consists of differentiated modes of consciousness is the great disclosure about its nature that has come about through science in our time. By our recognition of this, the development of the universe becomes a sacred story for us as well. Re-visioning nature, turning nature from an "it" into a "thou," will end our decimation of it. This revelation, and our responsibility for helping it unfold, is the part of the universe story that most concerns us as we enter the twenty-first century.

As the end product of the "story" of the Earth's development over 4.5 billion years, we in the West tend to consider ourselves the final chapter. Instead of seeing ourselves as the latest arrivals in a succession of fabulous creatures who have preceded and accompany us, we still think of ourselves as the crowning glory of evolution, with our wishes running the show and therefore the only ones worthy of consideration. While it is true that the continuation of many life forms on Earth now depends on us, with our recognition that everything in existence is an extension of the original fireball comes the realization that we can no longer treat consciousness simply as *human* consciousness. If we are to end the self-destruction we are inflicting on ourselves and on the planet, we must become sensitive to other modes of awareness.

Other beings in nature do not perceive Reality as we do, and for us to clear-cut a forest in the belief that our need for logs is the only allowable view, is to deny the validity of a whole community of other presences in that forest. To "forsake the garden" is to disallow their voices and close ourselves down to the wonder of communing with anything other than our own kind. The entire universe can be brought to consciousness through our penetration into its Reality, or we can miss the whole marvelous show because we're too self-absorbed to see it. It's a huge responsibility, and our awareness is everything. There's so much beauty for us to relate to and celebrate, but if we're not aware of it, it will remain invisible to us. Worse than that, we'll destroy it because it doesn't fit in with our limited picture of Reality.

The quantum physics view of the universe also reveals that everything exists in relationship to everything else. Ultimate Reality is not static, but develops through interaction and community—my "being" affecting yours, and your "being" affecting mine. Since everything vibrates its essence, we are all affected by the particular consciousness in every single thing around us. Interpenetration, in other words, is an axiom of existence. As the Buddhists say, there is no such thing as the separation of the self from the non-self. This is a physical as well as a psychic connectedness, since all things in the universe come from the same non-human elements. "A blade of grass is no less than the journey-work of the stars. . . ." said Walt Whitman.

For us to tamper with any part of this intricate web is therefore to damage the whole of it. The spiritual act of reclaiming our souls affects the Earth: "As within, so without." And vice versa: our souls are affected by any damage we inflict on the Earth, for the whole is reflected in each of its parts. "As without, so within." In our encounters with the natural world, we can enter the forest with reverence, or we can enter in order to brutally clear-cut it. In either case the interaction will change us, for, as Thomas Berry says, we do not live in a world separate from our surroundings.

Our salvation then seems to lie in our awareness that the world "within" and the world "without"—the psyche and the universe—are one, and in our willingness to play our roles in this huge cosmic drama of which our consciousness is such an important part. Our collective awareness of what contemporary science is revealing to us will enable the whole sacred story to come together.

Cosmology concerns itself with the origin and structure of the universe, but Thomas Berry and Brian Swimme's interpretation takes us far beyond hard science into the intrinsically numinous quality of the universe. Emily Dickinson expressed it exactly when she wrote: "What awaits us is the unfurnished eye." Unfortunately many of us do not see the radiance that surrounds us in the world because we are too encased in our own daily prisons of problems and desires. For most of us "the doors of perception" are not yet cleansed. But as Brian Swimme pointed out: "It is simply not human to live a life sealed off from all conscious contact with those powers at work throughout the universe and Earth and within every one of our cells." This is the same message Marion Woodman gives people at her workshops where all the participants learn to honor their body as the universe, the universe as their body.

Today, unconsciousness of our oneness with the natural world becomes reflected in the dreamless aridity of our hectic lives. In our society there is no cultural articulation of the childhood feeling that the Earth is a temple, that the Earth is sacred. All this disappears behind our need to control our environment; what was once sacred about nature is now God-forsaken and enters the realm of dream. We therefore need to honor "the dream of the Earth" within us if we would seek deeper communion with the informing energy of nature, so that it—and not we—might direct our journeys in the world.

What Thomas Berry conveyed to me in our talks is a sense of the Earth as a source of inexhaustible celebration. These feelings of love and reverence for the mysterious cosmos of which I am such a tiny part had been submerged in me for so long that it took many hours of meditation to bring them back. Out in nature on my cross-country skis, or hiking in the magnificent Rocky Mountains, I am now able to tap into those feelings of gratitude and wonder for the miracle of nature. I am also able to thank Thomas Berry in my heart for having brought me to that place.

Thomas Berry was born in North Carolina in 1914. After entering a monastery in Massachusetts at the age of twenty, he became an Asian scholar and studied both Chinese Taoism and the religions of India where, as he says: "The Divine is always immanent in the world of nature." In all his work he has emphasized Eastern religious thought and its relationship to the natural world. His published books include *Buddhism* and *The Religions of India.*

Thomas Berry is a Catholic priest who served for many years as president of the Teilhard Association, named after the great French scientist-priest Pierre Teilhard de Chardin. From 1966 until 1979, he directed the graduate program in the history of religions at Fordham University. He was also the founder director of the Riverdale Center of Religious Research in Riverdale, New York, from its inception in 1970 until he retired in the spring of 1995. Thomas Berry is also the author of *The Dream of the Earth* (1988), and co-author, with cosmologist Brian Swimme, of *The Universe Story* (1992).

Even though he is now in his eighties, Thomas Berry still travels the world addressing government, university, and general audiences about the requirements for our culture's transformation. His life-long interest in, and influence on, educational programs that seek to mitigate the destructive activities of the human community on the natural life systems of the Earth has earned him many honorary doctorates, as well as the James Herriot Award in 1992 from the Humane Society of the United States for his contribution to the ecological issues of our times. In 1995 his book, *The Dream of the Earth* was awarded the Lenin Prize for Literature for being one of the best ten books of the year.

NOTES

[1] CBC National Radio News, 6 p.m. edition, Thursday, Jan 8, 1998.

[2] Thomas Berry and Brian Swimme, *The Universe Story*, San Francisco: Harper Collins, 1992, p. 44.

[3] Ibid., p. 40.

[4] Ibid., p. 41.

[5] Ibid., p. 42.

[6] Thomas Berry, *The Dream of the Earth*, San Francisco: Sierra Club Books, 1988, pp. 202-4.

CONCLUSION

RETURN TO THE GARDEN

I BEGAN this book in an attempt to understand the psychological and spiritual dynamics behind the destruction of the planet and the illness in my own body. I am ending it with the proposition that ultimately there are no "solutions" to either the planetary crisis or our diseased states except those which involve our transformations at a bodysoul level. For as Ross Woodman said: "The state of the world mirrors our own inner state. We need to enter into a mutual love affair with it." We must therefore look within if we are to realize Blake's vision for humanity and enter into a healing alignment with the creative energy in the universe. Without that self-awareness, we become instead "part of the problem"; we end up damaging nature more than helping it.

The people interviewed in this book agree that we need to end the devastation of the planet through, as Thomas Berry says, "a change of consciousness that will end the patriarchal pattern of humans' drive to disturb the entire functioning of the globe." Marion Woodman tells us that we will only stop plundering our bodies and the Earth's body when we connect to our feminine roots and recognize the sacredness in all matter. Only then will we become what Laurens van der Post called "our journeying selves" who can once again build a bridge to the natural world which is our human heritage.

The life of the soul is contingent upon our recognition that we inhabit a numinous universe, and that our survival depends on learning how to commune with every part of it. This feeling of the soul's connectedness to the cosmos has seldom been more beautifully evoked than in this wartime recollection by Laurens van der Post:

> May I illustrate this from something that happened to me in the last war? [As a POW in a Japanese camp in Java,] I was standing at nightfall looking out of my prison. It was what I believed to be my

last night alive, and I had fully accepted that I would be executed by the Japanese in the morning. An enormous thunderstorm had broken outside and the heavy rain—which always, in my drought-conditioned African senses, brings feelings of relief and music—was falling. The lightning and the thunder were almost continuous. I thought I had never seen lightning more beautiful—it was almost as if I were in the workshop of creation where lightning is made—and it was so charged and intense that it seemed to overflow its own zig-zag thrust at the jungle and come more like a great stream of fire out of the sky and make a delta of flame in the black. But there were also great purple sheets of lightning in between, that swept like archangelic wings over my prison. But it was the thunder which meant most of all. I had never heard the voice so loud, so clear and magisterial. And suddenly, quite unbidden, a great feeling of relief came over me. "That's it!" I thought. "The Japanese are ultimately not in overall command. There is witness of a power greater than man which, in the end, will decide all."

[It was] one of the most overwhelming emotions I have ever experienced; and in that moment all anxiety left me and I was, in the deepest sense of the words, no more troubled. Through nature outside I had been reconnected with a kind of powerhouse inside myself of which I had been unaware.[1]

It is now nearly two decades since my body began to reject our contaminated surroundings, and my husband David and I traveled across the continent to start a new life in the luxuriant West Coast environment that is now our home. In my garden, the monks' hood, the Maltese cross, the cardinal flower, and the Canterbury bells transport my senses and nod their heads in agreement with me that this is indeed a sacred place. Medieval people, who probably named these plants, lived in a world of analogy, imagery, and allusion. In my imagination I conjure up a parade of holies who enter the garden to commune with the plants that bear their names. As I do so, I think of Thomas Berry in his monastery retreat of long ago, having fled, as I did, from the world of industry and commerce. I appreciate our rapport as I too withdraw to a peaceful place away from the poisoning of the world that he foresaw so clearly.

As I stand in my garden and look towards the sea, I am plunged into a world where the hues and scents of a multitude of flowers tantalize my senses. A neighboring artist wanders in to ask if she can paint this symphony of color "while the light is just right." The results express her joyous response to the play of light, and to the shapes and forms that give texture to the shimmering scene before her. Behind it all, the enormous Douglas firs and maples make a protective backdrop for this cloistered space.

In our conversations Ross Woodman said that a new healing myth for our time would envision "a marriage of the mind to nature." Now when I wander through my garden, I try to silence the incessant chatter in my head and tune my senses instead to nature's voices around me. I recall the time that Ross and Marion visited us on our island, and of how Ross lay back on the grass and "blissed out" on the smell of the earth and the sound of the sea. I remember also how Marion expressed her enchantment with the natural world she found here in a letter she wrote to us afterwards: "Your garden is etched in my mind in all its glory."

In my garden reverie, I also think about Laurens van der Post, who told me that it was through the "master pattern" within each of us that the possibility of metamorphosis lies. Like the butterflies in my garden, we are all in a process of continually evolving, "of becoming more than we even plan to become." Trusting in that "master pattern" is critical if we are to be cured of the hubris which is the bad "seed image" at the heart of our destruction of that larger garden, the planet.

These are the memories that are evoked in me by these four people as I write this coda to the journey we have all taken together. This is my legacy from them, a legacy which has had a profound effect on my soul and on my imagination. Like the dragonfly in its pond, or the bear in its temperate forest home, I now know that I too only make sense within the context of the natural environment. And like Thomas Berry's butterfly, who after generations away returns through unknown territory to a place it instinctively recognizes, I hope that I too am on a voyage that will eventually return me to the Garden.

Gradually, as I have learned to trust and befriend my psyche with its primary impulses towards wholeness, a new person has begun to emerge. My illness is still a concern. Why not? The Earth is still being poisoned by billions of pounds of chemicals which we dump onto it every year; I can't avoid those toxins in the air and food any more than anyone else. But as Ross Woodman said to me, "What we do, we first imagine." In other words, it's not the *old* health paradigm on which we need to focus, but the *new*—a metaphorical body, a bodysoul of the imagination. That's what being born in this present chaos means, and that is the new life I feel stirring within me.

The Newtonian clockwork perception of nature as a break-and-then-fix-it entity, as the basis for understanding how our world functions, underlies much of our current malaise. We still envision our bodies as machines. Thomas Berry says that it is the quantum model of reality which assures us that we are not just sophisticated biological mechanisms—there is a spiritual energy that animates us. This "informing principle" in the universe organizes and maintains the various constituents of our physical bodies, and turns them into living, breathing human beings. Our recognition that there is a soul in the machine is the real difference between the Newtonian perspective and the quantum model of healing.

What I've learned from Marion Woodman about the experience of illness is that any medical model that doesn't include our souls in its treatment will fail to heal us in any deep sense. Nor will it deliver us from our addictions, for addictions and loss of soul go hand-in-hand. Physical affliction is psychic affliction and vice versa. The things that I am pursuing to help myself—homeopathy, visualization, meditation, and bodysoul work—are based on the holistic wisdom of the feminine mode. The striving masculine principle enables us to survive, but the caring feminine heals.

Laurens van der Post believed that the illnesses many of us are experiencing today reflect the state of our sick culture, which has not found meaningful transcendent values since the diminishment of the Christian myth. People who are ill, therefore, may be mirrors in which the culture can recognize and acknowledge previously unknown aspects of itself. Within our struggle to restore soul-life to our sick bodies lies the potential for the whole culture to heal itself by regaining a sense of spiritual direction. In this context, I hope that my story has meaning for all who read this book.

In our popular electronic culture we are consistently being fed dead and destructive images that stupefy our consciousness and keep us from the healing imagery trying to reach us from the unconscious. Mercifully, at the heart of the chaos that we are now enduring lie the beginnings of new life, namely the rise of the new feminine consciousness embedded in the idea of the sacredness of matter. Whether the imagery here is of "the Great Mother," or "the conscious feminine," or "the great curvature of space," awareness of a feminine energy is being expressed today through different perspectives and disciplines which we all need to acknowledge for the sake of our survival.

There is also a recognition that matter cooperates with our own psychic, mental, and spiritual understanding and growth: a conscious Gaia will no longer tolerate rape and, as a part of Gaia, our bodies and psyches will not stand mutely by as we continue to mistreat our own souls and the planet's soul.

Feminine consciousness comes to us through the heart. Viewed from that perspective, I can see my disease—paradoxically—as a blessing as well as a curse. The solutions we environmentally ill have devised in order to survive force us to live lightly on the Earth. Raising our own vegetables in composted soil, joining in community efforts to save the land for future generations to enjoy, protesting the exploitation of our remaining wild spaces—these are caring endeavors that return us to our instinctual feminine roots in the earth, and nourish our souls far more than shopping trips in Wonderworld. Even so, they are only a few of "the ten thousand things" that we can do if we wish to join in the Great Work that is Thomas Berry's vision for our future.

During the course of our conversations, Ross Woodman said to me, "We can only save the planet by getting to the core of where God is. . . ." Getting to the core of where God and Goddess are, and relating my own sense of soul abandonment to the culture's loss of soul, has been the crux of the matter all along. It was when I started to look for a publisher for this manuscript that a cousin of mine threw some light on the question of God/Goddess-searching by saying, "Do you think that anyone's *really* going to want to read a book by a middle-aged woman sitting out in the middle of the bald prair-ee, searching for God?!" Suddenly, through the flippancy of that remark, the purpose of this book came into focus. Why indeed would anyone want to read my story? Perhaps because what I am searching for is what we are all searching for—a guiding personal myth that will heal our divided spirits and enable us to rediscover the sacredness of the natural world.

For myself, what I desire more than anything else at this stage in my journey is to be in a state of what Marion Woodman calls *kairos*, or integration with Reality. I want to believe that whatever I'm doing in my life, I'm where the universe wants me to be at that moment. I long to feel centered—consciously in touch with an embodiment of spirit which, by connecting me with the numinous energy in my psyche and in nature, gives my life purpose and direction.

Through the experience of writing this book, I have come to realize that in the surrender of my imagination to both the creativity at work in the universe, and the divinely sent images from the unconscious, lies my experience of the religious archetype. These are what inspire my reverence and my awe: the lawful universe, the lawful unconscious, and the capacity of humans for love. My need to find meaning in existence is the bridge that has enabled me to discover and enter those worlds. Through the compassionate wisdom and visionary scrutiny of Marion and Ross Woodman, Thomas Berry, and Laurens van der Post, I have been able to recover my lost ability to experience the numinous. In relating bodysoul to planet *without,* and to myth and dream *within,* I have finally begun to find new ways of being.

Marion Woodman said that in order to "return to the Garden" we have to travel around the entire perimeter of our psychic garden before attaining re-entry, through the original gate, to our center. Having relinquished our childhood innocence in order to experience and suffer our journeys to maturity in the world, we return to Eden and find Blake's "doors of perception" cleansed and open to receive us. The Quest for the Grail—for wholeness—is always precarious, but with our hard-won insights and understanding we are now aware of what the ceaseless "Mental Fight" has been all about.

To return to *our* garden is to consciously return to a place of fullness and naturalness of being that the modern world in its frenzied pace has threatened to obliterate. In the contemporary world, a garden becomes "home" to the alienated soul that has no home. It's a place where the lost soul can put down deep roots into the Source of his or her own being. This is not a place to try and conquer nature; we do not enter a garden in order to overcome or subdue it, but rather to allow nature to express herself through us. The garden is a metaphor for the soul—a place where the most important thing is to live and grow. To find ourselves in it once again is to find that part of ourselves that had been split off from our own deepest origins.

We all need a place in our lives where the flame does not flicker— where the soul feels connected to its Source. For me, that place is in the natural world. There my senses engage with the glories of Creation, and the unconscious works its magic. The animal psyche leads me on as, step after step, I follow with rhythmic strides. "I am," as Wallace Stevens wrote, "what is around me." In my imagination I am healed; in my dreams I, and the Earth, and the creatures of the Earth are once again made whole.

NOTES

[1] Laurens van der Post and Jean-Marc Pottiez, *A Walk with a White Bushman,* London: Chatto & Windus, 1986, p. 69-70.

ACKNOWLEDGMENTS

I would like to thank Brenda Rosen, Executive Editor of Quest Books, for supporting the publication of *The Forsaken Garden.*

I would also like to pay tribute to the editing skills of Dawna Page, whose tireless efforts and thoughtful input I gratefully acknowledge.

Also, my thanks to Sharron Dorr, Marketing Coordinator, for her hard work in bringing this book to the public's attention.

To Ross and Marion Woodman, Thomas Berry, and Laurens van der Post I extend my deepest gratitude for their unwavering support throughout the difficult task of giving birth to this book.

Without Jonathan Young's help I might not have been published, so I feel I have much to thank him for in the way of guidance.

Finally, to my dear friends Jean Strasser, Honor Griffith, and Meg Nicks, and to my niece Norah Ryley, I want to say "thank you" for listening, encouraging, and understanding.

BIBLIOGRAPHY

Abram, David. *The Spell of the Sensuous*. New York: Pantheon Books, 1996.

Abrams, Jeremiah, ed. *The Shadow in America*. Novato: Nataraji Publishing, 1994.

Argüelles, Jose A. *The Transformative Vision*. Boulder: Shambhala Publications, 1975.

Barrett, William. *Irrational Man*. Garden City: Anchor Books, 1962.

Bateson, Gregory. *Mind and Nature*. New York: Bantam Books, 1980.

Berman, Morris. *Coming to Our Senses*. New York: Bantam Books, 1990.

Berry, Thomas and Brian Swimme. *The Universe Story*, San Francisco: Harper SanFrancisco, 1992.

Berry, Thomas with Thomas Clarke. *Befriending the Earth*. Mystic: Twenty-Third Publications, 1995.

Berry, Thomas. *The Dream of the Earth*. San Francisco: Sierra Club Books, 1988.

Bly, Robert. *A Little Book on the Human Shadow*. San Francisco: Harper & Row, 1988.

Campbell, Joseph. *Myths to Live By*. New York: Bantam Books, 1978.

Capra, Fritjof. *The Tao of Physics*. Boulder: Shambhala Publications, 1983.

Dossey, Larry. *Recovering the Soul*. New York: Bantam Books, 1989.

Edinger, Edward F. *The Creation of Consciousness*. Toronto: Inner City Books, 1984.

———. *Ego and Archetype*. New York: Penguin-Viking Books, 1973.

———. *Encounter with the Self*. Toronto: Inner City Books, 1986.

———. *Transformation of the God-Image*. Toronto: Inner City Books, 1992.

Fox, Matthew and Brian Swimme. *Manifesto for a Global Civilization*. Santa Fe: Bear & Co,. 1982.

Hillman, James and Michael Ventura. *We've Had a Hundred Years of Psychotherapy— and the World's Getting Worse*. San Francisco: HarperSanFrancisco, 1992.

Hillman, James. *Re-Visioning Psychology*. New York: HarperPerennial, 1992.

———. *The Soul's Code*. New York: Random House, 1996.

———. *The Thought of the Heart & the Soul of the World*. Dallas: Spring Publications, 1993.

Jensen, Derrick, ed. *Listening to the Land*. San Francisco: Sierra Club Books, 1995.

Johnson, Robert A. *Owning Your Own Shadow*. San Francisco: HarperSanFrancisco, 1991.

Jung, C. G. *Analytical Psychology*. New York: Vintage Books, 1970.

———. *The Archetypes and the Unconscious*. Princeton: Princeton University Press, 1969.

———. *Modern Man in Search of a Soul*. New York: Harcourt Brace Jovanovich, 1960.

———. *Psychology and Religion*. New Haven: Yale University Press, 1938.

Lindbergh, Anne Morrow. *Gift from the Sea*. New York: Vintage Books, 1968.

Lonergan, Anne and Caroline Richards, eds. *Thomas Berry and the New Cosmology*. Mystic: Twenty-third Publications, 1990.

Macy, Joanna. *World As Lover, World As Self*. Berkeley: Parallax Press, 1991.

Marshall, Peter. *Nature's Web*. London: Simon & Schuster Ltd., 1992.

May, Rollo. *The Cry for Myth*. New York: W.W. Norton & Co., 1991.

McLaughlin, Corrine and Gordon Davidson. *Spiritual Politics*. New York: Ballantine Books, 1994.

Meier, C. A., ed. *Testament to the Wilderness*. Zürich: Daimon Verlag Press, & Venice: Lapis Press, 1985.

Neihardt, John G. *Black Elk Speaks*. Lincoln: University of Nebraska Press, 1961.

Oelschlaeger, Max. *The Idea of Wilderness*. New Haven: Yale University Press, 1991.

Page, P. K. *Hologram*. London: Brick Books, 1994.

Roszak, Theodore and Mary E. Gomes and Allen D. Kanner, eds. *Ecopsychology*. San Francisco: Sierra Club Books, 1995.

Roszak, Theodore. *Person/Planet*. Garden City: Anchor Books, 1979.

———. *The Voice of the Earth*. New York: Simon & Schuster, 1992.

Sardello, Robert. *Facing the World with Soul*. Hudson: Lindisfarne Press, 1992.

———. *Love and the Soul*. New York: HarperPerennial, 1996.

Segaller, Stephen and Merrill Berger. *The Wisdom of the Dream*. Boston: Shambhala Publications, 1989.

Seton, Ernest Thompson. *Wild Animals I Have Known*. Toronto: McClellend & Stewart, 1977.

Sheldrake, Rupert. *The Rebirth of Nature*. New York: Bantam Books, 1992.

Singer, June. *Seeing Through the Visible World*. New York, HarperCollins, 1991.

———. *The Unholy Bible*, Boston: Sigo Press, 1986.

Sjöö, Monica and Barbara Mor. *The Great Cosmic Mother*. San Francisco: Harper & Row, 1987.

Stevens, Anthony. *Archetypes: A Natural History of the Self.* New York: Quill Publishers, 1982.

Storr, Anthony. *The Essential Jung*. Princeton: Princeton University Press, 1983.

Suzuki, David and Peter Knudtson. *Wisdom of the Elders*. Toronto: Stoddard Publishing Co., 1993.

Suzuki, David with Amanda Mcconnell. *The Sacred Balance*. Vancouver: Greystone Books, 1997.

Swimme, Brian. *The Hidden Heart of the Cosmos*. Maryknoll: Orbis Books, 1996.

————. *The Universe is a Green Dragon*. Santa Fe: Bear & Co., 1984.

Tobias, Michael and Georgianne Cowan, eds. *The Soul in Nature*. New York: Continuum Publishing, 1994.

van der Post, Laurens. *About Blady*. London: Chatto & Windus, 1991.

————. *The Dark Eye in Africa*. New York: William Morrow & Co., 1955.

————. *The Heart of the Hunter*. London: Penguin Books, 1965.

————. *Jung and the Story of Our Time*. New York: Vintage Books, 1977.

————. *The Lost World of the Kalahari*. London: Penguin Books, 1987.

————. *Testament to the Bushman*. New York: Penguin Books, 1985.

van der Post, Laurens with Jean-Marc Pottiez. *A Walk with a White Bushman*. London: Chatto & Windus, 1986.

Whitmont, Edward C. *Return of the Goddess*. New York: Crossroad Publishing, 1984.

————. *The Symbolic Quest*. Princeton: Princeton University Press, 1978.

Wolf, Fred Allen. *The Dreaming Universe*. New York: Simon & Schuster, 1994.

————. *The Spiritual Universe*. New York, Simon & Schuster, 1996.

————. *Taking the Quantum Leap*. New York: Harper & Row, 1989.

Woodman, Marion and Robert Bly, *The Maiden King*. New York: Henry Holt & Co., 1998.

Woodman, Marion and Elinor Dickson. *Dancing in the Flames*. Toronto: Alfred A. Knopf, 1996.

Woodman, Marion and Jill Mellick. *Coming Home to Myself.* Berkeley: Conari Press, 1998.

Woodman, Marion with Kate Danson, Mary Hamilton, Rita Greer Allen. *Leaving My Father's House*, Boston: Shambhala Publications, 1992.

Woodman, Marion. *Addiction to Perfection: The Still Unravished Bride.* Toronto: Inner City Books, 1982.

———. *Conscious Femininity.* Toronto: Inner City Books, 1993.

———. *The Owl Was a Baker's Daughter: Anorexia, Obesity and the Repressed Feminine.* Toronto: Inner City Books, 1980.

———. *The Pregnant Virgin: A Process of Psychological Transformation.* Toronto: Inner City Books, 1985.

———. *The Ravaged Bridegroom: Masculinity in Women.* Toronto: Inner City Books, 1990.

Woodman, Ross. *The Apocalyptic Vision in the Poetry of Shelley.* Toronto: University of Toronto Press, 1964.

Zukav, Gary. *The Dancing Wu Li Masters.* New York: William Morrow and Co., 1979.

Zweig, Connie and Jeremiah Abrams, eds. *Meeting the Shadow.* New York: G.P. Putnam's Sons, 1991.

INDEX

Adam and Eve, 85, 117, 148-51

Addiction(s), 58, 61, 62, 86, 87, 107, 109, 116, 123, 220, 221; and self-destruction, 70, 72, 107, 111, 119, 183; to alcohol, 64; to drugs, 37, 62, 221; to food, 63, 83; to growth (*see* Myth(s), of progress); to money and profit, 65, 72, 201; to perfection, 69, 77, 80, 92, 122, 123; to possessions (matter), 65, 204, 209-11; to religion, 83; to work, 80, 83

Advertising, 71, 210, 211, 221; use of sacred terminology, 211

Afro-Americans, 158, 159

Allergies. *See* Environmental Illness

America, North, explorers and settlers, 225

Androgyne. *See* Inner Marriage

Anima. *See* Soul, feminine

Anima Mundi, 59, 195-97

Anorexia, 63

Apocalypse, 145

Aquinas, St. Thomas (1225-1274), 251, 262

Archetype(s), 19, 35, 56, 87, 95, 246-48; and culture, 247, 248; and genetic coding, 108, 247, 248; and the earth, 58, 109, 247, 248; as great powers, 19; Christ, 141; feminine (*see* Feminine Principle); forms visible in nature, 56; God, 58, 111-13; Goddess (Great Mother), 58, 66, 80, 112, 113, 188, 245, 248; masculine (*see* Masculine Principle); of the self (*see* Self); orphan (*see* Child, abandoned); patterns visible in the body, 56, 103, 108, 109; psychoid, 108; religious, 58, 278; *see also* Energy (ies), archetypal; Images

Art(s), 173, 174; metaphor in, 86; religious function of, 40; *see also* Creativity; Indigenous People, art and ceremony

Artists, and creativity, 41, 47, 48, 95, 254; and demoralization, 26; as shamans, 264; creating images of archetypal energy, 112, 113; *see also* Literature; Poets and Poetry; Romanticism

Asclepius, 48, 122

Awakening, 264

Awareness. *See* Consciousness

Baha'u'llah (1817-1892), 187

Banff National Park, Canada, 72

Bateson, Gregory (1904-1980), 240

Bears, 205, 243

Being. *See* Source of our Being

Berry, Thomas, 8, 235; as mentor, 4, 202, 271, 274; biography, 261, 262, 271; childhood, 261; dream about, 16, 17, 202; environmental ethics, 205; monastic life, 261, 262; mystical view of Nature, 203, 206, 263; rapport with indigenous people, 260, 261; *The Dream of the Earth*, 75, 202, 224, 225, 246, 263; *The Universe Story*, 204, 242, 244, 252, 253, 262

Bible, 252; *see also* Adam and Eve; Garden of Eden; Job; Shadow Energy; Satan

Biophilia. *See* Love, of the Earth; Wilson, E.O.

285

QUEST BOOKS
are published by
The Theosophical Society in America
Wheaton, Illinois 60189-0270
a branch of a world organization
dedicated to the promotion of the unity of
humanity and the encouragement of the study of
religion, philosophy, and science, to the end that
we may better understand ourselves and our place in
the universe. The Society stands for complete
freedom of individual search and belief.
For further information about its activities,
write or call 1800-669-1571, or consult its Web page:
http://www.theosophical.org.

The Theosophical Publishing House
is aided by the generous support of
THE KERN FOUNDATION,
a trust established by Herbert A. Kern
and dedicated to Theosophical education.